MY BROTHER GEOFF

Also by Tony Hamilton

Geoff Hamilton: The Complete Gardener

My Brother Geoff

The People's Gardener

Tony Hamilton

HEADLINE

First published in 2001 by HEADLINE BOOK PUBLISHING

Tony Hamilton would be happy to hear from readers with their comments
on the book at the following e-mail address: tony@pta-ltd.com

The extract from a television review by Nancy Banks-Smith,
published in 1990, is © the *Guardian* and used by permission

10 9 8 7 6 5 4 3 2 1

British Library Cataloguing in Publication Data

Hamilton, Tony
  My Brother Geoff
  1. Hamilton, Geoff, 1936– 2. Gardeners – England –
Biography
  I. Title
  635'.092

ISBN 0 7472 3284 9

Typeset by Avon Dataset Ltd, Bidford-on-Avon, Warks

Printed and bound in Great Britain by
Mackays of Chatham plc, Chatham, Kent

HEADLINE BOOK PUBLISHING
A division of Hodder Headline
338 Euston Road
London NW1 3BH

www.headline.co.uk
www.hodderheadline.com

Acknowledgements

DURING THE WRITING OF THIS BOOK I have been very fortunate to have been surrounded by a group of people who have inspired me, put up with me, fed and watered me, advised me and consoled me when times have been hard.

My grateful thanks go to all the people who gave up chunks of their valuable time to answer my questions and to build up a rounded picture of Geoff's professional and private life. In particular I should thank Geoff's dearest colleague, John Kenyon, who came to my house, ate a lot of my food, drank my cheapest red wine without complaint and told me many things I didn't know about my brother – most of which I've passed on.

I have depended a lot on Lynda, Geoff's wife, to recall some of the facts, to diligently dig out information without demur and, using all her teaching skills to best advantage, to 'mark' my work with her red pen. I ended up with a B minus, which is better than I did at school.

Celia Kent, the managing editor at Headline, bravely answered all my tedious telephone calls and cries for help with supreme calm and professionalism, though I suspect she received the final draft with a deep sigh of relief.

Heather Holden-Brown, the non-fiction supremo at Headline, has treated me with a courtesy I didn't deserve in the face of my upstart challenges and arguments, and I am grateful to have been let off so lightly.

My extraordinarily patient and forbearing wife, Carol, has kept my body and soul together, such as they are, for which she deserves a Queen's Award for Industry.

The most painful and difficult work has been done by my amazing editor, Anne Askwith, whose literary skills, formidable memory and minute attention to detail have served to put the book into some kind of intelligible order, to reduce my frequent lapses into rambling prose and to remove the endless repetition that always plagues my writing. I will be eternally in her debt.

Perhaps my deepest gratitude should go to Professor Samani and Mr Tom Spyt and their team, who managed to fit in a quick triple heart bypass operation during the writing of the book, so saving my life and ensuring that it was finished at all. They are unsung heroes to whom I owe more than I could ever express.

Contents

For Lynda, who made my brother happy

CHAPTER 1

London Days

THERE WERE NO MILITARY PARADES, NO fanfares, and no visits from the Queen on 15 August 1936 when Geoff and I were born in a small terraced house in Tollet Street in London's East End. In fact it appeared that the rest of London, regrettably we always felt, largely ignored the event, but in our little house there was much rejoicing and not a few 'ta-ra-ra-boomdeays'.

Many young couples lived with their families in those days, and our parents were no exception, living with our mother's parents and our elder brother Mark. Grandfather, Alfred Mark Abrahams, was Jewish and had been a music hall artist in his young life – hence the 'ta-ra-ra-boomdeays'. He was an ebullient, joyful man, who filled the house with optimism and laughter. He also believed, like all Jewish people, that the unshakable remedy for all illness, misfortune, depression and the like or, indeed, any cause for celebration, was food. So our poor mother, having just unloaded an aggregated fourteen pounds of identical twins, was probably nearly drowned in lockshen soup and stuffed to the gills with gefüllte fish. For those of you who have never had the good fortune to eat Jewish food, lockshen soup is chicken soup with noodles and gefüllte fish is chopped fish rolled into balls and fried in olive oil. Delicious, but very filling.

Geoff was born at 1.45 a.m., thirty-five minutes before me – a misfortune for me because, no matter how small the time period, being the elder gives you one invaluable commodity: *power*. And Geoff exerted this power over me, albeit in a largely benign way, for the rest of his life. You may find it incredible that by the time we'd reached our fifties thirty-five minutes of time so long ago could make any difference, but it did, as we shall see later.

But let me introduce you to the characters in our early lives. Grandfather was born at 13 Love Court, Whitechapel, in 1876, to Angel (a cigar maker) and Hannah Abrahams. Grandfather was a handsome man with a fine baritone voice. He began his working life as a ballad singer in the music halls in about 1900. His stage name was Alf Davis, a name he was obliged to use because in those days any music hall artist would be likely to suffer if he or she was obviously Jewish. He toured all the music halls in Britain, starting in London with the Hackney Empire and going to as many cities as he could on the west side of the country, ending up at the Glasgow Empire, where he always got the 'bird'. (Everybody got the bird at the Glasgow Empire. Booing and jeering were well-established Glaswegian pastimes.) Then he would pack his bags and visit every city on the east side of the country until he finally made it home. Major tours like this could sometimes take up to a year which, as he once said to me, 'rather puts the mockers on *affaires d'amour*'.

However, this predicament wasn't to last. During one of his 'resting' sojourns in London in about 1909, he met a strikingly beautiful woman, Harriet Setchel, with whom he was to conduct a tempestuous love affair for the rest of his life. Harriet, or 'Allie' as he came to call her, was born in 1888 at 40 Ramsey Street, Bethnal Green, to George and Harriet Setchell, and she eventually became his wife, despite a host of seemingly insuperable difficulties. Harriet was a Gentile and it simply didn't do for a Jew to marry anybody but a 'nice Jewish girl'. And Alf (whom we came to call 'Gramp') was not only a Jew but also a music hall artist. A Jewish music hall artist? For a Gentile, that's worse than being born in a handbag. But, with both their families declaring war, they blissfully ignored the fuss and became man and wife. It was to prove to be a devoted, steadfast relationship, but never without its ups and downs.

2

One of Gramp's steepest 'downs' was the day he was called up to fight in the First World War. Being a music hall artist was not considered to be work of national importance, so he had to go. Never a man to seek an ordinary job, he became a train driver, ferrying stores out to the Front. Geoff and I would sit at his knee, enthralled by the stories of his escapades. One day he told us of the time when he had inadvertently driven his train behind enemy lines. Looking out, he could see himself surrounded by German soldiers. Aghast and thrilled, we asked him, wide-eyed, what he did about it. 'Well,' he said, 'what would you do? I put the train into reverse, put my head down and drove it back again.' Fortunately, unlike so many, many others, he survived and returned home to try to rebuild his life.

Grandmother was a strong, upright woman renowned for her ability to help people out of trouble through sound advice and forthright support. She knew her own mind and she was utterly determined to see her principles through to the bitter end. For example, one day she was packing a suitcase for her new husband, who was about to embark on one of his long and arduous tours. Inside the case Grandmother, or 'Gram', as we knew her, discovered some sepia photographs of scantily clad chorus girls. Of course you have to remember that 'scantily clad' in those days meant that the ankle was showing, but this was enough to enrage Gram. She slammed down the lid of the case and shouted down the stairs for Gramp. He came sheepishly up the stairs, for Gram was not to be disobeyed, to find her brandishing the photographs and saying in no uncertain terms, 'I'm not having you associating with women like this. This is your last tour. When you get back we'll find you a different occupation.' Gramp didn't believe it, because he thought there was little else he could do. But he hadn't reckoned with the stern resolve of his wife.

Gram was a forelady in an aircraft factory, responsible for supervising the girls who applied canvas to the wings of aeroplanes, so she was relatively well paid. During the time that Gramp was away on his final tour, she scrimped and saved until she had enough to buy a black London cab, which was standing outside their house in Tollet Street when he came back. It was one of the very early motorised cabs, with no side windows for the protection of the driver and a huge brass hooter mounted on the side to warn off pedestrians, because it was capable of a speed of at least twenty miles per hour. 'That,' Gram said, adopting her Atilla the Hun stance, 'is your future career. Get on your bike and do the "knowledge". Make sure you pass first time and then start making us some money.' 'Doing the knowledge' was just a small matter of learning the name and whereabouts of every street in London. It is still a requirement for cab drivers today, although most of them now do it on a moped or in a car, but neither option was possible in those days. So poor old Gramp had to do it partly on foot and partly on a bicycle. It took him six months and at the end of that period he had to be examined. Perhaps more out of fear of our indomitable grandmother than respect for the examiner, he passed first time and he drove a cab for the rest of his working life. He did very well out of it, making enough money to make the family what Gram called 'respectable'. It was an unusual coincidence that years later, shortly after Geoff died and I appeared in a television series about his life, I received a letter from a Mr Ron Clarke, who now lives near Ely, telling me that he and his mother had had rooms at 30 Tollet Street and, even though he was only four years old at the time he can still remember Gramp taking him out for spins in the cab and allowing him to squeeze the rubber bulb of the great brass hooter. To befriend a little boy was typical of dear old Gramp; that was the kind of care and companionship he later gave to Geoff and me.

On 12 July 1911, our mother, Rose Abrahams, was born. It was a difficult birth but little Rose just opened her lungs, shouted her indignation and proceeded with dogged determination to thrive – a habit she never lost through eighty-four years on a road from some hardship to modest but undreamed-of success. She was to grow into a very beautiful little girl, adored but not spoiled by her parents, and thence into a young woman who caused heads to turn wherever she went.

Our father, Cyril Reuben Ham (he was later to change our name to Hamilton, God bless him), was born on 14 August 1905 at 112 South View Road, Hornsey, where his father, Reuben Hannaneal Elisha

Ham, and his wife Emily just about survived on Reuben's meagre wage as a fishmonger's assistant.

The story of how Reuben got this job is one that I don't know whether to believe or not, but since he was a fervently religious man (who wouldn't be with a name like his?) I'm quite sure he believed he was telling a true tale. During the great depression of the 1920s he, like millions of others, was unemployed. There was no Social Security to look after people who had fallen on hard times, so survival was extremely difficult and often the family lived on nothing but thin pea soup. Poor Cyril had to go to school with no shoes or socks, dressed in an old football shirt and a threadbare pair of trousers. He couldn't go to school on a Thursday, because that was the day his trousers were washed. One day they ran out of food altogether and Emmie, his mother, was at her wits' end. 'Don't worry,' said Grandfather, 'God will provide.' He went to sit in the park to think through a plan of action when, at the far end of the bench on which he was sitting, he saw a brown paper parcel. Nobody was in sight, so he picked it up and peeked inside. It was full of meat – steaks, kidneys, chops and all sorts. He had no conscience about taking it because he honestly thought it was a gift from God. So he hurried back home with his precious bundle and on the way he ran into an old friend he hadn't seen for years. 'Reuben,' the friend said, grasping his hand, 'just the man I wanted to meet. I've got a job for you in my fish shop if you need one. How about it?' Grandfather practically wept with gratitude and was able to stroll home to meet his worried wife with 'There you are, Emmie. I told you God would provide.'

I remember Grandfather as a kindly but strict man whose greatest eccentricity was that he wore a little quiff in the front of his hair, held in place with a kirby grip. Our cousin Kath, who is some sixteen years older than me, remembers that he would hang rows of bloaters on rails in the fish shop and when women customers came in and squeezed them to see which of them had a roe inside, Grandfather would growl at them, 'Keep your hands off my bloaters, you slut.' Such an attitude would not be thought of today as being in the best traditions of customer relations, but it was seemingly accepted in those days, for he was quite successful in his small way, eventually graduating to become a fully fledged fishmonger with his own open-fronted shop in the Commercial Road.

By the mid-1920s, Cyril – our father – was a young man, inclined to be a bit of a dandy and what they called in the East End 'street sharp'. In other words, he was always looking for ways in which he could make a little extra money. He never did anything that could be described as criminal, although he had a minor brush with the police over one of his enterprises – a scheme selling cigarettes from his father's shop. The parlour of the little shop was an ideal place for Dad to conduct his business. The idea was that customers came to the parlour and bought a packet of twenty cigarettes, and Dad would tell them that, if they brought a friend with them next time, they would get a free packet of ten. If they spread the net widely enough, they could smoke for nothing, and the same arrangement would operate for their friends. I think he had invented the first pyramid-selling racket. People streamed in and out of the shop, which eventually became full of cartons of cigarettes. Dad, of course, thought that this was all perfectly legal (and, sadly, it almost certainly was) and that he was on to a very good thing. But the police had other ideas. One evening there was a heavy knock on the door and Dad was faced by a large policeman who said, 'We know what you're doing and I'm here to tell you that if you don't stop immediately I'll have you inside before your feet have touched the ground.' As far as I know, the police never explained the legalities of the situation but Dad, having just a suspicion that discretion may be the better part of valour, stopped.

So Dad's dream of a fortune was dispelled and he went back to his day job as a foreman at the Eagle Pencil factory. He didn't much like his job, as it was boring and dirty; but he worked hard at it because he always felt he owed it to his employer. That work ethic stayed with him all his life and there is no doubt that Geoff inherited, or learned it from him. However, Dad's heart was set on greater things. He had left school (Silver Street High, he called it, because you had to go up a flight of steps to get in – a lousy joke but it amused him) at the age of thirteen, with no qualifications and only the ability to read and write and to do the most agile mental arithmetic I ever saw. Not enough, in his view. He knew the only way to achieve his ambitions was to educate himself, which he set out to do, spending every Saturday and Sunday in Highgate library reading philosophy, religion and politics.

What follows is a story that Dad told Geoff, Mark and me, three small, incredulous kids, which I am unable to verify and have always taken with a very large pinch of salt. Dad, like Geoff, was an inveterate embellisher of stories and could quite easily convince himself that they were true. He said he was browsing through the religion section of the library and took down a book written by Madame Blavatsky, who was quite well known at the time and wrote on the subject of theosophy, a mystic religion based on the sacred writings of Brahmanism and Buddhism. As he took the book from the shelf, he found a man standing at his shoulder, who asked him if he had read Blavatsky before. When he replied that he hadn't the mysterious stranger asked if he would like to learn more. 'Yes,' said Dad, cautiously. 'I think I would.' 'When you are ready to learn,' said the stranger, 'somebody will come to teach you. Follow me.' After a short walk, they arrived in a small house that was a cross between Dr Jekyll's laboratory and the film set of *Dracula*, where the teaching and philosophical discussion began.

Dad visited countless times after that and there he met many well-known thinkers of the day, with whom he argued and discussed and began to form a view that nothing in the world was impossible. One unlikely story he told us – although I think Dad really believed it had happened – concerned a demonstration of what Madame Blavatsky referred to as 'kinetic energy'. (Madame Blavatsky was very big in kinetic energy.) His mysterious mentor laid a large iron bar on the table and, without the aid of anything except the power of his thought, moved it so that it fell clattering to the floor. Well, that was the story.

It was not too long before Dad began to turn his thoughts away from religion and towards ethics and politics, although I discovered after his death that he was buying books from the Blavatsky Trust as late as 1976, which was shortly before he died. He was an intelligent man and soon became very knowledgeable. He wanted to share his new-found visions with everybody, so, being talkative, he would argue deep into the night with his friends or, indeed, anybody who would listen to him. He became, like Geoff in later life, a rabid socialist and even joined the Communist Party for a time. He also dispensed his knowledge and his radical views through the Workers Educational Association, for whom he frequently lectured all over London. No doubt influenced by him, when Mark, Geoff and I grew old enough to have opinions of our own we too would sit up into the small hours of the morning debating and arguing about ethics and politics. The example Dad set us was the bedrock of Geoff's passion for sharing his knowledge with people in an unassuming way. And it was because of Dad that Geoff knew that inside the majority of his viewers and readers there beat the heart of a Cyril Reuben Ham, East End kid made good, with a thirst to learn and improve his life.

During his time at the Eagle Pencil factory Dad was constantly looking for more congenial work. It was a very difficult time, but he landed a job with Kreitman's shoe factory, then one of the biggest footwear manufacturers in the country. He was put in charge of the dispatch department and became good friends with Hymen Kreitman, the tall, good-looking son of the owner, and a very sharp Jewish lad. Hymen eventually married Irene Cohen, a daughter of Jack Cohen, who owned a number of market stalls and open-fronted shops selling surplus NAAFI groceries, with a first-day turnover of £4 and a profit of £1. He was to go on to found the mighty Tesco empire and Hymen Kreitman eventually became chief executive. We still wonder what Dad's future might have been had Hymen offered him a job.

So Dad divided his time between the library, his job at Kreitman's footwear factory and the local boxing club. He was not the best boxer but he got as far as the first round of the ABA Championships. Sadly, he was knocked out in the first round by a man half his height, which put a decisive end to his boxing career. The fact is that he was not a good sportsman at all. He was painfully thin and lacking in co-ordination, which made it difficult for him to succeed in any sport. I can't tell you how many times, after we had moved from London, that Geoff and I were taken to watch Dad play for our local village cricket team, full of expectation, because he was the world's most avid optimist, only to see him bowled first ball and fumble his catches – but with an enthusiasm and good humour that were a joy to behold.

His great happiness at that time lay in working for the Kreitman family. They were, like many of the Jewish people I was later to meet, warm, friendly, generous-hearted people who treated all their staff like members of the family but seemed to have an especially soft spot for Dad. It was this experience, I think, which laid the foundation for his own solid backing of the members of his own family and the view he taught Geoff and me: if it's family, it's important and you must do anything to help them out of trouble and to show solidarity. Geoff took this philosophy to heart, to the extent that it would cause him sometimes no little heartache and often the expenditure of large amounts of money. But more of that later.

The only thing that was missing from Dad's life at this stage was what Hollywood would have called the 'love interest', but one momentous day in 1928 he was walking past the Pitman College for typing and shorthand in Southampton Row when he saw, walking out of the front door, a girl who took his breath away. He thought her so beautiful that he had to find out where she lived, so he followed at a discreet distance until she reached her house in Tollet Street. Remember that he had been imbued with the philosophy that nothing was impossible, so he bought himself a new suit and sent her a huge bunch of flowers, with a note asking for an introduction. His note went unanswered but he bought another huge bunch of flowers and this time sent it to Pitman's, with a similar note. 'Well,' he would say later, 'it seemed a pity to waste a good suit.' This went on for some time, with alternate flowers, chocolates and perfume. I don't know what Rose thought (he had discovered her name by charming the Pitman's receptionist), but find me a girl whose curiosity would not be aroused by such flattery and attention. Eventually he took up his courage and knocked on the door of 30 Tollet Street. He was reluctantly invited in, but he knew that, once inside, he could charm both the parents and Rose. His charm was founded in a simple expedient which he later taught to Geoff and me when our own hormones were beginning to stir. His advice was: 'If you want to get a girl interested in you, talk exclusively about her. She will then talk avidly and unceasingly about herself and come away saying what a good conversationalist you are.' Cynical you may say. Sexist even. But if you really want any people, male or female, to take an interest in what you have to say, give it a try. I can assure you it works.

Rose, nine years younger than Cyril, was an elegant graceful girl who, aware of her good looks, dressed in the latest fashions and cultivated perfect manners and style. She had been educated at Coborn School for Girls in Bow, which was considered to provide the best education in the area. It must have set our grandfather back a pretty penny, so he and Grandmother thought it was essential that she learned all the social skills that went with being a lady.

After leaving school Rose became a trainee shorthand typist, working for a small building firm called Charles P. Kitchen who helped to finance her through Pitman's College. Being a shorthand typist in those days was quite an upper-crust kind of job, especially for a girl from the East End, and, judging by some of the letters I still have from her boss, she was very well regarded, so she must have been conscientious and good at her job.

Dad simply fell madly in love with her and he determined that he would eventually marry her – but he knew it would be an uphill struggle. She was an only child, with doting parents and a Jewish father who, whilst not orthodox by any means, still felt that a nice Jewish boy would be better for his Rosie. But Father, undaunted, loaded up his powerful arsenal of charm and set to work.

He talked to the old man about taxis, routes round London and Jewish people he knew. He talked to the old lady about her cooking, her dressmaking and, of course, her beautiful daughter. He played cards and chess with the older fellows who came to visit Gramp and he never took a penny off them, partly because he nearly always let them win. Oh, he was a schmoozer, our Dad. Little by little he became accepted as a regular visitor. Our mother told us that he wooed her like Rudolph Valentino, with flowers and serenades and visits to the theatre and to the music halls, where they would sit and eat rejects from the local chocolate factory. He ingratiated himself further with Gramp by arriving at the house from time to time, usually on a Friday night, with a few bottles of stout and a carton of jellied eels or maybe a packet of salt beef sandwiches from the kosher restaurant in the Mile End Road, for a cockney supper and a game of cards.

Mother loved him because he was always well dressed and magnificently generous, although where he got the money from only he and his Maker knew. The only thing I can be sure of was that he came by his money honestly, because honesty was an obsession with him. 'Straight down the middle, boys,' he would tell us when we were older. Above all, though, she loved him because he was funny. He never stopped laughing all his life and the joy he spread around him was an instant attraction for an impressionable young girl. He also had the very good sense never to disclose how thin and stick-like his legs were! It was something that Geoff and I inherited from him and I can vouch for the fact that it is a feature best kept hidden.

He wrote the most mellifluous if florid love letters to Mother, which she kept hidden away all her life. I hope she would forgive me if I disclose an example. In one letter he says, 'Darling, when will you realise that you are my all and my one thought and desire? Why do I love you? God knows and God alone knows how helpless I am in your embrace. Sweetheart you are mine. You were ordained to be mine before you were born . . .' Well, if you think *I* have a florid writing style, you now know where I got it from!

Early in 1932, Cyril asked Rose to marry him and she accepted. Now there was cause for rejoicing, so out came the lockshen soup and the gefüllte fish and there was joy throughout the land – well, throughout 30 Tollet Street, anyway. On 31 July 1932 they were married. Cyril was a stylist, so he didn't want a honeymoon where every other cockney went – Southend. No, he took his bride to Bournemouth instead – in those days the height of luxury. Afterwards they came back to live with Rose's family in Tollet Street.

The person Cyril found he had married, when the initial romance had matured into love and regard (although the romance never died for the whole of their long marriage), was a resolute woman with a

11

sharp mind and a burning ambition to succeed. She would stand shoulder to shoulder with her husband until she had achieved her objectives. Together they made a formidable pair who, despite harder times than most of us ever get to see these days, seemed to be undaunted by anything. Cyril worked hard to build their lives together, forsaking the Highgate library at the weekend to work at a whole variety of jobs – selling coal 'on the knocker', as they used to call door-to-door selling in the East End, selling brushes for the Kleeneze Brush Company, even delivering greengrocery with a horse and cart. He had no pretensions about being anything but working class and he believed that the only way he would ever improve his circumstances was through hard work and just a little low cunning. For example, he would play cards and chess, knowing he was pretty good at both, with people whom he knew to be not so good, and place a small bet on each game. He usually won enough to buy a box of chocolates or a bunch of flowers, or even a carton of jellied eels, which would be enjoyed on Friday night with the family.

Their peaceful Friday nights were not to last for very long because on 25 July 1933 their first son Barry Mark was born and the endless round of sleepless nights and dirty nappies began, just as for any other parent. No amount of hard work or low cunning would stop these, and the flow of money now had to be increased also, so Cyril had to work even harder. By the time he was three Mark (he later dropped the name Barry and is known only as Mark, because he, like many people, disliked his name intensely) had become a handful; being an only child, with a doting mother and grandmother close at hand to attend to his every wish, he became demanding. For example, he would stand outside the toyshop window on one of the frequent walks his father would organise and scream for a toy. Something had to be done! So one day when he did this Dad warned him that if he continued he would leave him there and go home without him. The screaming continued. So Dad resolutely turned for home and left him there. When he arrived home and told her where he was, Mother was distraught at the loss of her little darling and ran up the road to find him. There he was, still weeping at the toyshop window, and Mother caught him up and rushed him home. When he saw Father sitting in his chair, he gave him the most resentful look a little boy of three could muster and murmured, through pouting lips, 'No toy!' But he never did it again. Of course nobody would dream of doing that now, but Father knew that his little charge was surrounded by people he knew in the street and that he would come to no harm.

Mark's only-child status changed, of course, when he was three and Geoff and I were born. Poor Mark was totally bewildered by our arrival and I am sure he found it quite difficult to handle, although now he has the good grace to deny that it had any effect on him at all. Our mother told us in later life how, when she walked out with Geoff and me in our double pram, people would stop and admire us with effusive compliments and pay no heed whatever to Mark, who later would appeal for attention with questions like 'Aren't I beautiful too, Mummy?' I can't believe that that kind of blow to a small boy's burgeoning self-esteem had no effect. Mind you, he was to grow up to be not only more beautiful but also more athletic, more intelligent, more musical and more talented in practically every way than either Geoff or me. Perhaps this was partly because our birth planted in his mind a feeling of intense competitiveness, which we were going to have to battle against for much of our later lives. Or perhaps there is a celestial arbiter after all.

I don't remember – and nor could Geoff – anything of our days in London, except lying in the big, black double pram that would stand in the hallway, where our mother would let us rest in the afternoon. At least, that was the idea. The rests, however, were punctuated by Geoff suddenly leaning forward, grabbing a tuft of my hair and pulling it out with a triumphant cry of 'Dot some!' I'm glad to say that these aggressive instincts towards me died down in later life but Geoff certainly had the more powerful personality, though he learned to use it for generous, good-humoured and protective ends.

One of Mother's ambitions was to live outside London and about eighteen months after we were born, Father decided that it was time to try to fulfil her wish. His income at Kreitman's shoe factory was rising and he felt he could afford to move. So he set out to look for a small house to rent somewhere in what he regarded as the country. He ended up in Broxbourne in Hertfordshire and, sure enough, true to the old man's inevitable luck, he found a modest semi-detached house at 34 New Road. Fearing that he might lose it if he delayed, he immediately signed the rental agreement and took possession of the keys. On the train on the way back to Liverpool Street station, he began to reflect on the fact that Rose hadn't even seen the house and he hadn't told her they were moving. She had never lived anywhere else but Tollet Street, except for a short spell in rented accommodation in Chingford, where Mark had been born, so he had some anxiety about her reaction to the news. In the event, she was furious. She insisted on travelling out the following day to see the house and her first reaction was one of complete repugnance. She disliked the fact that it was so quiet, she disliked the fact that it was so far from her parents and she had no idea how they were going to look after the large garden.

She couldn't foresee that she would grow to love the house, the area and the neighbours, that it would provide the perfect home for her three kids and that we would spend more than twenty idyllic years there. Just a few years after we had moved our kindly landlord, Mr Hodgkin, sold the house to Father for the princely sum of £400. The house and our family were to become the base that built the foundation of our childhood happiness. Geoff and I often used to reflect, when we got older, on what an enormous privilege it is to be born into a family that is warm and loving and to grow up in a house filled with laughter and music, as ours was. Money and material wealth will, of course, make you comfortable, but wealth alone will never make you happy, as many a rich or acquisitive man could confirm. We were small people with small aspirations and very little wealth, but our solidarity and care for each other gave us a life many will never know and gave us security and confidence that Geoff and I were to value all our lives.

CHAPTER 2

A Misspent Youth

BROXBOURNE, WHEN WE FIRST MOVED THERE in 1938, was a sleepy country village. At the top of our road, New Road, was Mr Frogley's farm and he would drive his cows past our house, No. 34, every day. The village was surrounded by fields and woodland, with lots of magical places in which little boys could construct adventures, live out their imaginations and so expand their minds and aspirations. Geoff and I began to live a kind of bumpkin existence that we both came to love, although as we had no memories of London, it was for us as though we had always lived in the country.

Geoff and I were, at this stage in our lives, inextricably bound together – we did everything together, we went everywhere together, we shared all our delights, our tribulations and even, later, our girlfriends although we did have a few fights amongst ourselves as well. His story is also my story, so I hope I can be forgiven here for appropriating bits of Geoff's biography, as it's impossible to separate the two.

Early memories are few, except for the traumas. Geoff and I had whooping cough at the same time and remembered it as distressing but attracting a plenitude of sympathy and comfort and therefore to be prolonged for as long as possible. Geoff had what Mother called 'scarletina', which he disappointedly saw as a less serious form of

15

scarlet fever, only to find, when he was a teenager and looked it up in the dictionary, that the two terms mean the same thing. Much to his regret, it was too late by then to attract suitable sympathy; nevertheless, because 'scarlet fever' sounded like a disease that Jim Hawkins might have contracted on Treasure Island it raised his level of pride considerably. It's strange that most people derive some form of self-satisfaction about diseases and surgical procedures from which they have recovered, as though some significant credit is due to them, and Geoff was no exception.

Geoff had, as I do, very clear memories of the Second World War and the effect it had on the family. We first became aware of the situation when blackout blinds appeared at the windows and pieces of hessian sacking were nailed to the top of the doorframes and hung down over the door. We were completely puzzled by this (we were only three years old), but we later learned that it was a device that would be soaked in water in the event of a gas attack, to prevent the gas getting into the room.

Geoff, Mark and I were put to sleep each night with our heads in the toy cupboard in the kitchen, with the table pushed up against it to protect the rest of our bodies, in case of a bombing raid. Mark remembers the very first air-raid warning. He reports that we had two visitors at the time, Ken and Betty Scorer, who were friends of our parents. When the alarm sounded, the response of the two women was hysteria – letting out shrieks and shouts that would themselves have provided an effective weapon against the Germans, crying, slapping each other on the face and lying in a heap on the floor. Meanwhile Ken and Father filled buckets with water and began throwing it at the hessian hanging across the door. We three boys, of course, thought the world had gone mad and were relieved when a sense of proportion returned to the house and things got back to normal.

Father, of course, had to register for the services or for war work, which he did immediately. When confronted by the registrar, he was asked what skills he had. 'Well,' he said, 'I've managed a shoe factory and been a salesman.' 'Not a lot of use for salesmen,' said the registrar.

'What did you do at school?' 'The three Rs,' said Father. 'What did you do with your hands?' asked the registrar. 'Well, I did a bit of woodwork.' 'Right,' said the registrar, 'skilled carpenter.' I never asked why he had not been called into the armed forces, but it was probably on medical grounds. He was still painfully thin and certainly didn't display signs of glowing good health. He was directed to work as a carpenter for the RAF, initially at Broxbourne aerodrome, a small airfield with a grass strip which was a repair base for Spitfires and Hurricanes.

Father was paid £5 a week for this work, which wasn't enough to keep a family of three in the lap of luxury, so Mother went to work in a small electrical and wireless shop in Hoddesdon, our nearest town. This meant that she had to find a way of dealing with the care of Geoff and me during her working hours, Mark by then being at school. So she found us a place in a nursery school in a priory in the town. We had no fear at all of the war, simply because Mother and Dad were there, which, quite irrationally, we translated as complete security. But we were terrified of the nuns. I'm sure they were kindness itself and I have no memories of any kind of physical or mental abuse, but to see these huge, black-clad creatures swooping down on us frightened us out of our wits. However, we survived and neither Geoff nor I carried any kind of nun-fixation into later life so the experience did us no harm. Geoff was later to landscape a new garden in the priory and he found it a most moving experience – not because of childhood memories but because the nuns were, in fact, not frightening figures but gentle people full of wisdom, compassion and (I hope you will keep this from the Pope) mischievous fun.

In 1941 it was time to go to primary school. Broxbourne School was a Church of England school on the edge of the village, about a mile from our house. Geoff and I would walk there each morning, past the big, affluent houses in Churchfields, across the main road, past the church and along the canal-side until we reached the school gates. I am quite sure that no parent would allow their five-year-old children to do such a walk today. What a pity that is. What adventures we had on that walk: sword fights with sticks we had picked up in the lane; running away from Jim Smith, the 'big boy' whose sole purpose in life, we were sure, was to beat us up (in fact he was a good-hearted lad of about ten and had no designs on us whatsoever); identifying the numerous German spies we were sure inhabited the village; and countless other flights and fights of imagination – none of which you could do strapped into the back of a Volvo, as kids are today.

Broxbourne School's policy was not only to teach facts but to teach poetry and literature and music and art and science – all with austerity money and nothing but dedicated teachers with kind hearts, left to get on with it in the best way they could. It seems to me, on later reflection, that Miss Cox, the headmistress, must have made a conscious decision that there were two other vital elements to good teaching. One was discipline, and she ruled with a rod of iron, and the other was happiness, which she found a way of distributing like confetti at a wedding. The school shaped our young lives in an atmosphere of respect and care. Geoff remembered it, as I do, with great affection and gratitude.

At the school we met Stanley Price, a remarkable boy, who could ride his bicycle backwards, sitting the wrong way round on the handlebars, and who could stand on the saddle without falling off. Geoff lived in awe of Stanley Price all his life; he ended his career a very successful man but, try as he might, he never learned to ride his bicycle backwards. We didn't keep in touch with Stanley Price but I hope he did well. He deserved it, although it is hard to think of an outlet for boys who can ride their bicycle backwards. There was Michael Lanchberry, who was prepared to stand in the playground beside the huge pile of coke we had for fuel, while we threw lumps of it at him. He was the finest coke-dodger in the business, for I never saw him hit. We had Freddie Simpson, the scourge of Station Road, who would terrorise small boys, but always steered clear of Geoff and me because he knew that if he took on one he would have to take on the other as well.

We also had a German school doctor. It never occurred to us to question the fact that a German was administering medicine to us, even though we were conditioned to believe that all Germans were evil. (It was good to learn in later life that this was propaganda and by no means true.) Had we had any fears, they would have been allayed by the fact that he never actually gave us any medicine. He seemed to have only one remedy for all ills. After your examination for suspected diphtheria, smallpox or bubonic plague he would pronounce in his strong German accent, 'Milk of magnesia – tell your mum.' I think a broken limb would have received the same treatment but fortunately we never had occasion to put it to the test.

It was at Broxbourne School that we began to feel the first stirrings of romantic love. During the lunch breaks, in the long, hot summers that were, of course, standard issue in those days, we would lie in the long grass beside the air-raid shelters, eating 'vinegar leaves' (sorrel – sweets were unobtainable), with Pamela Grist, Maureen Tyler, Janet Gardener, Brenda Gale, etc., expressing undying love for each other with a sincerity that was deeply felt but had, at all costs, to be concealed from Stanley Price and especially from Freddie Simpson. Our love was intense and innocent, unsullied by lust, although Geoff did once confess to me an overwhelming desire to touch Anne Sykes's knickers. I never discovered the truth about this, but I sincerely hope he achieved his objective. Janet Speller, a girl I actually fancied more than somewhat, recently told me that she felt we were far too good looking for her to set her cap at either of us. Oh, how misguided can a girl be!

The war was nothing but an excitement to us. At school we would get called out of lessons when the sirens sounded and file into the shelters, where we would play word games, sing songs or, if the teachers were in need of rest, play kiss-chase along the dark, dank corridors.

The greatest excitement of all came on the day we captured the German pilot. Well, we didn't exactly capture him with our own bare hands, but we were certainly instrumental in his apprehension. We were standing one day on the top of the shelters watching a dogfight between a Spitfire and a German fighter, urging on our side as innocently as if we were at a football match. We all read comics like the *Rover* and the *Hotspur* and were very familiar with the exploits of Rockfist Rogan, ace pilot. The stories always started with lines like,

'Rat-tat-tat-tat-tat – Rockfist thumbed the button of his Browning cannon and watched in satisfaction as a stream of bullets tore into the Hun fighter ahead and it spiralled down in a cloud of black smoke.' So we were confident that the Spitfire would win the day and, sure enough, the German fighter was eventually hit and we watched it falling to earth. The pilot baled out and we saw him parachute to the ground beside the river. Then, as we watched, he filled his parachute with stones and threw it into the river, with the clear intention of making his escape. We ran to Miss Cox and told her, whereupon she phoned the police and we rushed back to the shelters. The German pilot was still there and before many minutes had elapsed we saw a black police car coming down the towpath to capture their man. A couple of days later a police sergeant came to the school to thank us for our patriotic efforts and we all felt as though we had just won the war single-handed. Rockfist Rogan strikes again!

At home, as the war ground on we grew too big for the toy cupboard, so we were transferred to the cupboard under the stairs, which was very exciting because we could clearly hear the wireless in the kitchen, which made us more aware of the progress of the war. This still didn't seem to induce any feelings of fear, even though we could hear the buzz bombs. These would drone overhead and suddenly stop; then, after a moment of silence while they dropped to earth, we would hear the explosion, which fortunately for us, was usually distant. Nevertheless we occasionally went into school to find that one of our friends was missing and we were then given a sombre announcement in the school hall.

One night, at about 2.00 a.m. we were suddenly woken by a thunderous knocking on the front door. This time we were afraid. We lay trembling in the cupboard, fearing German soldiers at the door, and Father came running down the stairs to open it. There on the doorstep were our grandparents, covered in soot and dirt from head to toe and clutching small suitcases. With a quirky little smile, Gramp said, 'We've been bombed out. Can we have a room for the night?' They had been in an Underground station when the bomb dropped and in fact the house in Tollet Street was only partially damaged, so they were able to gather a few belongings before they came to our house. There was no transport, so they had had to walk the twenty miles or so from Stepney to Broxbourne. On the way they had agreed that living in London had now become too dangerous to be sensible. So, completely undaunted by what he regarded as a minor setback, Gramp went off the following day, found a house to rent close by and bought himself a bicycle so that he could get to his cab, which was undamaged. He couldn't get the petrol to drive to and from London, so for the rest of the war he cycled there, twenty miles there and twenty miles back, every day. He had the kind of Jewish stoicism born of thousands of years of persecution and there was no German who would ever cause him to slacken his stride.

Geoff and I caused a little consternation on the day we found an unexploded bomb. Walking home from school one day, aged about seven, we found a bomb lying under a hedge. Geoff, of course, immediately took command and ordered *me* to guard the bomb and to keep civilians away, while *he* ran home to get Dad. He was always the general in our little army and a superb strategist, particularly if it kept him out of trouble. When he arrived home, breathless, and told the story, Dad, filled with alarm, left his meal of sausage and mash and tore back to the site of the bomb on his old bicycle, to find me marching backwards and forwards, keeping civilians away. We were surprised to see him bend down, pick the bomb out of the hedge and wave it angrily in our faces. It was the ball off a ball-cock valve from a lavatory cistern. Well, it looked like the bombs in the *Beano* and the *Dandy*. It just didn't have 'BOMB' written on the side.

The war caused privations for everybody, rich and poor, but it was certainly worse for the poor. Even with Mother's wages, Father simply couldn't provide for his family, so he did what he had always done – he worked longer and harder and smarter than most. Because of the restrictions of the war he couldn't do anything very adventurous, so he set himself up as an odd-job man, doing bits of carpentry, gardening, repair work, etc. On one occasion he was asked to repair an antique bed for an extremely rich, noble lady who lived in a huge mansion close to Broxbourne. He explained that it would take a week to dismantle it and reassemble it with the faulty parts repaired, although he knew that it actually only needed gluing and cramping to make the joints solid again. It took the first night to complete the work and he spent the remaining four nights sitting in the room, occasionally banging on the floor with his hammer to give the impression of work, and the following Friday he collected a week's money. When we were older, we were inflamed by the injustice of his action but, when we tackled him about it he said, 'My family had no money and she had plenty. I did a good job, but just charged a little more. Think of it as a redistribution of wealth.' Well, he was a socialist and he felt no guilt about what he had done, although when times were better he would not have dreamed of doing it again.

To save the family money he dug up the whole of the garden so that he could put it down to vegetables. He dug up the lawn, the flowerbeds, the little rose arbour – everything. He built a chicken house at the end of the garden and from then onwards we lived well, on vegetables and eggs which supplemented the meagre rations allocated by the Ministry of Food. This, I believe, was where Geoff's love of gardening began because, although we were diminutive creatures, we were pressed into weeding, sowing and harvesting duties, and we loved it.

So for six years of our young lives Geoff and I knew nothing but war – hearing the crump of anti-aircraft fire and the scream of incendiary bombs, sleeping in shelters, listening out for the ominous wail of the sirens and breathing sighs of relief at the 'all clear', becoming used to the sight of barrage balloons and portentous notices warning that 'Careless Talk Costs Lives'. But for us this was all the life we had known, and it did not worry us or impinge on our happiness.

At the height of the bombing in London, around 1943, Father was posted to an RAF station at the Lizard in Cornwall. He worried greatly about being away from us all at such a hazardous time, but there was little he could do about it. But he was able to arrange for us to stay at a farmhouse owned by Mr and Mrs Jeffreys, near Porthleven for the whole of one summer. It was an enchanted summer, filled with excitement and peace and unforeseen delights. There were two children in the family: Jim, who was about fourteen and worked on the farm, and Thelma, who was about a year older than us. Geoff fell in love with Thelma at first sight, but then Geoff fell in love with any number of girls at first sight at that age. We would spend the lovely hot days searching for eggs the chickens had laid about the yard, helping to hand-milk the cows, fishing with Jim in his small boat, wandering the high-banked, flower-covered lanes or just lying in the long grass talking of pirates and spies and adventures to come. It was a small, poorish farm, but the quality of the Jeffreys' lives was high and Geoff and I came back with some childishly romantic but firmly rooted views about how we wanted to live in the future.

To supplement the family income, Mother and Dad decided to take in a lodger, Fred Taib, who owned the shop where Mother worked. He never entered an air-raid shelter for the whole of the war, partly I believe because he seemed to be perpetually and terminally tired and it was simply too much trouble. So he pulled his bed away from the wall about two feet and he put a double mattress and pillows underneath. When the siren sounded he would roll out of bed, still half asleep, drop on to the bed beneath and sleep through the raid. As soon as we heard the sirens wail, we three boys, lying in the cupboard under the stairs, would wait expectantly for the thump as he fell to safety, when we would collapse into giggles.

Fred had other little eccentricities, which he would practise on us. He persuaded us to leap on to chairs when Mother entered the room, raise our arms in supplication and shout, 'Madame Pompadour!' He would wait until we were in bed and whispering softly to each other in the dark, and then slowly open the door a fraction and slide his hand over the wall, as though looking for the light switch – a ghostly, terrifying sound which made our blood run cold. Then he would glide silently away, leaving us wondering what or who our intruder had been. He also taught us to play chess, listen to good music and make crystal wireless sets. But his most exciting ploy happened on Christmas Day each year he lived with us. He would stand on the landing at the top of the stairs and shout 'Scramble' as he tipped a large box full of small change and another full of sweets, and then watch us scrabbling for our share in the hall below. He must have saved the money from his shop during the year but where he got sweets from I don't know, because there were none in the shops. If it was black marketeering it was the most generous kind there could be.

As well as Fred Taib's constantly entertaining presence we were surrounded by many unusual, almost surreal people. There was Mr Wentworth who would come to play his violin to entertain us. Geoff and I would watch in fascination as he contorted his large chin into the most extraordinary shapes as his emotion got the better of him, silvery strings of saliva slowly emerging from his tortured mouth. There were Rosa and Stephen Hobhouse, she a poet who came be-caped to the house, quoting poetry as she strode up the path, and he a tall, thin ascetic who wrote impenetrable books on philosophy and would argue with Father for hours. Mother always claimed he willed himself to die, but we were never able to prove it. There was lovely, kindly Mr Small, small in stature as well as name but not in heart, who would bring his cello from his house across the road to make up a trio with Mr Wentworth and Mother, who played the piano.

But the element that affected us most was the ever-present laughter, which seemed to shape our lives with optimism and confidence. Geoff's sharp and wicked sense of humour came, without a doubt, from our dear old dad. He was constantly playing tricks on us, joking with us and occasionally having jokes at our expense, the meaning of which we didn't always realise until years had passed. For example, one day we ran down New Road and into Churchfields to meet Dad, who we knew would be cycling back from the aerodrome where he worked. It was a cold winter day and, when we met him, we saw that he was holding his handlebars with one hand and had the other behind his back. We understood later that it was because he only had one glove and he changed them over from time to time, keeping his spare hand as warm as he could by holding it behind his back, but it puzzled us. So Geoff, ever the forward one, said, 'Dad, why do you ride with one hand on the handlebars and the other behind your back?' Without a smile he said in grave tones, 'Son, never let your left hand know what your right hand's doing!' and pedalled on with no further explanation, leaving two perplexed little boys behind him. We

24

now know, of course, that the old devil was making the joke for his *own* benefit, a thing Geoff came to do as he got older.

Dad would fool our mother with 'literary quotations' which came entirely from his own head and had only a tenuous foundation in literature but which poor old Mother would accept with her good heart and a proud smile. For example, after a meal Mother would say, 'Have you had enough, dear?' to which he would reply, gravely and gratefully, 'Sufficient is enough unto the day thereof,' with a sly wink to us when Mother wasn't looking, and she would be entirely taken in.

On 8 May 1945, the armistice in Europe was signed – VE Day. There seemed to be an endless round of parties – parties at school, parties in the street, parties in our friends' houses – and such a buoyant air of optimism it was hard to be anything but ecstatic.

VJ Day, 15 August 1945, was the final end to the Second World War and our ninth birthday. By this time Father had a car, an old Morris Isis, which he had bought for £1 from a farmer who was keeping chickens in it. Father cleaned it out and got it going, with the help of his friends, and it became the family car. The Morris Isis was the Rolls-Royce of the Morris range, a small limousine, so we thought ourselves pretty lucky. Father needed it because by this time he had been posted to De Havillands in Hatfield; it was too far away for him to cycle there, and he was allocated a ration of petrol because he was engaged in war work. So, as a birthday treat, he took us all up to London to join the VJ Day celebrations. We travelled through the utter devastation of bombed buildings and cratered roads, but in the centre of London the scene was unbelievable. The streets were so crowded with people it was almost impossible to get the car through – servicemen in uniform, office girls in tin hats, kids in Mickey Mouse gas masks, all waving flags, shouting, dancing, bands playing, people drunk on booze and people drunk on joy. When we stopped the car and joined them we clung tightly to our parents but were nevertheless assailed by good-hearted people giving us lemonade and sticky buns, American soldiers giving us chocolate and chewing gum, street sellers giving us fruit, until we felt we would burst with the wonder of it all.

Gradually the euphoria wore off for our parents, as it did for everybody else, as the post-war austerity began to bite, but it is to their great credit that Geoff and I had no inkling that life was hard. Somehow they managed to feed and clothe us just as well as the better-off kids in the area – a signal of status that was very important to Mother. She was utterly determined to shake off the cloak of her East End background and her three boys were her badge of success. As long as we were healthy, looked good and behaved like perfect gentlemen she could hold up her head. Oh, if only she knew what we got up to when she wasn't around!

Our most abiding memory of being young after the war was of the extraordinary freedom we were given – to roam the countryside, to go on long hikes or bicycle rides to faraway places, to mix with people of all ages and kinds without restriction, even to take the train, alone, to London to buy coveted items from the Scout shop in Buckingham Palace Road or to see other exciting places. Our parents loved and protected us with great tenderness and care, but they were careful not to smother us and restrict our adventures. That freedom gave us a self-reliance and independence that both Geoff and I came to see as their most important gift to us.

Gradually our days of innocent romance – we could fall in and out of love with little girls faster than you can blink – gave way to longer attachments, even though we were still very young indeed. One of my earliest memories of Geoff's domination of me was when we were riding our bikes down St Michael's Road one day, at about the age of nine, and he put it to me that it would be much more convenient if I was in love not with Pamela Grist, my current heart-throb, but with Janet Cleverley, who was a friend of *his* girlfriend. And even then he had such charisma that I immediately and dutifully fell in love with Janet Cleverley. As it happened I stayed in love with her for a long time, until her father, a pig farmer, caught us in the back of his very smelly van, talking quite innocently, and suggested, in the friendliest possible terms that if he caught me with his daughter again he would break my back. I was always one to see the logic of a well-expressed argument, so I complied with astonishing speed.

★ ★ ★

One of our great delights was reading. Geoff and I would spend many a Saturday morning browsing through Loveday's, the junk shop in Hoddesdon, going through the second-hand books and carrying back prizes like *The Last of the Mohicans* or *White Fang*, and of course we devoured all the Arthur Ransome books, including *Swallows and Amazons*. This, I think, gave us not only a life-long taste for good literature, but also a taste for adventure. We desperately wanted to live like Red Indians or Canadian trappers or explorers so, from the age of about nine, when our friends were playing rugby or cricket, neither of which were we good at, we would spend a lot of our time in the woods, watching birds and animals, lighting fires and cooking meals, and generally emulating our heroes as much as we could.

Our discovery of the Boy Scouts put a whole new perspective on life and gave us a new set of heroes. I was put into the Owl Patrol, where I had the great good fortune to have a patrol leader called Keith Sinclair, whom I still thank for making a marked impression on the lives of both Geoff and me. Keith was the kind of person in whom one could have implicit trust. He was a big chap, a smallholder's son, whose work had given him huge, rough, capable hands and a personality to match. No matter how hard the conditions or tough the position we found ourselves in, it would be OK because Keith was there. He was an excellent leader who took his duties seriously and would often organise adventures in the woods and the fields, camping, hiking, and playing what were then called 'wide games', which usually involved getting from A to B without capture, or finding your way over difficult terrain in the dark or hunting for treasure through the interpretation of clues. Through his towering intelligence and courage he taught Geoff and me to face life's trials with self assurance, which stood us in good stead for the rest of our lives. I wish there were more Keith Sinclairs about and more groups like the Owl Patrol, to build the same spirit into all kids.

Geoff, on the other hand, had the misfortune to land in the Badger Patrol, led by our elder brother Mark. At the time we didn't get on too well with Mark, so poor old Geoff suffered a bit. During the early stages of our childhood, up to our early teens, our relationship with

Mark was not good. I think Mark felt a deep resentment of us because we were so close and because we attracted people's attention simply because we looked alike. It certainly was not because we were naturally more attractive than he was: we weren't. He was well built, athletic and attractive, while we were skinny, weedy and ordinary. But we had the invincible strength of union and we used it unmercifully. I still remember, with deep feelings of guilt, planning an attack on Mark with the words, 'You get him down and I'll kick his boil!' We were pretty unfeeling in those days and I don't wonder at all at Mark's antagonism. He and his greatest friend, Jack Christie, once declared war on us and, during the negotiations of the rules of war, we declared that this was to be a 'deadly war', with no holds barred. Geoff and I established our HQ in an air-raid shelter at the end of the lane which ran along the back of our house, where we stored huge piles of cabbage and Brussels sprout stalks to hurl at the enemy from the hatch in the top of the shelter. Mark and Jack would ambush us as we returned home and charge us with boughs of hawthorn trees that they had trimmed from the hedges in the lane, but our great triumph came when we crept up to their HQ, which was in the chicken house that had been used during the war, and tore down their rules of engagement. I confess that I can no longer remember all the rules but the first one sticks in my memory – 'Fires will be dowsed at seven o'clock.' We capitalised on that one for years and even in our adult years we would creep up to Mark, particularly if he was engaged in conversation with a beautiful girl at a party, and whisper, 'Fires will be dowsed at seven o'clock.'

I don't think Geoff or I ever achieved the same degree of closeness with Mark as we had with each other. He was very independent and thus isolated. This was always one of the greatest sorrows and frustrations of Geoff's life and still worries me. We seem now to have tacitly agreed a truce and agreed to live apart but in contact and as friends, which is as close as we are going to get, I'm afraid.

When Geoff and I joined the Scouts, however, our sibling rivalry was at its height, so Geoff joined me and the Owl Patrol on many of our activities outside the regular weekly Troop meeting.

Before long Mark moved on to the Senior Scouts and Geoff eventually became patrol leader of the Badgers and I of the Owls. Now we could run both patrols on the lines that Keith Sinclair had taught us and we entered into the spirit of the job with tremendous enthusiasm. In fact, Keith inspired us not only to pursue the outdoor life with the Scouts but also to have ever more adventurous times on our own, but always together. Often, at the weekends, we would walk the five miles up to the woods on 'survival' trips. We would take no food, cooking utensils, sleeping bags or other items of comfort and safety, just a knife, an axe and some rope. We would build a shelter, fill it with bracken to provide a warm comfortable bed, and live off berries, nuts, rabbits and even hedgehog, an old gypsy dish which, if baked in the embers of a fire tastes a bit like chicken. I would not recommend this practice now, however. I'm on the side of the animal lovers now – but then we were surviving, remember.

One of our more romantic outdoor adventures was set in a lovely area of steep valleys, woods and streams called the Pollards, about three miles from home. It was owned by Admiral Bingley, who had commanded the fleet in the defence of Malta during the war. In a field close to his home was a small blacksmith's forge, now disused but in good repair. It had an old brick floor and a huge fireplace at one end – the ideal place for winter camping. But how to approach the great man to ask his permission? Geoff and I asked ourselves what he would have done himself in such circumstances and, remembering that he was a war hero, we plucked up our courage and knocked on the door of his beautiful old farmhouse to ask if we could use it. I remember him as a big, bluff man with a deep voice and a weather-beaten look, the archetypal admiral – Horatio Hornblower from the top of his tricorn hat to the soles of his knee-boots. He smiled at our impudence, ruffled our hair and immediately agreed – as long as he could come to see us from time to time. And so we would spend the summer months camping in the surrounding fields and the winter in the forge, where we would build a big log fire in the fireplace and sit round it, cooking our food. Don Speller, a member of Geoff's Badger patrol, remembers wonderful nights with us there, sitting round the fire, singing songs and telling stories. I don't think the old admiral ever knew what value we placed on his generosity. It is a sad irony that, having come unscathed through one of the most vicious wars in history, he died in his garden from a bee sting.

Now we were Scouts our new hero was Lord Baden-Powell, our founder and Chief Scout, and we devoured all his advice unquestioningly. For example, in *Scouting for Boys*, our bible, he advises observing the pattern of nails in the boots of tramps and vagabonds sitting at the roadside, in case they are criminals. It never occurred to us that there was a distinct lack of tramps and vagabonds in middle-class Broxbourne to observe, so we kept dutiful eyes open and instructed our patrols to do the same. I still have a book by Baden Powell called *Rovering to Success* (a truly inspiring title), in which in a chapter headed 'Women' he gets as close as his Victorian morals will allow to advising about sex and tells of a Scout who is getting married – to a Girl Guide. 'I see promise in this,' he says, rather tersely. Geoff and I would have hung on his every word at the time. It was only later in life that we marvelled at our naïve acceptance of some of his teaching. Disillusionment set in many years after our scouting career, when we discovered that Baden-Powell had been the original inventor of the concentration camp during the siege of Mafeking. But there is no doubting the immense value of the work he did with the Scout movement, and Geoff and I acknowledged the character-building effect his teaching had on us.

Simultaneously we both won the Queen's Scout award, the highest that could be achieved at the time. Mother was immensely proud, and Father said, 'No more than I would have expected,' which we later saw was a compliment, cleverly phrased to keep our heads to a normal size and our feet on the ground. We were two amongst the first small group of Queen's Scouts ever appointed. Though we boasted about this, there was little credit due to us for this; it was down to the fact that the King had the good grace to die at the opportune moment. We continued scouting for many years as Senior Scouts and Rover Scouts, and finally jointly running the local Cubs pack and then both the Cubs and the Scouts Troop, an experience we both enjoyed and valued. Don Speller remembers us at Gilwell, the inspiring – indeed magical – training centre in Essex, showing small boys how to build shelters and generally take care of themselves in the wild – and also telling them horrifying ghost stories in the twilight hours, before sending them to bed trembling with terror. Perhaps not in the true spirit of comradeship, but we felt we had to get our pleasure where we could.

Running concurrently with our scouting exploits was our membership of St Augustine's Church choir. Mother was quite an accomplished pianist and taught us all to sing. We would gather round the piano and sing ballads and Broadway songs in four-part harmony – enjoyable but never very professional. Though Mark was later to become a professional jazz musician, neither Geoff nor I had much ability with instruments. In fact, when Geoff played (or rather 'scraped') his renowned 'Bluebells of Scotland' on his violin the dog would run howling to the bottom of the garden. However, when Mother made us join St Augustine's choir (when we were seven), although there was much weeping and wailing and gnashing of teeth at the time, both Geoff and I came to be very grateful for her wisdom and foresight. The church choir gave us our first introduction to good music and, if you will allow me to pontificate for just a moment, nothing is more calculated to embed an appreciation of the inspiration and joy of good music than to be surrounded by it at an early age. We were at once engulfed in the towering sounds of a good church organ, the amazing range of *Hymns Ancient and Modern*, and the glory of anthems and oratorios by Handel, Bach, Mendelssohn, Mozart, Haydn, Stainer and dozens of others. We still liked Bing Crosby and Frank Sinatra and we still listened to jazz and swing, but St Augustine's choir introduced us to hitherto unknown treasures.

The church choir was led by Mr Jenkins, or 'Jenks', who was not only a superb musician but also had the ability to inspire and motivate his choir to produce music far beyond their innate capabilities. He had a way of making us laugh or weep, as well as sing, which I believe is the secret of inspirational music. There were about twenty boys in the choir and a dozen men and I can't describe the joy Geoff and I experienced in working together with them to make music.

But I'm afraid that we transgressed. Although we found the singing wonderful, the sermons were invariably boring and dull for little boys. We began throwing paper darts from side to side of the choir stalls, but the vicar soon stamped on that. So Geoff and I sank to the depths of criminality and stole some small books from Woolworth's. They used to do a pocket series of stories on *Sinbad the Sailor* or *The Three Musketeers* and the like, too expensive to buy with our sixpence-a-week pocket money, but if one of us created a diversion it was easy for the other to pinch a book. In time we built up a little library, which we secreted in the choir stall and which kept the whole choir entertained throughout the dreary sermons. I have left an instruction in my will that, when I die, the cost of the books shall be returned to Woolworth's and I can only hope that I shall be forgiven at the Day of Judgement.

As choirboys we wore black cassocks and white surplices, with little white ruffs at our necks. We felt a bit silly in them at first but soon discovered their considerable pulling power as far as the girls were concerned. When we left church on Sunday evening we would usually be greeted by a small entourage of little girls and we would walk them over the river bridge to the Recreation Ground, where we would carry out dark deeds. Actually, looking back on those exploits I blush to say that our deeds were not nearly as dark as they could have been, so perhaps we missed an opportunity there.

The golden gift the choir gave us of the joy of song laid a foundation for lives that were filled with music. In fact Geoff continued to sing all his life, right up to the day he died, and it gave him almost as much pleasure as his gardening.

Another defining moment in our lives came when I was cycling along the towpath of the River Lea, where we used to swim and fish, and a sculling boat from the rowing club on the opposite bank came by. It was being sculled by Tony Scarrow, our scout master, so I made some facetious remark as he passed. He stopped and smiled and asked why Geoff and I didn't join the club. He knew we were skinny little chaps but explained that the club was short of coxswains and we might enjoy it. He suggested that we should meet him at the clubhouse the following evening, and he would introduce us to the captain of boats and propose our membership.

So Geoff and I cycled down, with some trepidation, to meet the captain. His name was Jimmy Dunsmuir and he was a quiet, pipe-smoking man of very few words. 'OK,' he said, 'try them out with Tom Dymock and Geoff Fairs.' Geoff got his namesake and I got Tom. I thought at first that I'd got the thin end of the deal because Tom's language was straight from the barrack room and was a whole new education for me but, in the event, he turned out to be a good-hearted man who became a great friend. Although most of the oarsmen were only in their twenties we, at thirteen, were completely in awe of them, but it was good to be in adult company and it was good to experience the unique pleasure of being in entirely male company.

I think Geoff and I became quite good at coxing, which was appreciated by the people we looked up to so much. They treated us like kings, in the kindliest ways possible, whilst putting up with no nonsense in the boat. If we were rowing we were there to win – none of this 'honour of competing' business. They used to take us to regattas all over the country and buy us meals and sometimes a bed for the night. Each year, for instance, we would enter Worcester regatta on Bank Holiday Saturday and move on to Evesham regatta on the Monday. Travel was difficult in those days, so if we could fit two events into a single journey that was a great advantage. One year we had made an arrangement with Worcester rowing club that they would leave the key of the clubhouse under the doormat for us, so that we could sleep on the clubhouse floor, but when we arrived, late at night, there was no key. We had no phone numbers, so there was no alternative but to sleep in the stands at Worcester racecourse, which was near by. It was cold and uncomfortable and made no better by the fact that we could feel rats scampering all over us. Needless to say we were knocked out in the first heat the following day.

When we got older Geoff and I began to row ourselves and we were probably the most mediocre oarsmen in the history of the sport.

Technically I think we were both reasonably good and, since we rowed every evening and later worked physically every day, we were certainly fit. But we were skinny, and at nine stone six we were never going to make the grade. It is true in rowing that a good big'un will always beat a good littl'un, so while we won now and again, it was much more frequently the case that we trailed home with our tails between our skinny little legs. But the joy of doing it was immense. It was so satisfying to train hard all winter and to greet the spring with a great optimism and a view that this year was going to be our year. It never was, but the pleasure and anticipation never diminished.

Don Speller, our old scouting buddy, was a member of the crew that trained all winter and travelled to regattas during the summer. He recalls that, because we were too young or later too poor to own a car, we would travel either with Mr Beresford-Smith or Harry Sykes. Beresford, as everybody called him, had been practically crippled during his time as a Japanese prisoner of war and he rowed to try to get fit again. He was a great character, with a tremendous spirit, but he had a habit when driving of stretching his game leg by putting one foot on the accelerator and the other on the clutch, and we travelled with him to regattas with spasmodic bursts of the noise of the engine racing so hard we thought we were about to take off. Harry Sykes was no better. A very short, wiry little man with a huge Buick car, he could hardly see over the steering wheel. He was also totally unconcerned about his recklessness, on one occasion getting round a slow-moving lorry by driving through a garage forecourt, on the inside of the truck, emerging just in front, to the sound of furious honking from behind. Harry also became famous for an embarrassing episode at a dinner, when we were guests of the mayor at Sudbury in Suffolk, after a regatta. Sudbury at the time was seriously stuffed with civic pride and the dinner was attended by all the local dignitaries, and one was definitely expected to eat with ones little finger in the raised position. We had been to the pub before the dinner for the traditional filling of the silver pot we had won at the regatta, so we arrived a little late, in itself a serious offence. It was made a little more serious when Harry, who had attended from the start shouted at us, as we were trying to creep to our seats unnoticed, 'Don't eat the fish, boys. It's 'orrible!' We tried desperately to look as though we weren't with him but to little avail, I'm afraid.

We had only one moment of discord in the rowing club that I can remember and Geoff took care of it in his usual exuberant way. We had trained all winter in a four. We weren't good, but had become passable and we had some hopes of winning something. Then one evening in late spring we assembled for a practice and, just as we were getting into the boat, one of our crew told us that he would not be available to row during the summer. Now it's not easy to row a four with only three people, so this was a shattering blow. Nevertheless he condescended to row with us for one last time. Geoff was in the bow seat and, as our reluctant crew mate stepped into the boat Geoff took a small and silent stroke, which swung the boat away from the landing stage just enough for our 'friend' to step not into the boat but into the river. It was a masterstroke and the perfect end to our relationship.

Some years later, Geoff, who continued to live in Broxbourne after I had moved away to work, took up sculling (usually done alone with two oars) and became very good. He won a number of significant races, achieving 'senior' status, and, but for a judging error, would have won the Boston marathon, which is a thirty-six-mile race from Lincoln to Boston and is a tremendous trial of stamina and technique.

After Geoff's death I went back to the rowing club to film a short piece for a television programme on him. It was a Wednesday, which is designated 'Old Fart's Night', so a number of our old friends were there. I met one, John Francis, who explained as he greeted me in the car park that he was now in his seventies and deaf as a post, and I'd have to shout. So I shouted my pleasure at seeing him again and told him I'd see him in the bar later, when we had finished filming. Imagine my surprise when, ten minutes later I saw John carry his sculling boat from the boat shed and watched him scull off at twice the speed I could have managed when I was eighteen. I vowed to get myself fit again – and some day I will.

★ ★ ★

By the time we joined the rowing club we had, of course, left our primary school. Geoff and I passed the eleven plus examination and moved on to Hertford Grammar School, a half-hour bus ride from home. At primary school we had been considered clever, Geoff consistently being top of the class and I being second. It was therefore quite a shock to arrive at grammar school and discover, to our horror, that there were boys who were much brighter than we were, and we began to slide closer and closer to the bottom of the class. Faced with opposition like John Tydeman, who became the head of BBC drama, and David Gentleman, who is now a prominent artist and for many years designed some of our most admired postage stamps, we became disillusioned and our work rate slackened. We tried to work, but our predisposition for mischief, coupled with the fact that we were identical twins and masters couldn't distinguish between Hamilton 3 and Hamilton 4, distracted us far too often for us to do well. Our antics gave us a lot of joy but not a little grief as well. I can remember Geoff's ashen face as he travelled home on the bus at the end of one term with a school report in which – we had steamed the envelope open in the biology lab, as most boys did – the headmaster's remarks contained the single sentence, 'Hamilton is the buffoon of the school!' I thought I saw just a glimmer of a twitch at the corner of Father's mouth as he read it – he was probably remembering that he was exactly the same at school. Nevertheless, Father was not pleased and several weeks without pocket money and being 'gated' until the garden was dug throughout ensued.

We also had to contend with people like 'Biff' Clouting, our fearsome physics master, who would pride himself on the fact that he could get every stroke of the cane in exactly the same place; and 'Sid' Palmer, our woodwork master, who could throw a small offcut of wood with such remarkable speed and accuracy that it was a foolish boy who risked his wrath. Then we had the real characters, 'Jimmy' Irwin, the English master, who would chastise boys in Shakespearean terms. He only had one arm and he would point the finger of his hand and you would tremble as he said, 'Thou coxcomb, thou monkey, settle or thou shalt suffer!' He was also known to walk steadily up and down the rows of desks, swinging his arm to clout the cowering boys and chanting, 'You're wasting your time and your parents' money.' We had 'Drip' Taphouse, our Latin master, who was obsessed by the Roman army and, if you played your cards right, you could get him to talk about them for the whole lesson, so diverting him completely from the task of teaching Latin. The odd thing about him was that he would speak using Latin grammar, and say phrases such as 'the having-been-beaten Romans'. But Geoff and I owed most to our headmaster, Tom Bunt, who loved his school and loved his boys. In spite of being a strict disciplinarian he ruled in the kindliest way possible. I remember that before he chastised you he would stretch out his arms, so that the sleeves of his gown flapped like the wings of an enormous bat, then slowly bring his arms in and straighten your tie – whether it was already straight or not. Everybody respected and admired him and he was a fine example of how the leader of a school should conduct his business.

Parents' Day was a big day at the school, with lots of ceremony, including the presentation of a pair of white gloves to the mayor, with the speech made by the head boy, in Latin, a tour of the school and a sumptuous lunch, all rounded off by the Masters v. the Boys cricket match. One year Geoff and I, who were not good enough cricketers to play for the school, crept into the music room and 'borrowed' some instruments. Geoff chose a trumpet and I a French horn. We secreted ourselves in the bushes at either side of the field and, just as the match was reaching a climax and one of the most fearsome masters was running in to bowl, Geoff blew a thunderous blast on the trumpet. Immediately a group of masters jumped up and ran to the side of the field from which the sound was coming. I waited until they were nearly there and then let rip with the French horn. The group stopped in their tracks, turned and began to run towards the other side of the field. This time Geoff waited until they were nearly there and blew another blast on his trumpet. Confusion reigned, with masters running this way and that, boys collapsed in laughter and parents wondering what kind of school they had sent their children to. I regret to say that this was a prank we didn't get away with. We were caught and dragged before the headmaster the following day to explain ourselves, but to our delight Tom Bunt just smiled at us in a weary sort of way and said, 'Get out, boys, and try to behave.' It was a sample of his excellent psychology because we felt we had let the school down and we didn't do anything so public again.

Nevertheless, the reprimand didn't stop Geoff from filling the bowl lampshades in the biology lab with tadpoles, with the result that when the lights were switched on the room was filled with ghostly moving shadows. Neither did it stop us enticing a group of eight prefects, including the head boy, out on to a balcony, locking the door and going home for the evening. They got back inside eventually, but they were very cross the following day. We formed a small syndicate, in fact, made up of a group of boys whom Geoff and I liked to look upon as inventive, but who would now be viewed as anarchists and probably excluded. We would each put sixpence into the kitty for an 'assignment' so that whoever was brave enough to do it would earn about half a crown. I remember winning the half crown and a good beating for riding a bicycle round the corridors whilst lessons were in progress and Geoff dressing up as an Arab, taking several copies of the score of Gluck's *Orfeo*, which we were singing in the choir at the time, and standing on a corner in Hertford in the middle of the day ringing a bell and shouting 'Gluck's *Orfeo*, buy your Gluck's *Orfeo* here.' He didn't sell a single copy, but he got some very strange looks.

Thus our schooldays were filled with fun and laughter and I blush to admit that Geoff and I did most of our homework in the bus going to school. Brinkmanship, I think they call it. We were not an entirely lost cause, though, for we were both in the 'A' stream and both got a respectable six subjects at O level. We both opted for sciences rather than arts when the time to choose came, our favourite subjects being botany and zoology. We actually became quite good at dissecting earthworms and dogfish and were eventually to take these subjects at A level. However, we both ended up with a couple of miserable A levels, when three was the standard for entry into university. We regretted it later, because we knew we could have eaten it had we tried, but life was just too good at the time and in any case by this time

Geoff, from his small beginnings in our garden at home, had become consumed with an interest in horticulture and was determined to go to horticultural college, and I wanted to study agriculture, so we didn't have the incentive. Well, that was our excuse, anyway.

When we were thirteen, I can vividly remember sitting on the number 310 bus with Geoff and Mother, going to Hertford. Father, who was now working as a salesman for a company that sold industrial supplies, was away in Scotland, and he only got home on occasional weekends, but he had to do it, as jobs were hard to come by and we needed the money. Mother looked distressed and puffy-eyed, as though she had been crying and we asked anxiously if she was OK.

'No,' she said, 'I'm not. I've just discovered that your father is having an affair with a woman in Glasgow and it's making me very unhappy.' 'How do you know that?' we asked, with utter disbelief. 'Because I found a letter from her in his jacket pocket, that's how.' Geoff and I were dismayed. Our dad, the rock and mainstay of our young lives, having naughty secrets from the rest of the family – it was too ghastly to contemplate. 'What are you going to do about it?' said Geoff. We saw Mother's mouth harden and her chin begin to jut. 'I'm going up to confront the bitch,' said she, her indomitable spirit beginning to reassert itself. 'You can't do that,' we said in chorus. 'You'll get into terrible trouble.' 'Can't I?' she said. 'Just watch me.'

So the following day we were packed of to Gram and Gramp down the road and Mother got on a train to Glasgow. When she arrived she got a taxi to take her straight to the fancy woman's house. She had the address because it had been foolishly put on the letter. Mother knocked on the door and it was opened by a woman she later described as a kind of gangster's moll. She always had a taste for the dramatic, did Mother. Cowering in the background, looking terrified, was poor old Father. The woman, whose name we never learned, must have realised who this angry-looking woman was because, without a pause, she felt in her handbag, pulled out a pistol and pointed it at Mother. Mother, God bless her iron-clad socks, utterly unfazed by this, held out her hand and said in her sternest voice (and she could be stern), 'Don't be bloody ridiculous. Give me that gun,' at which the woman meekly handed it over. Mother tucked the gun into her own handbag and said, 'Come on, Cyril, get in the car, we're going home.' And that's exactly what he did.

After that little episode Dad was covered in guilt and contrition, and for literally years after that he would come home loaded with presents for us, presents for our grandparents and, above all, presents for his courageous wife, who never mentioned the episode again. They actually loved each other dearly all their lives and I think she recognised that the old boy had just been lonely and sought some female company to compensate. I can vouchsafe that he never did it again.

When Mother died, I had the mournful job of clearing her house and while doing so I took home a box of papers relating to her personal life. When I began to do the research for this book what did I come across, hidden at the bottom of the box, but the gun – proof of the story that she had told her two wide-eyed little boys on her return from Scotland all those years ago. I reluctantly handed it over to the police because, although it was a fascinating piece of family history I didn't want to risk having three years to contemplate it while I languished in jail.

Geoff and I had a lot of friends at school, but one of our greatest pals was a chap called Robert Browning. We looked on him at first as one of the toffee-nosed kids, because he had been to St Christopher's private school in Broxbourne, which was regarded by eleven-year-old hard cases like us as a school for the weak and wimpish. It was a matter of days before Bob proved us wrong. He was a tall, blond, good-looking boy, a superb swimmer who eventually swam for the county, and a good rugby player, cricketer and athlete. It was infuriating that he was also clever and accomplished. Nevertheless, his saving grace was that he was almost as bad as we were in terms of mischief. It was he who invented the game of bringing a brick into the class room. As soon as the master turned to write on the blackboard, we would hear a whispered 'Hamilton' and look up to see the brick flying dangerously towards us. You then had one of three options: to let the brick drop and disclose to the master that you were involved in a prank, to allow the brick to hit you and suffer pain and suffering or to catch it so that you could eventually throw it back. Catching it was by far the best option and our efforts to do so were frantic and often hilarious. It was Robert Browning who organised the whole class to move seats every time our master turned his back, thus confusing the hell out of him each time he turned around to find that nobody was where he expected them to be.

So we warmed to Robert and, since he also lived in Broxbourne, we began to spend more time together. One day he introduced us to his great friend Clive Darlow, whose father, a prosperous businessman, was also the secretary of Broxbourne aero club, which was sited at Broxbourne aerodrome, where our father had worked during the war. He would occasionally take us for short flights in a De Havilland Rapide, which gave its name to the Rapide Club, a small assembly of four – Geoff and me, Clive and Bob.

The Rapide Club was formed in serious vein, with a serious purpose. We had a written constitution and democratically elected officers – a president, a secretary, a treasurer and a member. These posts were exchanged on a weekly basis, a system we believed would have been appropriate for the government of the day. We would meet on Friday nights in a four-foot by eight-foot trailer, on to which we had built a plywood superstructure, the four of us squeezed uncomfortably round a small table. When we met we would give each other the courtesy of the Rapide salute, the index finger of the right hand placed smartly over the right eye, and sing the specially composed Rapide song. First the minutes of the last meeting were read and then the serious business of the club would commence.

The primary purpose of the club was to assess the female talent of the village on a scientific basis, as required by the constitution. To do this we drew up a large chart, with the names of all the girls we knew along the top axis and desirable qualities down the side. The qualities began with the obvious physical ones and we went on to consider how much they talked, their vacuousness quotient, the frequency with

41

which they tucked their dress into their knickers to do handstands, and their political and spiritual leanings – all important and closely linked factors which went to make up a girl's real worth. You must remember that political correctness was yet to come, and I doubt if it would have made any difference in any case. We would then debate the various factors we considered important and give points for each girl, the average score being recorded in the appropriate place. There was some doubt, however, about the validity of the survey, which may have ruled it out for publication in *Nature*, because if one of the club members had a current girlfriend she always seemed to attract top marks from the member concerned and no marks from the remainder. This led to some argument, but when the attractions of bachelorhood were fully explored the matter was usually resolved.

After the weekly assessment we would often hold a séance. This consisted of playing the ouija board to make contact with 'the other side' or spreading our hands on the table and, through the power of concentration, trying to raise it from the floor. The necessary air of mystery was difficult to establish as, two minutes after beginning the session, in the dark and closely squashed together, we would feel somebody's knee beginning to shake as they tried not to laugh and we would all collapse in a heap on the floor laughing.

Another of our good friends was Don Feast, who was an amiable and jolly person and good to be with, and who had one other attraction that none of our other friends had: a Dansette gramophone and a collection of Jo Stafford records. We would go to his house, be spirited up to his bedroom, wind up the gramophone and lie back to indulge our deep and everlasting love for Jo Stafford. 'Shrimp Boats are a Comin'' would raise goose pimples and evince deep sighs of romantic love. How much you lose as you get older, your hormones begin to settle and responsibility sets in! Don remembers one of the first signs of Geoff's environmental awareness. While he and Geoff were out together one day in Broxbourne woods, a magical place of deep, dappled shade, musty smells and the sound of scurrying animals, Don felt the need to relieve himself, which he did over the fallen branch of a big tree. Geoff was beside himself with outrage, pointing out that somebody might want to sit on that branch, stopping poor Don in mid-stream and directing him peremptorily to a patch of undergrowth.

They were memorable days, which taught us the value of really close companionship and the joys of human contact. Geoff was particularly outgoing and good at forming relationships with all kinds of people, while I was more introspective and less confident.

As we got older, of course, we began to be more emotionally involved, and our young loves became as important as our other exploits. Geoff's girlfriend at the time was an astonishingly beautiful girl called Marilyn Early. She had raven-black curly hair and a vivacious, animated personality which Geoff revelled in. She was a member of the sailing club, which operated from the same site as the rowing club, so he saw a lot of her. We all expected this to be a childhood romance that would end in marriage, but sadly it seemed to fade and die as they each became involved in other interests. Not, however, before it had caused me a good deal of embarrassment. One Saturday I had met a girl at a dance in Hertford and I had arranged for her to meet me off the bus at a certain time. Unbeknown to me, Geoff had also arranged to meet Marilyn, who lived in Hertford, at the same bus stop at the same time. By a cruel stroke of fate I missed the bus and had to catch the next one, five minutes later. My new girlfriend saw Geoff alight from the bus and approached him, thinking it was me, only to find him ignoring her and greeting another girl, giving her a kiss and walking off. I got to Hertford just in time to see my new girl walking away and then found myself trying to persuade her that I had not just met another girl, parked her up the road and come back for our assignation. In fact I had to take her home to see Geoff before she would believe me. The relationship didn't last long.

By the time we left school we had each won a place at the Essex Institute of Agriculture, as it was then called, at Writtle, near Chelmsford, Geoff to study horticulture and I to study agriculture. A precondition for entering the college was a year's work experience, so while I got a job on a farm Geoff went to work for Jack Alison, a tomato grower in the Lea Valley. At the time, Geoff felt that tomato growing was what he wanted to do and he had romantic and totally unrealistic ideas of starting his own enterprise when he left college. Jack was a good employer, who recognised Geoff's desire to learn and invested a lot of time in teaching him all he knew. But while we looked forward to college with great enthusiasm, we knew that our days of freedom were about to come to an end, for hanging like a dark cloud over us was the spectre of National Service.

CHAPTER 3

Detained at Her Majesty's Pleasure

I T WAS LATE IN MAY 1955 that the dreaded brown envelope with the fearsome 'OHMS' on the outside dropped with a deceitfully benign plop through the letterbox. Right up to the time we tore open the envelope we both harboured vague and naïve hopes that some kind officer in the Ministry of Defence would find it in his heart to grant us an exemption: on what grounds we couldn't say, but we hoped nevertheless. But no, it was an order that we were to report to the local office to register for National Service.

We both wanted to get into the RAF because we had heard that it was the 'cushiest number'. The navy was all bull, discipline and seasickness, and the army was all bull, discipline and more discipline. Most people went, without choice, into the army. I think we have our brother Mark, who had already done his two years penal servitude, to thank for getting us into the RAF because he advised us about the induction interview. 'Tell them,' he said, 'that the family has a long history in the RAF, both your father and brother having served, and if this doesn't swing it, add that you believe it to be the finest fighting force in the world.' It worked.

The next step was to choose a 'trade' that we would pursue

throughout the two years of our service career. Geoff asked if he could please be a gardener, but that got a short reply. There were, in fact, only two trades on offer at the time – cook or air wireless mechanic. We were both horrified by the thought of cooking for two years, so we chose the latter, not really knowing what it meant, but knowing that it had to be better. The medical was quite amusing – fifty young men, all stark naked, standing in a row being examined in the nether areas with the most advanced equipment known to medical science at the time – a bicycle lamp and a pencil. We all passed, of course. You had to be pretty close to death to be rejected. Geoff's memories of the inspection for 'social diseases and infestation', as they were called, caused him great amusement when on holiday in America many years later. He brought back a photograph, because he didn't think we would believe him, of a huge roadside sign pointing to a fish restaurant with the slogan 'Surprise her with crabs'.

After registering we went home to await news of our fate. The RAF had a very ill-judged policy at the time of keeping twins together. It was based on the firmly fixed but entirely erroneous belief that they would expire if parted and failed to appreciate that it opened up undreamed-of opportunities for deception and subversion. So the next brown envelopes to arrive contained identical instructions for Geoff and me to report to RAF Cardington in Bedfordshire, shortly after our eighteenth birthday.

There we were kitted out and given our first haircut. Haircutting at reception camp was just a trifle unsophisticated. No scissors were used, just a set of electric clippers run over the whole head in two minutes flat. Geoff and I with no hair looked like prisoners of war, and that's exactly how we felt. But on our first evening, just as depression was setting in, we were rescued by the Rapide Club. The door of our billet suddenly burst open and there stood Clive Darlow, a big smile on his face and the index finger of his right hand firmly affixed over the right eye. He was accompanied by our old mate Don Speller, who was also in the RAF and had been posted just a few miles away. What a boost to morale that was!

The most interesting part about our induction into the RAF was the opportunity it gave us to meet the most extraordinary set of people, all mixed up together in close proximity, and to see their reaction to one another. We had a 25-year-old solicitor who had had an exemption to complete his studies and who cried himself to sleep each night with homesickness; we had a farmer's son from five miles outside Dundee, who had never been further than Dundee and whose journey to Cardington had been his first introduction to a train; we had man who, in a grotesque and unsettling way, would sleep with both his mouth and his eyes open, and another whose proudest boast was that he had never read a book or a newspaper and who read only the *Beano* and the *Dandy*. This motley but largely good-hearted crew was certainly our first introduction to life in the raw. It was noticeable that Geoff formed relationships with them all, much more easily than I did. Confident and self-possessed, he seemed to have an ability to draw out the more interesting sides of their characters and to make firm friends quickly.

We stayed at Cardington for no more than a week, after which we were dispatched to our basic training, or 'square-bashing', camp at RAF Hednesford in Staffordshire. We drove into a bleak, dismal place with rows and rows of wooden huts that was to be our home for the next eight weeks. As the coach that was carrying us drew up to the grass verge outside our hut, we were greeted by a small, terrier-like drill instructor, the peak of his hat steamed down so that it almost obscured his eyes, back ram-rod straight and his stick carried tightly under his arm. Before any of us could alight, he was screaming at us, 'If anybody steps on that grass they'll be on a charge!' Well, there was no alternative but to step on the grass, so we simply stayed in the bus. This resulted in a display of pyrotechnics the like of which I don't wish to see again, so we got off the bus and, after a manic lecture on what 'horrible little men we were' and how if we transgressed we would wish we'd never been born, together with some well-chosen words about where he could put his stick, we settled into our beds. Grown men wept and called out in their sleep for their mothers, but Geoff and I had our Mutual Benefit Society working for us, so we coped pretty well.

Basic training consisted of being taught how to march and rifle drill, learning how to use a Bren gun and gaining experience in how to be shouted at by a primeval creature with an inflated sense of importance without resorting to physical violence. It was only a matter of days before Geoff and I began to lose our fear and to see the whole exercise as futile. As wireless mechanics we were not going to be doing a job that required marching and we certainly wouldn't be issued with a rifle, let alone a Bren gun. And why could we not be treated like human beings who would respond to intelligent treatment? There was no escaping the experience without being shot at dawn, so Geoff and I resorted to Dad's fundamental premise – if things look black find a way to laugh yourself out of it.

This got me into trouble and Geoff was obliged to get me out of it. I had become known by the drill instructors as 'Laughing Boy', because I couldn't keep a straight face when confronted by the antics of our chimp-like instructors. One day, when my amusement got the better of me, the corporal in charge bawled out for me to take two paces forward, which I smartly did. Putting his face right into mine, he shouted, 'You're bleedin' Laughing Boy, aren't you, airman?' Knowing that Geoff would support me, not through any kind of telepathy but through an inbuilt confidence, I said, 'No, Corporal.' His face reddened, his voice rose an octave and several decibels, and he screamed, 'Yes you are. You're bleedin' Laughing Boy.' 'No, Corporal,' said I. As the corporal's face turned almost black with rage, Geoff stepped two paces forward and said, quietly and calmly, 'I'm Laughing Boy, Corporal.' Well, the corporal's face had to be seen to be believed. He looked at me and then at Geoff and back at me and he just couldn't believe what he saw. He hadn't realised there were two of us and he was completely floored. He stopped the training session and we returned to our billets in triumph.

One of the noblest failures at our square-bashing camp was Pateman. Every intake has a Pateman. Pateman was the kind of man who could never get his beret to lie down at the side – it always stuck out like a flying saucer; whom it was quite beyond to march in step; and who dropped his rifle more times than we could count. Part of our training was the barbaric process of bayonet practice, in which we were asked to run, screaming abuse, down a hill and plunge our rifles, with bayonets fixed, into a sack of straw strung up on a wooden frame. Pateman, a quiet and diffident lad, found it impossible to scream and made a kind of bleating sound as he ran, poking the sack in his normal friendly, quiet fashion. Well, that wasn't good enough for the instructor, who sent him back up the hill to do it again, amid a shower of abusive language. This time Pateman drew on all his modest reserves of courage and came down the hill like a wailing banshee. He plunged his bayonet into the sack, let go and the bayonet, rifle and all went straight through, leaving Pateman standing looking at his empty hands in puzzlement and the rest of us in helpless laughter. Pateman lived on in affectionate memory for the rest of Geoff's life. When Geoff's sons, Stephen, Nick and Christopher, were little their favourite bedtime story was always a story about the exploits of Pateman.

After eight weeks of enduring a cross between a Gilbert and Sullivan opera and *Dad's Army* we finally 'passed out' and were posted to Yatesbury in Wiltshire for our trade training as air wireless mechanics. This was a lot more civilised, with very little 'spit and polish' but some long, dull days learning very little about wireless.

However, there was a new feeling of freedom and a number of bright spots, perhaps the brightest of which was the riding club, which Geoff and I joined as extremely raw horsemen, having had two or three lessons at home. But the excellent instructors taught us the rudiments in a short space of time and it was not long before we were able to ride out on Gordon Richards' gallops, which was a stretch of wonderful downland opposite the camp. The RAF had invested in some racehorses that hadn't made the grade, and riding them was the most exhilarating experience. There was only one mishap, which could have been more serious than it actually was. We had one horse that was fractious and highly strung and thus avoided by everybody, but one day Geoff arrived late for our gallop and this was the only horse available. We had ridden off without him and were about a mile ahead when Geoff's horse spotted us. He put his head down, bit between his teeth, and set off at a mad gallop. Geoff saw barbed wire looming ahead and was preparing for a nasty accident when the horse took off and cleared it in a bound. Geoff hadn't learned to jump, but somehow clung on for dear life. When the horse reached us we turned round just in time to see it stop dead and do a ninety-degree shuffle, and Geoff flew up into the air, reins in hand. Miraculously he landed on his feet, still holding the reins, and, trying to look as though he had meant to dismount, he mumbled, 'Well, you might have waited for me.'

By the time we reached Yatesbury our pay had risen to the princely sum of sixteen shillings a week (eighty pence in today's money). This didn't exactly give us access to a libertine lifestyle. In fact, the coach fare home was exactly sixteen shillings, so we were always obliged to hitchhike if we wanted to spend any money on our girlfriends at home. This meant walking to the main gate and joining the three thousand or so other hitchhikers all aiming for the same destination – London. The trick, we discovered, was not to be the first out of the gate, but to be the last, since that would make you first in line for a lift. It was a bit hazardous but it was fun.

But oh, the pain of returning after the weekend, deeply in love, as Geoff and I both were (although thankfully not with the same girl), and about to be parted. How well I remember being taken to Hanger Lane station on the North Circular Road by our parents and getting on to a coach with thirty other world-weary airmen, only to be bombarded by weepy love songs on Radio Luxembourg sung by Peggy Lee and Ella Fitzgerald. (Those were the days of good popular music – or am I getting old and crabby?)

But Geoff and I kept each other's spirits high and our amusement quota satisfied through the little tricks we could play on innocent officers, NCOs and instructors, who hadn't realised there were two of us. If put on 'jankers' (punishment for straying from the paths of military righteousness), which usually consisted of having to wash greasy pots in near-cold water in the cookhouse, we would simply take it in turns, one night on and one night off. On one occasion I had had some treatment for a very minor inflammation of the eye and to test the efficiency of the medical officer Geoff went for the check-up the following day. The MO was surprised and puzzled, and actually appeared to be disappointed to find such a complete recovery, calling in one of his colleagues for a second opinion. However, he was happy the following day to find that the inflammation had returned and tell me to resume the eyedrops. Puzzlement returned the following day, however, with a seemingly sensational recovery, followed by a distressing relapse the following day. We stopped after that. We felt that we had squeezed enough fun out of it and the MO was beginning to suspect.

After nine seemingly endless weeks we had to sit final tests and we were amazed to find that we had passed with rather low-flying colours. The thought that unsuspecting pilots would now be in our hands filled us with dread, not for us but for them. Who would knowingly fly an aircraft that had been serviced by the likes of us? And what had happened to Pateman? We never found out, but neither did we hear of any disasters attributed to him, although *we* had some near misses. The next step was to get a permanent posting that would last for the rest of our RAF career. It goes without saying that we all hoped for a home posting, although Geoff and I put ourselves down for Singapore and the Far East as alternatives – anywhere more exciting than Europe. And what did we get? We got Europe.

We were both posted to RAF Wildenrath in Germany, close to the Dutch border. The RAF showed great sensitivity to the morale of the troops by shipping us there on the day before Christmas Eve. Our troop ship, which sailed from Harwich, seemed like an early slave ship, with bodies packed in so tightly that it was difficult to move, people being seasick all around and a steaming temperature, even in the winter. It was not a pleasant experience. But it was only to be for a night, so that wasn't too bad. The following morning we clambered up on to deck, expecting to see the Hook of Holland, our first sight of foreign lands, only to find that the ship had developed engine trouble in the night and we were now back at Harwich, facing the awful prospect of going through it all again.

Finally, after a long train journey, we arrived at Wildenrath, another bleak camp, but this time darkened by pine trees glowering in the dusk. There was a thin powdering of snow on the ground and we saw the railway line disappearing into the pine forest. Geoff said that he fully expected to see a train towing cattle trucks filled with prisoners of war emerging from the gloom, but I'm happy to say that didn't happen. We were then marched to our billet, to be greeted by a corporal at the door. As each man entered he was asked, 'Girlfriend?' If the answer was 'Yes', we were told, 'Right, choose a bed at the far end.' When we asked why we were being separated like this, he explained that he didn't want the rest of the troops kept awake by the weeping when the 'Dear John' arrived. A 'Dear John' was the service term for the letter one inevitably got from one's girlfriend saying, 'Dear John, I love you but I can't wait for two years.' We nearly all got them eventually, even the handful of airmen who were married.

The following morning we were marched down to our squadron to take up our duties. Geoff and I were assigned to a communications squadron that flew personnel and hardware backwards and forwards to the UK in old Second World War Ansons, which were light bombers. Some of the older planes were covered in canvas and we noticed on that first morning that one had small patches stuck on to the canvas at regular intervals along the fuselage. When we enquired what they were, our grizzled old flight sergeant explained that, at the start of the war we were very short of fighters, so the Ansons would carry a dozen or so soldiers, armed with 303 rifles. They would then poke a hole in the side of the fuselage so that they could shoot at the enemy. How successful they were was never disclosed, but it's little wonder that Hitler was so confident.

Life on the squadron in those early days was extremely boring. The majority of the people on the camp were supposed to be assigned to a squadron of Canberras, but they hadn't arrived, so there was an immense surplus of staff to service the few aircraft the camp did have. Thus there was little to do except loaf about in the workshop – until we had found our feet and realised that there was a lot of fun to be had despite the rigours of service discipline.

Geoff and I put our entrepreneurial instincts to the test by starting what became affectionately known as the 'tea swindle'. We saved our meagre wages and bought a huge electric kettle, some mugs, jars of coffee and packets of tea. At ten thirty every morning a kind of hot dog wagon would roll into the hanger where we worked, blowing its horn to announce the NAAFI break, and it would be surrounded by eager airmen anxious to get a cup of tea or coffee. But after we set up in competition they would rush into our workshop instead, because we were a good deal cheaper, and the poor NAAFI man would drive disconsolately away. As our capital increased we added cakes and savouries, and eventually even the officers and NCOs would dine at our establishment. It was at this time that we were put on to opposite twelve-hour shifts, so our tea swindle became a twenty-four hour operation. We put up a notice saying 'We never close' and we did a roaring trade.

Being on opposite shifts opened up excellent opportunities for subterfuge because, since nobody could tell the difference between us, we could change places at will. The shifts never comprised twelve solid hours of work; in fact if we worked four or five hours that was considered a hard day. This made it possible for one of us to disappear on a jaunt while the other simply did both shifts. As a result we each saw a lot of Germany, Belgium and Holland.

We were allowed to hitch a lift on an aircraft that was going to the UK, on condition that you were entitled to some leave. But this rule didn't need to apply to Geoff and me. If either of us felt the need of some time at home we would put into practice a well-tried routine. Both of us would walk out to the aircraft, dressed in our 'denims' RAF overalls – each carrying our tool kits with us, ostensibly to service the aircraft. Once inside, the one going home would take off his denims to reveal civilian clothes underneath. The denims would be stuffed into the tool bag and carried back by the other, who would then take on both shifts until the wanderer returned, when the process would be repeated in reverse. The only real difficulty came at pay parade. The troops would be assembled in ranks in front of an officer, who sat at a table with the wage packets ranged in front of him. He would call out the name of the recipient of the wage packet, who would reply by shouting out his name and number – in Geoff's case '2758996 LAC Hamilton, sir!' He would then march up to the table, salute and collect the wage packet. The difficult part was the fact that Geoff's name and my name came in quick succession. So, if I was 'absent without leave', or AWOL in service parlance, Geoff would stand unobtrusively in the rear rank and, when he'd been called, he would march smartly up to collect the first pay packet. He would then march quickly to the rear rank again, while one of the boys in the front (they were all in on the scam) would have a violent fit of coughing, or faint on the ground – anything to create a diversion. By the time order had been restored Geoff would have gathered himself for the next sortie to collect the second packet. We were never suspected and continued this dubious and undoubtedly criminal practice almost to the end of our service careers.

Free trips eventually ended and we had to take commercial flights home. Geoff and I continued our subterfuge, but it became much more risky. However Geoff found a simple and elegant way to make it safe. One Christmas he decided to go home, with me covering for him, but when he got to Düsseldorf airport he was confronted by a military policeman with a clipboard on which was a list of all the people who had applied for leave. Now if you were a serviceman you didn't need a passport; you could simply show your identity card or '1250', as it was known. The MP was stopping all passengers who looked young enough to be servicemen and asking for their 1250 to check against his list. If you had a 1250 and were not on his list you were for the high jump – and Geoff knew he wasn't on the list. So when he got to the MP, he simply told him he was a civilian and had a passport. 'OK,' said the MP, 'passports over there.' Geoff went to the passport desk and when the German official asked for his passport he said, 'No, I'm a serviceman,' and showed his 1250. Piece of cake really.

After Geoff and I had endured about three months of intense boredom, I wandered up to the station pig farm. Most RAF stations had a pig farm, to supply meat to married quarters, and I thought I'd take a look. It was run by a dour Yorkshireman, Bert Clitheroe, who, I discovered during the course of our conversation, was due to leave in about a month, and no replacement had yet been found. So I hurried to the officer in charge of the farm and convinced him that I was the man for the job.

This job opened up an infinite new freedom for me and a great source of fun for Geoff. The farm had been carved out of the pine forest about a mile from the centre of the camp, so I moved out of my billet and into an old hunting lodge built like a log cabin. It had huge fireplaces and raw wooden walls and I was back in my element again. But the most appealing part of running the farm was the lack of management control and the most extraordinary concessions I was given. For example, I was able to go to the station stores and draw any amount of food that took my fancy. So Geoff and I, with all this sumptuous food, would organise parties at the farmhouse, asking anybody who was invited to bring a bottle. Then I persuaded the officer in charge of the farm, who knew nothing about farming, that the only reliable remedy for a sick pig was a nip of brandy, so he gave me a 'chit' which entitled me to draw one bottle of brandy every week from the stores, so with a little prudence enough brandy could be saved to preclude the necessity for people even to be asked to bring a bottle. Part of my job was to take finished pigs to the slaughterhouse, which was also on the station, so not only did I normally get a nice joint for myself but I got all the pig's trotters. These I would remove to the farm and boil for hours in a huge cauldron, and then I would invite the boys up for a game of poker. We would often spend most of the night playing poker whilst gnawing on pigs trotters and drinking RAF brandy, all for nothing. I had the greasiest pack of playing cards on the station and a reputation for being 'King Rat'.

I blanch at the thought of things Geoff and I did on the farm at that time, because both he and I grew to have a respect for the law and now would be horrified at the thought of transgressing. But at the time it seemed that anything went. I would draw rather more tea and coffee than I needed from the stores, for example, because they were known to be in short supply in Holland. We would get our two German workers, Hans and Willie, to take them over the border on their bicycles and sell them. We gave them 20 per cent and it was years before either of us made as much money again.

Perhaps my worst transgression was when I stole the German pig. I was just about to go out to the farm after my lunch when I got a telephone call to say that one of my big sows was loose in married quarters and was terrorising the neighbourhood. I immediately jumped on to my tractor, my only form of transport, and drove at high speed to the camp. I knew which sow it would be because I had one who could jump anything. I had considered entering her for the National but decided she may not be accepted. She had a high fence around her sty and another around her yard, but still she managed to escape. However, when I got to married quarters there was no sow in sight. I searched high and low and eventually wandered out of the back gate of the camp, where there was a small German farm with some loose boxes, half-doors open, fronting the lane. I looked over one of the doors and there was my sow. What a nice thing to do, I thought; the farmer obviously found my sow wandering and locked it away to await my call. I went round to the yard to thank him, but I could find nobody so I decided to take the sow back and come back to thank him later. Anybody who has tried to drive a sow will know that it's no easy matter and I had a mile to go with this one. Three times she escaped my stick and legged it back to the German farm, so three times I had to start all over again. But eventually, exhausted, irritable and dirty I got the animal into the yard, closed the gate and opened the door of her sty, intending to lock her in for a while – only to find my sow inside, lying peacefully asleep. It had not been my sow that had escaped, but the German's! So now what? Was I going to go through the whole awful process of driving the damn thing back again? Not on your life, I thought, I'll keep it, justifying my despicable action with jingoistic thoughts about who won the war, anyway. The poor German never found his sow, which eventually died for Britain, so I guess I have another act of compensation to write into my will, although I think there is a certain poetic justice about the whole sordid incident.

Geoff would frequently come up to the farm to see me and to help with the work. We both loved to be outside and Geoff liked the fact that even if had no garden he could at least become involved in growing, because on the other side of the camp we had a few acres of land where we grew corn crops to supplement the animal feed. One day his enthusiasm very nearly got him into trouble. We were muck spreading on our arable land, which meant loading up pig muck back at the farm and transporting it by tractor and trailer to our land across the camp. The only trailer we had was an old bomb trolley, which was very long, low and without sides, so we had to stack up the muck on it as best we could in a great steaming, stinking heap. This apology for a trailer then had to be driven right through the station, using the main thoroughfare. When Geoff got to the middle of the camp, he discovered that the route was lined with airmen, bulled up to the eyebrows, with white webbing belts, white rifle-slings, the lot. They were rehearsing for an impending visit from a senior member of the royal family and, just as Geoff got there, they were given the order to present arms. So there was Geoff, driving a huge load of dung between two rows of airmen, giving him the royal salute. I'm afraid Geoff's irrepressible sense of humour got the better of him and he stood up on the tractor and gave a gracious, queenly wave of the hand all the way down the ranks – until a large, formidable flight sergeant bellowed out, 'Airman, come 'ere.' Geoff stopped the tractor and walked meekly over to the flight sergeant, whose voice rose to a scream as he shouted, 'What the bloody 'ell do you fink you're doin', airman?' Geoff spread his hands in supplication and said, 'Come on, Flight. If you were presented with an opportunity like that what would you have done?' A glimmer of a smile appeared on the flight sergeant's face and he said in exasperation, 'Oh, bugger off, airman. And don't ever come back!'

Geoff came up to the farm one day to tell me that life on the squadron had taken a sharp turn for the worse, with the appointment of a new warrant officer – the disciplinarian of the station. He was determined, it seemed, to impose a new regime and his first action was to organise an inspection parade, a thing we hadn't done since square bashing, which we would have to attend, all polished and shining. Then Geoff told me of his plan to strike back. The warrant officer was possessed of a small, scrubby moustache, so Geoff circulated the whole of the squadron with the suggestion that we should all grow small, scrubby moustaches, which without exception we did. When the parade took place we could all see the realisation dawn on the warrant officer's face that he was being ridiculed – but there was nothing he could do because it was within Queen's regulations that an airman could grow a moustache. His face reddened and he asked a few people what the growth on the upper lip was supposed to be. 'Growing a moustache like yours, sir,' was the standard reply. We didn't have another inspection parade after that.

Geoff would also take terrible risks, not with the safety of a plane he was servicing, but with his own security, for the sake of some fun. One night we were all anxious to go to see a visiting jazz band – Tony Crombie, if I remember rightly – who were appearing in the camp cinema that night. But Geoff was on duty and he had one more aircraft to come in before he could get away. If it had a fault, he would have to stay behind to fix it that night, even though there would be plenty of time the following morning. So he walked out to the plane as it arrived and walked back with the pilot. 'Any snags, sir?' he said. 'Well,' said the pilot, 'I thought the radio compass seemed a bit dodgy and I'd be glad if you could check it for me.' Geoff saw Tony Crombie disappearing over the wide blue yonder if the pilot reported it, so, thinking quickly, he said, 'Did you fly over the Channel, sir?' knowing that there was no other route. 'Yes,' said the pilot. 'Fairly low?' 'Yes, fairly.' 'Ah,' said Geoff sagely, 'damped oscillations. It's the humidity, you know.' 'Well,' said the pilot, 'you know more about it than I do. I won't report it then.' We all enjoyed Tony Crombie and Geoff fixed the fault the following morning.

There was a modicum of hard work in our life in the RAF, but there was a lot of responsibility as well. We were constantly aware of the fact that the standard to which we did our work could mean the difference between life and death to an aircrew, and we took that very seriously.

It was also interesting and absorbing work – there was just too little of it and too much sitting around wasting one's life. But as well as being able to explore Germany, Holland and Belgium, Geoff and I enjoyed entirely polite and courteous relationships with a couple of local families, frequently having dinner and conversation with them in our halting and schoolboy German, as well as adventures which would have attracted less approval from Mother.

There was the competition for the favours of the 'fourteen-year-old barmaid', Hannalora, who was the daughter of the owner of the Arsbeckerhof, the local hostelry. Of course she wasn't fourteen – that was just our childish fantasy; but neither was she as naïve as we first thought her. After some months of frenzied serial courtship by most of the RAF men who frequented the bar, during which she was bought copious amounts of rum and Coke in an attempt to win her attention, we realised that, although she charged for rum and Coke, she only ever poured the Coke. She simply waited until either our patience ran out or we were too blotto to notice and she slipped quietly off to bed. Her father must have been very proud.

I also remember a night of outrageous depravity on the German festival of Rosen Montag, Rose Monday, which takes place in February and when it appears that anything goes. German inhibitions are sometimes almost as difficult to break down as the British variety, but on this one night the community gives its permission for unbridled revelry and, by golly, do the Germans take advantage of it. One year we went to Cologne, where the festival is all highly organised, with floats and street musicians and 'oom-pah' bands – all very enjoyable, but not a patch on our little village affair, which we went to the following year. We went to a dance in the village hall, where it is the custom to dress in national costume and also to wear masks – not of the kind we are used to seeing in old films of masked balls, but full-face masks of Mickey Mouse or Donald Duck. So if you asked a girl to dance you had no way of knowing if she was a girl or an old matron – it was all a matter of pot luck. Geoff, in those days much less sedate than he appeared later on television, tried to solve this problem by lifting the mask to have a look, but he was frequently repelled by a sharp crack over the knuckles with a small bunch of twigs that are part of the national costume. Becoming exasperated by this, he pulled out his cigarette lighter and set fire to them. Very shortly after that, I came out of the bar in the village, where I had been unsuccessfully trying to persuade the fourteen-year-old barmaid to come to the dance with me, to see Geoff running down the street with a large German woman in hot pursuit chasing him with a bunch of flaming twigs. With a sigh of resignation, I trotted off to rescue him and to try to prevent an international incident. 'Well,' said Geoff when I chastised him later, 'what could an English gentleman do in circumstances like that?'

National Service ground on through its two long years, with us all marking off each day on a 'demob chart', like the Count of Monte Cristo – although it was actually a lot more enjoyable and instructive than we ever could have hoped. Just before demob we were sent back to the UK to do two weeks of civil defence training in Chorley in Lancashire. This was tremendous fun because it was devoted almost entirely to fire fighting and there is a great deal of boyish pleasure to be had from squirting hoses and, if you have the courage, running up and down sixty-foot escape ladders.

Eventually we were sent off to our demob camp at Innesworth in Gloucestershire, where we were able to meet, for the first time since enlistment, the people we had met at our reception camp at Cardington. Most had changed, seeming to acquire a new self-confidence and independence. The solicitor who used to cry himself to sleep we were amazed to learn had signed on for another five years, so he wasn't there, but the man who slept with his eyes open was and he hadn't changed. The most remarkable change was in the farmer's son from Dundee, who had been diffident and withdrawn. Because he could drive a tractor he had been posted to a unit that built and repaired airfields, and driven an earthmover. He had been all over the world doing this – Europe, Malaysia, Australia, Canada, everywhere – and now he was entirely different: he was self-assured and talkative to the point of cockiness and he knew *exactly* what he wanted to do and how he was going to do it – and it wasn't in Dundee. I hope he succeeded.

At last, after endless rounds of paperwork and bureaucracy, we were drummed gratefully out, still in our uniform, because we would be on the reserve list for several years to come, and put on the train home, to some pretty uninhibited celebrations. When Geoff and I looked back on our service careers we both agreed that we were extremely fortunate to have been obliged to do it. Not only was it great fun, but it stiffened our already burgeoning self-reliance and taught us a few tricks that were to stand us in good stead in the years to come. Not everybody had this experience; for all rookies basic training was just a brutal and pointless waste of time, and it broke the spirit of some people. Those not lucky enough to be posted abroad usually found themselves in tedious, boring jobs which dispirited them further. But Geoff and I carried our mobile support system with us, and not only were we sure that it was this that had sustained us but we were now confident that it was there for ever.

CHAPTER 4

Striking Out

COMING OUT OF THE AIR FORCE was like coming to Shangri La. Free from all the restrictions and irritations of service life, we revelled in the company of our friends and family. We were both excited by the thought of going to college in a few months' time, but it was not long before the meagre funds we had managed to save from our niggardly RAF wage ran out and we suddenly realised that we would have to buy all kinds of things to see us through our time at college. Father was already faced with paying our accommodation fees, as our grant only covered tuition, so we didn't feel we could ask him for any kind of allowance. In the event he gave us ten bob each (fifty pence in today's money), which, with beer at about a shilling (five pence) a pint and petrol at half a crown a gallon (twenty-five pence) went a long way. But we knew it wouldn't finance the book budget, the clothes budget or the girlfriend budget. Additionally we both smoked. We had both started smoking in the RAF, where cigarettes were a shilling for twenty. We started for the reason that most young people start – because we thought it looked sophisticated – but now we simply couldn't afford sophistication. We couldn't afford cancer or heart disease either but the cigarette manufacturers hadn't chosen to tell us about those dangers at the time. We both gave up when they did choose to tell us, and we both felt resentful about the subterfuge.

Geoff and I had done some work during the school holidays for a young Dutchman who had started one of the country's first garden centres on the land that used to belong to Mr Frogley, at the top of our road. His name was Cornelius van Hage. He was struggling to establish himself, but, although he couldn't afford to pay us a lot, he kindly took us both on again to fill in the time until we went to college. Cor, as he was known by customers and employees alike, was, and I'm glad to say still is, a tall, well-built, handsome man with a line in charm that would have made even Ann Widdecombe go weak at the knees. Whilst I, a potential farmer, would be put to work weeding or digging, Geoff shadowed Cor and, in the process, learned a great deal about plants, their names and habits and how to propagate and grow them.

Cor built an almost full-size Dutch windmill on the site, which was a most eye-catching feature and a great marketing ploy, particularly as the garden centre was on the edge of the busy A10 London-to-Cambridge road. Of course, busy in 1957 was not like busy in 2001, and neither was gardening as rampantly popular as it is now; nevertheless customers poured in, in a constant and ever-expanding stream. To cope with the numbers Geoff was pressed into service, dealing with customer enquiries and helping them to solve their gardening problems. In those days there was a much more friendly and helpful atmosphere than exists in many garden centres today, with an opportunity extended to anybody to just come in and conduct their own personal 'gardeners' question time', even if they bought nothing. Cor drilled into his staff, including Geoff, the need to answer customer questions in a helpful and friendly way. His argument was that if people know where to come for advice they will know where to come for plants. So Geoff began his education about the eccentricities and the joys of the Great British Public at Van Hage's. Cor says that he was always polite and patient, never talking down to people and accepting even the most fatuous question as though he valued it, and saw that it needed a serious, sympathetic answer, simply because it was a serious issue for the person who asked it.

Cor was full of bounce and energy and humour, which was an

inspiration to Geoff and me, although Cor's humour occasionally got him into trouble. We often used to recall the time when a man came into the shop, having bought a large number of trees and plants, asking for them to be delivered. Cor asked for his name and address and as soon as he said 'Mr Glasscock' Cor had to hand over to Geoff, and go outside, from where we heard a muffled explosion of laughter. For days afterwards we would find him laughing about the incident. I don't remember Mr Glasscock returning but I do hope that he or any other Mr Glasscocks who may be reading this are not offended. Cor was an endearingly childish man – and still is, God bless him.

But, despite Cor's highly successful windmill idea, he made one marketing error. In our house we were very amused one breakfast-time by the arrival of the latest catalogue from Van Hage's. It was a two- or three-page affair that had been typed by Cor's wife, with some crude hand-drawings, obviously done by Cor, before duplicating on a not-too-clever Gestetner machine. Some of the illustrations showed the small range of concrete garden ornaments he stocked at the time – which I'm sure he wouldn't countenance now. The one that caused hilarity around our breakfast table was entitled 'Frog on Rock' and next to it another drawing entitled 'Frog without Rock'. Father immediately dictated a letter to Mother, who acted as his secretary, which said, 'We were excited by your catalogue showing 'Frog on Rock' and 'Frog without Rock', but were extremely disappointed to find that the product we really wanted to buy was not listed, namely 'Rock without Frog'. We would be extremely relieved to know that this is, in fact, available.' I seem to remember the catalogue improving the following year – and you should see what they have now.

Cor was an extremely shrewd businessman, seeming to know exactly what plants to stock and in what quantity without putting undue strain on his cash flow; he knew exactly how to get the customers to want to come back time after time; and, perhaps because of his Dutch roots, he knew how to provide them with plants that were strong and healthy, with clear planting, positioning and growing instructions so that they would perform well for their new owners. Eventually he went on to establish the Van Hage Garden Company at Great Amwell, near Ware, which is a 125-acre site and a multi-million pound business. Unfortunately though, Cor's business acumen was the one thing that Geoff failed to learn from him, which caused him much trouble and distress later.

In spite of our most enjoyable job at Van Hage's, Geoff and I could see that we were never going to make enough to finance ourselves fully so we were faced with the problem of making some more money.

In crises like this we would always call on our life-long mentor and adviser – Father. He was a salesman, so his first suggestion was that we should find something to sell. When he was our age, he had sold goods from door-to-door each time he had found himself short of money, and he saw no reason why we shouldn't do so also. 'What you need,' he said, 'is a product that people need to replace from time to time and will often find that they have none in stock. Most of all it needs to be cheap, because if it's cheap enough the customer will often buy it, just to get rid of you! So off you go, put your heads together and come up with something.' It was Geoff, of course, ever inventive, who came up with the idea – electric light bulbs. Father not only approved of the product, but he also knew of a small electrical wholesaler in the East End who could supply us. So the following day he took us out to a small shop that bulged at the seams with electrical devices, to strike a deal. Geoff and I put our total capital together, five shillings, so that we could each have one sample, a 100 watt for one shilling and sixpence and a 60 watt for a shilling, which we carried home in triumph.

Now Father charged us with coming up with a 'story' to tell the customer. 'No lies,' he said, 'but it has to be convincing and that means it has to be different from similar products.' 'But it isn't different,' we protested. 'It's an electric light bulb!' 'No, but it can *sound* different without the need to lie about it. When the customer comes to the door tell them that you are introducing this bulb into the area. You aren't going to ask them to buy a lot but you thought they would like to try one of each. Sell them at 100 per cent mark-up, five bob for one of each wattage, which will be about the same as you can buy them in the shops.' 'And suppose they ask us what's special about this bulb?' we asked. 'Well,' he said, 'tell them it has a toughened tungsten filament and is gas filled.' 'But isn't that so for every light bulb?' we asked. 'Yes,' he patiently replied, 'but they won't know that. You're just putting your product across in the best possible way. You've said nothing untrue and you are not selling at an inflated price. They probably won't have any spares in the house, so you're doing them a service. You have absolutely nothing to be ashamed about. If they do know that what you're selling is the same as they can get in the shops you just say "Good afternoon" and leave it at that.'

The next job was to confirm the legality of what we were going to do, so we phoned the council for advice. They were surprisingly helpful, telling us that either we had to take orders for later delivery, to give people time to change their minds, or for direct sales we needed a Tinkers' and Peddlers' Licence. We thought we'd try to avoid the delivery part of the work, so we opted for a Tinkers' and Peddlers' Licence. Rosie – as we called Mother – was incandescent with rage. She wouldn't hear of her boys going to the local post office to ask for such a thing. What would the neighbours think if they got to know? She would have died of shame. She fumed and foamed to the extent that we thought she was in danger of an apoplectic fit, so we dropped the idea and settled for the delivery job and a quieter life.

Good old Rosie, though, did lend us her car for our first sortie into the world of Tinking and Peddling. We realised that we would have to work fast if we were to make any serious money, so we rushed from house to house at high speed, avoiding all offers of cups of tea or conversation as we were acutely aware of the fact that every minute was precious. By and large the customers were a delight, although we did get our fair share of 'Not today, thank yous and Geoff even got one gorilla of a man who let him shoot his story and then said, 'If you're not off my doorstep in five seconds I shall punch your posh little teeth right through the back of your head!' Geoff, remembering Father's advice, drew himself up to his full height, looked this giant of a man straight in the kneecaps and said, 'Good afternoon.'

Most people, though, recognising our financial plight, warmed to a little enterprise and parted with five bob to help us on our way. After all, they had nothing to lose. The most embarrassing moment came when Geoff knocked on a door and was asked the dreaded question, 'So what's so different about these bulbs, then?' Geoff trotted out our by now automatic reply, 'They have a toughened tungsten filament and are gas filled.' A glimmer of a smile flitted across the face of the man at the door, who said, 'Look, I work at the Osram factory just up the road, and I *make* electric light bulbs. I know that *every* light bulb has a toughened tungsten filament and is gas filled.' Geoff, desperately trying to maintain his dignity, coughed out a hurried 'Good afternoon', but the chap called him back and said, 'Well, I can't fault your cheek. Give me two,' and he thrust five bob into Geoff's hand. The world is full of nice people if you look hard enough.

Each Saturday we had the arduous task of delivering the bulbs. This meant setting off early for London to get our supplies (Dad financed us for the first Saturday, on the strength of the hundreds of orders we had taken), and then going back to each house, running backwards and forwards from the car to the houses, like a political canvasser, and putting the money into a box in the back of the car. At the end of the first Saturday we came home exhausted but with a huge box full of money, which we tipped on to the table and counted, with mounting triumph. We'd made a small fortune. In fact it was to be ten years before either of us made as much money again. Mind you, neither of us would have gone through all that turmoil again – we wanted to do something more satisfying – but if ever things get tough for me in my old age I know exactly what I shall do. If you, dear reader, feel a pressing need for some light bulbs, which have a toughened tungsten filament and are gas filled, just give me a ring.

The next memorable milestone in our lives was our twenty-first birthday party. Father had told us after our seventh birthday party in 1943, during the war, that that was the last birthday party we could expect until we were twenty-one, I imagine because he saw the war stretching endlessly forward, and he was a true man of his word. So we were pretty hungry for one by 1957. To give them due credit, Rosie and Cy really pushed the boat out. (We felt that now we were twenty-one it was acceptable to call our revered father Cy – you'll remember that his Christian name was Cyril – and we were a bit surprised to find that he really liked this familiar address. In fact, I once overheard him boasting to one of his friends, 'My kids call me Cy.') We all spent the week before the party in feverish preparation. Rosie was baking and cleaning and cooking and Cy, Geoff and I spent the time making the garden look like Kew, building a little arbour for the use of any couple who felt the need to do the necessary, and putting up strings of soft lights, so that the whole place looked like fairyland.

When the morning of the great day arrived, Cy came into our bedroom to wake us with his usual greeting, drawn unashamedly from *The Rubáiyát* of Omar Khayyám. He would fling back the curtains and shout majestically, as if he were Sir John Gielgud, 'Awake, for morning in the bowl of night hath flung the stone which put the stars to flight, And lo, the Hunter in the East . . .', by which time we had usually sprung out of bed and tackled him manfully to the floor. Once we were washed and dressed, we went down to breakfast to find, propped up on the table, an envelope, obviously written by Cy. We opened it and inside was a birthday card and a small strip of flat metal, like a screwdriver with a tiny metal handle. We couldn't work out what kind of a joke this was, and the old man wasn't going to tell us until we had eaten. So we bolted our food, which was nothing new, and demanded to know. 'Come with me,' he said, and we all trooped down to the bottom of the garden and into the garage. There stood an amorphous shape, covered with a large tarpaulin which, with a theatrical flourish, Cy whipped away – to reveal the neatest, most delicious, little Morris Eight Series E convertible, built in 1936, the year we were born. The small piece of metal was the ignition key. Our reaction was an almighty '*Wow*' of delight, in unison. (We did everything in unison.) Father had bought it for £15 locally and, although it needed some attention, it was the very best thing he could possibly have done. It was also very generous, because £15 was quite a lot of money in those days and we knew that the old chap was quite hard up. In we jumped, side by side, backed it gingerly out of the garage and spent the whole morning driving round and round the country lanes, singing and shouting with joy at this great new addition to our freedom.

The party was a riot, not literally, although it nearly became one when I caught Geoff in the little arbour with Skin McCubbin's sister, a strikingly beautiful girl with long blonde hair and a number of other endowments in addition. I have always wondered about Geoff's preoccupation with love seats and arbours in later life and I'm pretty sure I know what sparked this obsession. All our friends came, and a few we'd never met before, but, as long as they brought their bottle they were welcome. We were showered with generous presents and just couldn't believe our luck. I can't honestly claim to remember how the party ended, not because of my advancing years; I couldn't remember the following morning. Geoff couldn't remember either, but he had a sneaking feeling that he'd done something dire, so he felt the need to ring round to test the water in case he owed somebody an apology, but I don't think he did.

Once the party and the two giant hangovers were over we decided that we just had time to renovate our new car before we went to college. After a close look at the bodywork we found that one wheel arch had rusted and could be seen from the inside of the car. Of course we had no welding equipment and we didn't want to break into our hard-earned money set aside for college expenses, so we decided to do it ourselves. What we needed was a strip of metal, preferably rustproof, but we didn't have any. I am inordinately proud of my brother Geoff, but I do sometimes have to blush at his cheek and his slightly criminal tendencies. Outside the sweet shop in the village stood an enamelled metal sign advertising 'R. White's Lemonade'. 'That sign,' said Geoff, 'is eminently pinchable and it's exactly what we want.' So that night we stole round to the sweet shop and pinched the sign, carrying it back between us, to cut it up and bolt it into place over the rusted spot. We took care to preserve the words 'R. White's Lemonade', which we left proudly showing on the inside of our car, still advertising the product, but also, alas, advertising our misdemeanours.

Next we removed the engine and rebuilt it, replacing all the worn parts. For this tricky job we recruited the services of Ralph Bateman, a friend and amateur mechanic of dubious reputation. He had acquired this reputation after building a wooden body on to an old Riley chassis that he had bought for a few bob somewhere. He, like us, had no access to welding equipment and there were not enough R. White's Lemonade signs to go round, so he built a sturdy frame of two-inch by one-inch timber and covered it with plywood. As he was driving through Broxbourne one day, on the A10, the whole body fell off into the road, like something out of a Laurel and Hardy film. 'My God, Ralph,' we said, 'what did you do?' 'Well, what *could* I do?' he replied shamefacedly. 'I drove on!' But he was a good mechanic and he had the tools, so we made a pretty good job of the engine.

We also decided to make the car more secure by fitting an immobilising switch into the ignition circuit, because it could be switched on with a screwdriver or a penknife. This we hid under the dashboard, and in the event it turned out to be a very useful innovation because, if out driving with a fanciable girl one could drive close to a convenient layby and secretly switch off, causing the engine to die. Then the ploy was to look grave and apologise profusely, before taking the opportunity to do whatever business we felt we could get away with, which I regret to say, was usually surprisingly little in those days of a less liberal society. Then it would be a matter of jumping out of the car, lifting the bonnet and pretending to make adjustments. A further secret flick of the switch and the engine would burst into life, thus greatly impressing the girlfriend and setting up a possible small expansion of the business next time.

We hand-painted the rather ropy bodywork, changing it from black to a bright red, trying to create the illusion of a Ferrari. It didn't look good, but it was the best we could do. The final touch was to replace the hood, which by now had become more collapsible than convertible and I have to confess to an underhand and cruel move, in pursuit of this objective, that I have regretted ever since. I knew of a girl who quite fancied me (yes, there really was one), who was also a good needlewoman. So we bought some black canvas and I persuaded her to make us a hood, at the cost of going out with her a few times. The relationship didn't last for much longer after the hood was fitted. I hope she's forgiven me by now, though that would be more than I deserve.

By now the car was superb. Forty miles an hour top speed if going downhill with a following wind, but even that was exciting because the suspension was so hard that it bounced about all over the road and we came close to landing in the ditch several times. My most frightening experience was caused entirely by Geoff, who clearly had every intention of striking terror into my heart. It had been my turn to use the car and I drove into London to buy something for college. Unfortunately I broke down at the top of Stamford Hill, so I rang Geoff at home and asked him if he would borrow the old man's car to come out and tow me home, which he agreed to do. When he arrived, we attached the tow rope to each car, but I felt that it was really too short to be safe. Since it was all we had, I asked Geoff to drive slowly and carefully to ensure that I could stay in control. Stamford Hill was cobbled at the time, so the surface was extremely rough, but Geoff set off at breakneck speed with me streaming out behind, bouncing all over the road and blowing my horn like fury. I could see his face in the driving mirror of Cy's car and he had a demonic little smile on it. He ignored my frantic hooting and drove like that all the way home, with just the occasional, infuriating wave of encouragement. When I got out, I felt a nervous wreck and he stood smiling at me. 'You bloody idiot,' I said, 'you nearly killed me.' 'Ah,' he said wistfully, 'but I didn't, did I?'

Shortly after this dramatic demonstration of fraternal affection it was time for us to take up our places at Writtle to start our courses. We were lucky enough to be the first students in the brand-new Strutt Hall of Residence, a lovely building, but with shared bedrooms. Geoff and I didn't want to share with each other, so we took pot luck, like all the rest of the students. I got a very quiet, but pleasant lad called David Corry, who was unfortunately afflicted with the most terrible stutter, so making conversation was difficult to say the least. Geoff was fortunate to share a room with a chap called Paddy Barker, who came from a large fruit farm in the romantically named village of Gamlingay in Cambridgeshire. His father was one of the pioneers of the 'dwarf pyramid' fruit tree, grown through a combination of a dwarfing rootstock and a rigorous pruning regime, so he was already very knowledgeable about fruit and helped Geoff a great deal by passing that knowledge on to him. But the most endearing thing about Paddy was that he was a warm, humorous rascal who joined in many of our pranks and dangerous escapades.

It was at this point that Geoff and I began, for the first time in our lives, to pursue separate paths. Although we shared some good social evenings together, I saw nothing of him during the day and we found different friends and different interests to fill our leisure time – not that there was much of that. Students had to work hard in those days and, with the exception of the odd prank, we were both too absorbed in our studies to spend much time together.

Geoff's curriculum for the National Diploma in Horticulture was demanding, covering the whole range of horticultural activities. This involved not only lectures, often delivered at lightning speed, with students scribbling feverishly to take notes, but also a great deal of good solid practical work. This included glasshouse work, learning all aspects of the production of garden plants, but also commercial crops like tomatoes and cucumbers. Outside he covered the whole range of market gardening, fruit and flower production, all in meticulous detail. He was even subjected to instruction in flower arranging – not his favourite subject, but the tutor, a man who had come from Constance Spry, a very fashionable name in flower arranging at the time, was such an engaging personality and loved Geoff's cheeky sense of humour so much that he enjoyed even that. Not that I ever saw him arrange any flowers at home, however.

Geoff got a bit of a reputation as a lively contributor to lectures, often arguing the toss with his elders and betters and not always getting it right. For example, on one occasion the discussion had turned to water divining and its strange power. He left the class in convulsions of laughter by, in all seriousness, proclaiming that he had read of a diviner who didn't need to use a divining rod of any kind because he had a painful muscular spasm every time he passed water.

Most evenings were spent catching up with the notes that had been taken during the day, revising the information and getting them into some sort of readable order. There were also assignments set by seemingly vindictive tutors, which kept our several noses closely applied to the grindstone. During the evenings and weekends, Geoff could often be seen wandering round the extensive gardens at Writtle, memorising the Latin names for plants and their descriptions, with the result that by the end of his two years at college he had an almost encyclopaedic knowledge of plant names. This was surprising, since the sum total of his knowledge of Latin at school extended to *amo, amas, amat, hic, haec, hoc* and, of course, 'the having-been–beaten Romans', which he could only say in English and which knowledge could not be said to have served him well in later life. He also came with me on my expeditions into the countryside, looking for wild flowers and agricultural weeds, which we had been charged with collecting, pressing and identifying. We did the identification with a wonderful book called *Flora of the British Isles* by Clapham, Tutin and Warburg, which enabled us to recognise any wild plant through the most elegant process of elimination. The book was very expensive, paid for with our electric light bulb money, and Geoff and I would spend hours poring over it and the specimens we had collected, labelling and pressing until we had a huge collection. A very satisfying occupation, which I am determined to resume when I am old and doddery and good for little else – in a couple of months' time.

Geoff's great love had always been his greenhouse, ever since we went with Father, when we were aged about ten, to buy a second-hand dilapidated structure for £2, which we transported home, with great difficulty and no little danger, down the A10 on the Boy Scouts' hand cart. He and Cy had erected it, repaired it, fitted it out and stocked it on hardly any money but with a lot of inventiveness and pleasure. He would grow enormous mop-head chrysanthemums, carnations and fuchsias as well as border plants and vegetable plants for me, as I had been designated vegetable supremo.

So imagine his joy when he was first given sight of the spacious glasshouse complex at Writtle, in which he was to begin to gather a confident knowledge of glasshouse practice. Glasshouses were all wooden structures in those days and not equipped with the modern gadgetry for environmental control that now exists, so people had to find other ways to create the optimum conditions for growth. Ian Lambert, the tutor responsible for the glasshouse unit reported in 1959, Geoff's final year, that, 'We can now produce three crops a year. Long days are artificially produced using ordinary light bulbs and short days can be produced by using black plastic sheeting.' A far cry from today's commercial techniques, but more than adequate at the time. Geoff loved to work in the glasshouses and began to develop an ambition to make this his life's work. But this was a commercial undertaking, without the diversity and interest of his little greenhouse at home and it began to dawn on him that he could be faced with a lifetime of tying in tomatoes and pinching out laterals. So, whilst he maintained a passionate interest in the work, his focus for the future gradually began to shift away to pastures new. His view of the possible boredom of work in a large commercial glasshouse enterprise was reinforced when he and I, during one vacation and between bouts of selling electric light bulbs, got a temporary job with Thomas Rochford, then the biggest indoor plant grower in the country. They had 200 ft by 50 ft glasshouses devoted entirely to one type of plant and he and I were led into one house on our first day to be greeted by literally thousands upon thousands of aphelandras, standing in serried ranks as far as the eye could see, potted into six-inch pots. 'There you are,' said the foreman. 'Pot those on into nine-inch pots.' 'What, all of them?' we said, aghast. 'Yes, all of them,' he said, and added with a little grin, 'You've got all day!' Neither Geoff nor I have ever bought an aphelandra since and personally, if they were to find their way on to the endangered species list, nobody would be more relieved than I.

When Geoff returned to Writtle for the following term, although he was still ravenously hungry for knowledge about fruit and vegetable growing, as well as glasshouse work, his real attention turned to ornamental plants and garden design. And this was where our identical genes seemed to play tricks, because he discovered a positive flair for design and for planting in pleasing combinations of colour and form, whilst I plodded away with my lack of creativity burning like a beacon before me. It was perhaps fortunate that I had decided to become a farmer rather than a gardener.

Faced with this mountain of work and both determined to do well, we had little opportunity for a social life, but by golly, when we did socialise we really did socialise. However, most of it had to be free of charge, so we turned our minds to pranks and wheezes. We had a tutor who had been giving us a bad time, with grumbles, suggestions that we were not doing as well as we should, and punishment with the imposition of extra work, so Geoff and I decided that something had to be done. The tutor had an old banger of a car, which looked like a Model T Ford, so we decided to carry out a 'spectacular', as any terrorist group would have called it. We gathered together a group of young men whom we knew to be equally foolhardy and intemperate and, led by Geoff, we all agreed to meet at 2.00 a.m. outside the Strutt Hall of Residence. Some extensive building work was going on in the grounds, so our first move was to liberate two or three long ladders from their site and to put them up against the front wall of the college. We then quietly pushed the car to the foot of the ladders, carefully tied some ropes to it, taking care not to damage it, climbed to the roof and hoisted it up so that it was sitting astride the parapet at the eaves of the roof, some thirty feet above ground level. We then replaced the ladders, hid the ropes and slipped gratefully into bed. In those days the only entrance to the college was via the front drive, so next day each arriving tutor could not fail to see the car sitting aloft in all its glory. We were gratified to see groups of puzzled tutors standing beneath, scratching their heads and wondering how to get it down. We were exultant to see the tutor to whom it belonged jumping from foot to foot in fury. Nobody ever discovered who was responsible and, if I knew Ben Harvey, the principal, he would have enjoyed the prank as much as we did.

We aimed for a 'spectacular' at regular intervals, just to keep the staff on their toes. The next was to steal a hot-dog stall from Chelmsford, tow it to Writtle and set it up outside the main doors of the college with a large sign on it saying 'Ben's Hot Dogs'. I'm not sure Ben Harvey took that one so well, but it was a joy to see one of our tutors sheepishly towing it back to Chelmsford with one of the farm tractors, escorted by a black Wolseley police car, ringing its bell to warn the traffic.

Our next adventure took us to the traffic island in the village. It was a large island with a garage built on it, so it was not possible to see over it. For this little jape we borrowed some traffic signs from a contractor who was working on the road in the village and positioned them so that the traffic was directed round and round the island in a never-ending and more and more congested stream. We then sat back to admire our work and to witness the increasing frustration of motorists.

Our final triumph was directed at our warden, who had developed an unsociable habit of checking that we had arrived back at the hall by 11.00 p.m., as stated in the rules. So again, led by Geoff, an inveterate scoundrel, we decided to 'doctor' his car. Vandalism would not have entered our heads in those days, so damaging it was taboo, but inconveniencing the owner was OK. In the dead of night we assembled again. We had just had a new, modern dining hall built and it had a single door with a large glass panel adjacent to it, all mounted in a hardwood frame. This we carefully unscrewed and, with the help of the giants from the rugby team, manhandled the whole assembly to one side. We were then able to quietly push the warden's car into the middle of the dining hall and replace the frame. It was a surprisingly innocent bunch of students who gathered for breakfast the following morning to discover a group of tutors earnestly discussing how we had got it in and how on earth they were going to get it out! Well, boys will be boys!

Of course our academic work was punctuated by some inordinately long holidays, which we had to spend largely working to earn enough money for the following term. Nevertheless we revived the Rapide Club meetings, rowed every evening and had time for romantic interludes of the sweetest kind. I often think that the awful blaring sounds of the discotheque have completely killed the age of romance. No longer can you whisper in the ear of your beloved, 'My word, you look lovely tonight, Miranda' – that just isn't the kind of thing you can shout at 300 decibels.

The holiday we awaited with the greatest anticipation was Christmas. Christmas in our house was the only time when we three boys would all get together and, often to the chagrin of our parents, and later our wives, we set out to laugh from morning to night. We would have quizzes, card games, board games, etc., just like any normal family, and we would also sing and play guitars together. Our brother Mark was a very accomplished guitarist, Geoff was passing fair and I could create harmonies to any tune, so we had the raw material for some good, old-fashioned fun. We would record our work on Cy's huge reel-to-reel tape recorder, subsequently playing it back to politely appreciative parents. Oh, the guilt now when I think back to the pain we inflicted on them, assuaged to some extent by memories of Cy creeping in when Rosie's back was turned to add his basso profundo to the choir.

All this was, to our everlasting shame, accompanied by an excessive consumption of alcohol, as a result of which the laughter gradually got more coarse and the jokes more ribald. There is no doubt that our greatest joy arose from the limerick game, which we would often prolong to the early hours of the morning. The game was not carried out in the normal way, with each person contributing a line at a time; in our version each person was given a first line and could then retire to think about it, returning with the completed rhyme. Invariably they had us laughing uncontrollably. Most of them were too rude to print but perhaps a couple of examples will give you the flavour. The first was one of mine. When I returned to tell it to the other two, I simply couldn't stand for laughing and had to crawl into the sitting room. It then took about twenty minutes to actually recite it.

A chubby young stripper named Gertie
Had an act indescribably dirty.
The sight of her paps
Would intrigue all the chaps,
'Cos she didn't have two, she had thirty.

Geoff's most printable effort caused him some consternation when he first received the challenge and he retired grumbling at the difficulty of the line, which was 'A hairy gorilla from Rheims'. He returned, however, with:

A hairy gorilla from Rheims
Was subject to erotic dreams.
He said it's no good
To keep pulling my pud,
I'm coming apart at the seams.

We continued with 'A medical student named Martin', 'The dirty old bishop from Crewe' and many others, none of which are printable, but could be sent in a plain envelope for a small fee.

Back at college our work continued, with rising panic as the time for our final examinations approached. In the event they turned out to be less intimidating than we had expected, although both Geoff and I were convinced that we had failed. The last days of the final term were passed in a dream. No more academic work, no more exams, just an endless round of fun and frolic – and big, agricultural young men can be unusually frolicsome when they try. Raids on Longmeads, the women's hostel, were not infrequent and noticeably not repelled with the enthusiasm one would have expected from polite young ladies. I can remember taking part in a football match with Geoff, in blazing sunshine, that took literally all day, at the end of which we were utterly exhausted and stiff in muscles we didn't actually have. Oh, for that kind of energy now!

On the final day of term the college staged a ball, in a huge marquee pitched on one of the extensive lawns. We all brought girlfriends, dressed up to the nines and danced all night to the music of the Geraldo orchestra. It was a memorable way to end our college career. Then all we had to do was to await our results, which came surprisingly quickly, before we left for good the following day. Both Geoff and I passed with distinction. Our first job was to phone home to tell the folks. We found Cy to be quite downbeat and unexcited but when we got home it was quite clear that he was excessively proud of his two prodigal sons and the fatted calf was duly consumed. So now that Geoff and I had our certificates, what we each needed was a job.

CHAPTER 5

Geoff's First Faltering Steps

W^{E HAVE TO STEP BACK A PACE} to 1958, when we were still at college, to find the place where the next momentous stage of Geoff's life began. It was at a party in, of all unlikely places, Stoke Poges in Buckinghamshire. Alan Higginson, who had been in Geoff's Badger Patrol in the Scouts when we were boys and had also attended the same course at Writtle, invited us to a kind of house-warming, since he and his sister Joan had moved there from Broxbourne with their parents. The party was in full swing when we arrived and it was immediately clear that, like most young people's parties of the day, it was to be based on jazz, swing and alcohol. The final crucial component was, of course, flirting with the girls.

Geoff set to work immediately but in the crush of people it was some time before he noticed a strikingly beautiful but retiring girl, sitting alone at the side of the room. When he plucked up the courage to ask her to dance (beautiful girls suffer from the disadvantage that they are often not asked because of men's fear of rejection), he was bowled over by a reply in a strong, delightful French accent. She was Colette Joulin, a French milliner, in this country to learn the language. It may sound a cliché to call her a French milliner, but that's what she was. She worked for a very exclusive company in London, and her design and millinery skills were little short of miraculous.

Colette remembers Geoff as a funny young man with very untidy hair, which is about right. He remembered her as a princess, which is also about right. I can't remember that night very well because, having been unsuccessful with the flirting, I had resorted to the jazz, swing and alcohol. All I can remember is that, after they had poured me into the front seat of our old Morris, I woke to find Geoff, in a haze of euphoria, driving the wrong way down a dual carriageway at two o'clock in the morning. Fortunately, at that time of night and in the period before every family had eighteen cars, there was no traffic on the road and we had encountered no danger and no policemen, so I was able to advise him diplomatically of his mistake and, with a cherubic smile he turned the car round and went back to the next roundabout.

So Geoff engaged in weekend courtship until we had graduated from college. During this time Geoff told me of some of the embarrassments caused by Colette's imperfect mastery of the English language, the worst of which was the evening he took her to the cinema. While they were sitting in the dark, munching their popcorn, Colette dropped her glasses on the floor and, with typical Gallic panache, exclaimed loudly to Geoff, with her strong French accent, 'Oh, Geoffrey, I have lost the testicles.' I'm glad to report that her English has improved greatly since that night and that no damage was done either to spectacles or testicles.

Geoff was always optimistic about every aspect of his life and he could convince himself that all would be well, whatever the circumstances. Accordingly he was unshakable in his belief that a long and happy future lay ahead of him with Colette. So, with no prospects of a job, an income or a place to live after he left college, he proposed to Colette and she accepted, much to the delight of our parents, who were equally bowled over by her charm.

After he had graduated from college, more in desperation than by design, Geoff approached Jack Alison, the Lea Valley tomato grower he had worked for before, who fortunately was able to offer him a job. As this entailed Geoff stepping back to pinching out laterals and tying in plants, which he had decided he didn't want to do, despite Jack being a good, constructive employer Geoff was far from satisfied. But uppermost in his mind was not his job but the fact that he was to be married in December.

Before he could do that he had to meet Colette's parents, who lived in St Mandé, a suburb of Paris. Neither of them spoke English and Geoff's French was, to say the least, a bit 'schoolboy'. His only boast was that he could find his way to the station, could book a room for up to four people and had never lost the pen of his aunt. But this was not enough to make good conversation, so Geoff was expecting a hard time. In the event Colette translated with consummate ease, Geoff did his best with the smattering he did have and all in all it was a great success. He also demonstrated his commitment by taking instruction to become a Roman Catholic, but I'm afraid his religious conviction didn't last long.

They were married twice, in fact, once at St Pancras Register Office on 14 December 1959 and again at Colette's church in St Mandé. We had been used to our beautiful but rather humble low church in Broxbourne and Geoff was quite unprepared for the Catholic richness of ornamentation, robes, music, language and ceremony, and I felt for him as he went through a bewildering service, conducted in a language he didn't understand. The reception was held at the home of Monsieur and Madame Joulin and was made memorable by the staggering excess of French hospitality. The meal took four hours to consume, with lengthy breaks between what seemed like dozens of courses (no fast food in the Joulin household) and the champagne seemed to come from a bottomless vat. We all found it possible to converse, albeit falling about laughing at each other's silly mistakes, which only heightened the enjoyment of an unforgettable occasion.

But once Geoff and Colette came home from their honeymoon the realities of life began to bite. They began their married life in a little flat in a leafy suburban road in Broxbourne but soon found a house to rent in Ware Park called the Old Vicarage. It stood in several acres of parkland and was an idyllic place to be, but since Geoff had very little money he found it difficult to furnish and heat adequately. Soon the pressure of lack of money began to take its toll. Geoff had, by this time, decided to set up on his own in garden maintenance but he was, as I have already intimated, perhaps the worst businessman in the history of commerce, a problem he had all his life, although after his writing and television success he had enough money to hide his inadequacy completely. At that time he would disregard financial problems and, like Mr Micawber, hope that something would turn up. If brown envelopes came through the letterbox he would ignore them, particularly if they had 'OHMS' printed on the front. He would do the same with those which had Barclays Bank printed on the front, which led him into all kinds of difficulty. There came a stage when, as he had done nothing about his increasing overdraft, the bank stopped honouring his cheques. In their efforts to get his finances settled, they would write to him, but he would not reply, so the bank manager would visit his house in the evening to confront him, but Geoff would see his car coming through the park and hide. In the end Geoff's despair became so apparent that Cy dug deep and baled him out. His problem arose because he wasn't earning enough, but neither was his work satisfying him, so the family held a council of war to decide what to do about his precarious position.

The result was that early in 1960 he took the plunge and set up as a landscape gardener, with a second-hand Rotovator, a bunch of old tools he'd scrounged from Cy and a clapped-out pick-up truck. He also moved house to a cheaper property in Wharf Road, Wormley, just a stone's throw from Broxbourne. It was a tiny house with two small bedrooms and an outside lavatory, so it wasn't exactly the kind of luxury he would have liked to present to his new wife, but they both realised it was all they could afford. Geoff also realised that he had a huge financial hill to climb if he was ever going to pay Cy back, so he now set to work with a vengeance.

He was good at getting work because Geoff didn't lack charm, so he could persuade people to undertake much more ambitious schemes than they had originally envisaged, thus turning small assignments into big ones. He was an inspired garden designer and he would produce beautiful coloured drawings that would immediately excite the imaginations and desires of his potential customers. He could also execute the work with great skill, with the result that the finished product looked like something straight from a glossy magazine. Consequently his reputation gradually began to grow, and so did his order book.

He was an extremely hard and dedicated worker, often working twelve-hour days, even working by the headlights of his truck to get a job finished. He rented a small plot of land close to his home and on it he erected his very first polytunnel, which he used to propagate and grow plants for use in his business, thus improving his profit margin. So his income began to climb and his life began to stabilise.

But as his workload expanded he realised that he could no longer manage alone, so as well as enlisting my help when my own job as a farm manager allowed, he began to take on staff. This was the cause of his next round of business disasters. Geoff's boundless optimism and constant cheerfulness were unquestionably great assets – they made him good to be with and gave his customers confidence; but they also led him into the most staggering acts of foolhardiness. When he began to look for help he didn't look for one person, he looked for three, because he was convinced that he had the work to keep them employed, which at the time was probably true. What he hadn't considered was the fact that his staff had to be paid during inclement weather, when no work could be done, and during the periods when work was light. He found his profit margin falling and, because he felt obliged to buy materials up front and refused to ask for advance payment, his cash flow began to suffer as well. This was exacerbated by the fact that people didn't pay him on time – particularly rich people. So the dreaded letters from the bank started to reappear and Geoff's worries began to mount again, but he soldiered on regardless. Something, he was sure, would turn up.

He did some wonderfully inventive work throughout Hertfordshire and Essex, as well as the odd assignment in Chelsea, Kensington and even Mayfair, so his reputation for the quality of his work began to spread, but his cash-flow problems began to rise in direct proportion. However, he was enjoying the work and his greatest joy was to take a piece of land covered in brambles and nettles and turn it into a beautiful garden where the owner could relax and escape from what Geoff rather cynically thought of as the tribulations of making very large amounts of money. One such owner was a bookmaker, who lived in Broxbourne and who gave Geoff the job of redesigning his very ordinary garden. One day he arrived home to his palatial house and, climbing out of his car, Geoff noticed that he looked tired and world-weary. Ever concerned about the people around him, Geoff asked him if he was OK. 'No, I'm not,' said the bookmaker irritably. 'I've just lost sixty thousand pounds on the Boat Race.' 'Oh my God,' said Geoff, having visions of his payment disappearing as the bookie went broke. 'What are you going to do?' 'Oh, don't worry,' he said with a little grin, 'I'll make it up again next week on the Grand National.' And he did, and he paid, and he did it on time, and Geoff and he stayed firm friends thereafter.

Geoff's landscaping career also gave rise to a mass of funny incidents, many of which Geoff embellished outrageously in the telling, but I know this one is true because I was with him at the time. He had enlisted my help to clear a pile of rough old soil which needed to be removed to a landfill site. By this time he had graduated from his clapped-out pick-up truck to a clapped-out tipper truck. This was an extremely small truck and the tipping mechanism consisted of a handle which was wound from one side of the body. In order to save time Geoff overloaded the truck to about twice its normal capacity, so that it was right down on the springs. This brought the front wheels up, making the truck very light on the steering. 'You'd better come with me to give us a bit of ballast,' said Geoff, as though my meagre nine stone six was going to make any difference. So in I got and we set off, with the truck meandering all over the road as we went over bumps and pot holes. We had just got into the centre of Hoddesdon, our local town, when a policeman stepped out into the road, holding up his hand to stop us, even though we were travelling at no more than twenty miles per hour. Geoff cursed at his bad luck and suddenly remembered that, because of his financial problems, he hadn't taxed the truck. So, quick as a flash, he jumped out and leaned nonchalantly against the bonnet, with his hand on the windscreen, obscuring the tax disc. 'Excuse me, sir,' said the constable, 'but do you realise that your truck is grossly overloaded and you represent a danger to the public?' 'Yes,' said Geoff, 'but I have to finish this job today or pay a large penalty clause, which could bankrupt me. I was rather hoping you'd forgive me under the circumstances.' 'Well, I might,' the constable replied in measured tones, 'but what do we have under here, sir?' And with that he began to prise Geoff's fingers, one by one from the obscured tax disc until the whole awful truth was revealed. It is to the constable's everlasting credit that he charged us with nothing but asked Geoff to present his new tax disc in five days' time and not to overload his truck in future. It was, in fact, a profitable day for Geoff because he learned not only that he should obey the law but also that the police are, by and large, observant, intelligent and humane. For ever after he would be inflamed by people who, on the basis of no general evidence, would claim otherwise.

One of Geoff's incurable weaknesses was also one of the characteristics which made him such good company. It was his passion for a joke. He would do outrageous things, often without a thought for the consequences, just to bask in the pleasure of other people's laughter. From time to time his desire to make the joke would not take into account the feelings of the person he was joking about, but he was such an engaging character that this rarely upset anybody. However, joking often got him into trouble. On one occasion at about this time he was with the boys from the rowing club in a restaurant in Leicester, having dinner together after a particularly successful regatta they had been to. The waitress was extremely pretty and, as she served Geoff, he said, 'What would it cost for me to persuade you to come out with me?' 'More than you've got,' the waitress replied. 'OK,' said Geoff, 'but I'm very rich.' 'Well, what about a million pounds?' said the waitress, a wise and level-headed girl. With that Geoff whipped out his chequebook and wrote a cheque for a million pounds, which he gave to her. She tucked it into her bodice and disappeared, amid much laughter. But the next day she presented it to the bank. Geoff got a stern phone call from the bank manager, who asked him to come to the bank immediately, where he sat, head bowed in contrition, while the manager pointed out the error, and indeed the fraudulent nature of his action. Geoff left with his tail between his legs, a good lesson under his belt, and fortunately his tiny balance intact.

One of Geoff's business weaknesses was that he never developed 'an eye for a deal', as Cy used to call it. Perhaps it was linked to his innate desire to treat his customers fairly, to do a first-rate job and not to overcharge, but I'm sure that this integrity led him away from some profit that other landscape gardeners would have snapped up with alacrity. This was exemplified by a job he was asked to quote for in Chelsea. It was a big house and the owners were clearly very wealthy indeed, but it was just a small job, worth about £90. Although £90 was a lot of money in those days, he had plenty of other, more local work on and the thought of driving in and out of London didn't fill him with enthusiasm. So he asked me what he thought he should do and I advised that, if he really didn't want the job, he should price himself out of the market. 'Put in a huge price,' I said. 'You never know, they may even accept it!' So he quoted £900, ten times what he thought it was worth, and then forgot about it, with no intention of following up such a ludicrous quotation. He was surprised and delighted to receive a letter a few days later, accepting the proposal. That helped the cash flow quite a lot – but it never caused Geoff to stop and question his pricing policy. He based that judgement on what *he* would pay for the work he did and I'm afraid he had too low an opinion of his own abilities. I begged and pleaded with him to try inching his prices up, but stubbornness was another of his failings and he resolutely refused, despite the disastrous writing on the wall. It was always a puzzle to me that Geoff never really regarded himself as a success, even later when he had so clearly become one. Gay Search, who worked with him and befriended him during much of his television career, says that she regarded him as something of a lost soul, with a great, blustering charm on the outside but a sense of

Geoff and his faithful friend Moss, who died a week after his master (*Stephen Hamilton*)

Cyril, the Whitechapel dandy, aged twenty-seven

Rose, demure and beautiful, was an irresistible attraction for Cyril

Cy, and Rosie, as they came to be known, still looking sprauncy in later life

Gram (Allie) and Gramp (Alf), out for the day with Rosie and Mark, in 1935

Geoff (left) Mark (centre) and Tony (right) looking angelic as they try desperately to suppress the devilish giggles within

The twins proudly receive their Queen's Scout badges. Geoff confident as usual, while Tony can't quite believe it

Mop-headed Geoff, aged sixteen, tending his favourite mop-headed chrysanthemums

Geoff and Tony pose in what they believed to be deep sophistication during National Service in Germany

There was a vague similarity about Geoff and Tony in RAF uniform, a disguise that was to fool the entire military establishment

Rebels at Writtle celebrate a less than academic achievement, which was shortly to dismay a tutor (*Writtle College*)

A very youthful Geoff with his enchanting French bride, Colette

Geoff endlessly advised the customers in his tiny garden centre, one of the many factors that caused its eventual downfall

Times were improving for Geoff when he attended the 'Twinning with Paris' celebration. Seen here with Carol, his first employee and Nancy, a good friend

Anglia TV's *Gardening Diary* was Geoff's first sortie into the world of television. Here he presents a programme from the Chelsea Flower Show (*Anglia TV*)

The doughty team at Top Cottage, the first Barnsdale. Carol (left), Geoff (centre) and Rod (right)

Carol, the diminutive diva (left) and Geoff, the basso profundo, singing outside with the Exton singers, one of the happiest collaborations of Geoff's later life

One of Geoff's first broadcasts from Top Cottage, a desolate sea of mud that was somehow transformed into entrancing television by its brilliant producer, John Kenyon

Television cameras record Geoff's advice on deep beds during an early *Gardener's World*, in its new, more practical format

The second Barnsdale – the house which excited Geoff's imagination and was to become the source of his great contentment

insecurity on the inside. He was a person who greatly needed the love and approbation of others and although, with a few notable exceptions, he was much admired and loved for his work, he had that black dog of doubt resting constantly on his shoulder.

Nevertheless he continued to work hard and creatively, determined to trade his way out of his troubles. By this time two of his three children had been born. Stephen Jean-Marc was born on 30 January 1961, just ten days after my own daughter Kate, so it is not difficult to imagine the joy in the Hamilton households with two new grandchildren and the volume of babies' head wetting that went on. And there was a repeat command performance for Geoff sixteen months later when Nicholas Pascal hove kicking and bawling into view, on 30 April 1962. Stephen and Nick were to be joined later on 26 January 1964 by Christopher Daniel. But when the the initial euphoria began to fade, Geoff realised that he now had a lot to provide for and very limited resources to do it, a position which I know caused him deep anxiety. Unfortunately then came the winter of 1963, when it snowed and it snowed and it snowed. The snow carpeted every job that Geoff had started for three months, making any attempt at work impossible. What he should have done, and indeed, what I advised him to do, was lay off his staff and hope that he could pick them up again when the weather improved. But Geoff knew that this would cause them immense hardship and his conscience wouldn't let him do it. So he went on paying them, and his overdraft mounted and mounted. Unfortunately he chose to ease his troubled mind with his friends in the rowing club, which in turn began to put pressure on his marriage, so for both Geoff and Colette it was a tough time, although none of his kids was aware of any problems and each remembers their time at Wharf Road with great happiness and affection.

By the time the snow had gone and spring began to show its face, the financial hill was back, glowering over everything Geoff did and during the next few years seemingly impossible to climb. This pressure seemed to affect his morale, not outwardly, because he still appeared to be his old bouncy self, but I could easily see that he had internalised his problems and was, once again, unable to face them head on. I would occasionally drop into our parents' home in Broxbourne and I would often find Geoff there, drinking coffee and arguing some philosophical or political point with Cy, when he should have been out working. The consequences were inevitable and in 1967 he was obliged to close down the business, with the loss of all he had.

At that stage he could have gone on the dole, but that just wasn't Geoff's style. He had always worked hard and now he searched around for something which would earn him enough to keep his family. He decided that he had to do anything that presented itself, so during the day he would go picking potatoes or Brussels sprouts or topping carrots, and in the evening he would do the odd bit of garden consultancy or design. These were desperate times for Geoff and they inevitably reflected sadly on Colette as well, though she continued manfully to hold the fort and take care of her three lively little boys.

Eventually in 1970 Geoff succumbed to Cy, who had been suggesting for months that Geoff should go to work for him. Cy could not afford to pay him wages but he would let Geoff take all the profit from any sales he made. Well, this seemed like a tempting offer, so he agreed to go for a week of training with Cy, whose East End background had made him a superb salesman, making quite a lot of money from selling industrial boiler parts – mainly gasket material for plates and pipe flanges. Geoff's romantic and bucolic nature was not exactly inspired by plates and pipe flanges, but being in dire need, he really had no option.

The first stage of the training was to teach Geoff the 'story'. They sat together for the whole of one day practising it until Cy was convinced that Geoff had it right. Then it was out on the road to try it for real. Geoff's first call was organised by Cy, who drove him to a small factory and said, 'OK, try your luck.' Geoff went in, and with great trepidation asked for the engineering manager. When the man arrived, Geoff shot the well-learned story, but noticed that his potential customer was becoming more and more incredulous. But he listened patiently until Geoff had finished and then he said, 'Do you know what we make here, son?' 'No,' said Geoff, with a growing sense of misgiving. 'We make candles,' he said, 'by hand! We wouldn't have any use for your stuff in a million years.' Calling on his light-bulb-selling experience, Geoff said, 'Good afternoon,' and walked regally away. He got back in the car and he could only say to Cy, 'You bastard!' Cy smiled at him and said, 'Geoff, you've just learned your first sales lesson. Always find out what your customer does before you try to sell to him.'

After that things got easier. He didn't take to the work, and never matched Cy's sales figures – Geoff was amazed to see how silver-tongued Cyril could coax orders out of his customers, but he made just about enough to keep his several bodies and souls together.

Cy was a hard act to follow. On one occasion Geoff introduced himself to the engineering manager in a large and well-known company and, at the sound of the company name, he stopped Geoff in his tracks and, taking him silently by the hand, led him across the shop floor to the stores. It was *built* out of gasket material. 'I had one of your people here about six months ago,' he said, 'and he sold me enough to last me two hundred years. We built the bloody stores out of it just to get it out of the way. Don't you dare come back here trying to do it again.' 'What did he look like?' said Geoff. 'He was a distinguished-looking bloke with a grey moustache,' said the manager. 'Good afternoon,' said Geoff, and beat a hasty retreat.

On another occasion he called on a very large company and asked for the engineering manager again. The receptionist asked for his name and when he told her she said, 'Ah yes, Mr Hamilton, we were expecting you. Would you care to join the others in the board room?' Geoff, bemused, was given a badge with his name stylishly printed on it and directed to the board room, where he found himself participating in a presentation about the company. He was then asked to join a party of people who were being shown round the factory, but Geoff, being short of time and quite unsettled by now, asked again if he could see the engineering manager. 'No,' he was told, 'the managing director would like to see you first.' So he was shown into the managing director's office, introduced as Mr Hamilton and put into a plush leather chair.

'Scotch?' said the MD. 'Well, yes,' said Geoff hesitantly. 'How's your wife?' said the MD. 'Oh, fine,' said Geoff, getting more and more puzzled. 'And the kids?' 'Yes, they're fine too.' 'Another Scotch?' 'Well, yes,' said Geoff, feeling the situation getting quite surreal. 'Good health,' said the MD. 'Been on your holidays yet?'

Geoff decided he could take this no longer and said, 'Look, who do you think I am?' 'Well,' said the MD, taken aback, 'you're Mr Hamilton of Hamilton Brushes, aren't you?' 'No,' said Geoff, 'I'm just Mr Hamilton and I've come to sell you some gasket material!'

The managing director's mouth dropped open and, after a lapse of a second or so, he burst into uncontrollable fits of laughter. 'Oh dear, oh dear,' he said, 'I've entirely forgotten what the bugger looks like. He must be out there on the interminable factory tour. Come on, this is too good not to warrant another Scotch.' So Geoff, who was also giggling maniacally, sat and drank copious amounts of Scotch, had a wonderfully funny conversation but sold no gasket material at all. But then, as he was half full of Scotch that didn't seem to matter too much. Mind you, he had to sleep in his car for three hours before he dared drive home, but he felt it was worth it.

Geoff found the job more and more tedious and dispiriting, but he was still in Mr Micawber mode and knew that, sooner or later, something would turn up. Sure enough, one day in 1970 he was prompted to take an action which was to change the whole course of his life although he had some further trials to go through before the celestial goods were properly delivered.

During an interview with Radio Leicester he was quizzed by John Florence about this period in his life and he said:

I believe that up there in the sky there's some lady who looks down at me and says, 'Look we've got to give this guy a break,' and she looked down that day because there was I doing this terrible job and it was a lovely sunny day and I was in the country, driving towards Birmingham. I saw, standing outside a gate, a pile of turf, a few boards, a barrow and a rake and I looked at these things and I said to myself, 'I've *got* to become a landscape gardener again. I've got to get back into it.' So I went into the first nursery I came to and asked if I could please borrow the trade magazines. The chap lent a magazine to me and in it there was an advertisement for a piece of land for rent that could be turned into a garden centre. It was in Kettering. It was under a box number and it said 'a mile off the A6 in a thriving Midlands town'. So I went back home and phoned the magazine and said, 'Can you give me the telephone number of this box number?' They said, 'No, we can't. That's what we have box numbers for.' So I said, 'OK, so you phone the owner and give him my number and tell him I'm interested.' I then got in my car and I drove up the A6 and I went a mile up every road in every town in the Midlands until I found the place, so that I could say to the owner, 'Yes, I'll have it.' And so I rented this small garden centre from this chap.

It was about five acres of land with a small, single-storey building on it, which would do for a shop, and a small range of wooden out-buildings behind. It was ideal for what Geoff wanted. It was also close to where I lived. As he drove home, his excitement mounted. He telephoned the journal as soon as he could, to ask if they would release the name of the vendor, but they wouldn't, so he asked if they would get the vendor to phone him so that they could discuss the proposition. He got a call that very evening and, after that conversation and the subsequent signing of a few papers, he became the proud owner of a business called the Hamilton Garden Centre in Weekley, near Kettering. He had no money to finance it, no stock and no customers but he did have an unshakable faith and a spirited, though somewhat dubious optimism that all would be well.

First of all he went to see the bank manager who, much to Geoff's surprise, fell over himself to offer him money. This, of course, was the 1970s when the banks were lending money for business indiscriminately to every Tom, Dick or Harry who asked for it, whether or not their business had a chance of succeeding. I can remember being approached on the street with an offer of a Barclaycard. No checks, no credit rating, nothing. So Geoff got his money, without having to provide a business plan or a cash-flow forecast or any evidence of his ability to succeed. I thought, and I still do think, that the granting of such loans was a heinous crime for the banks to commit, but commit it they did and of course, being banks with huge political clout, they got off with it scot-free, leaving countless ill-advised small businessmen and women to lose their all.

Geoff immediately plunged himself into the establishment of his new business with an enthusiasm that only he could muster. (Well, perhaps there were a few others – Captain Scott, Edmund Hillary, Winston Churchill, etc. – but there weren't many.) He started by refurbishing the shop and landscaping the area immediately outside it, and at the same time he bought stock and built a large area with paved or gravelled paths for lining out hundreds of trees, shrubs and herbaceous plants. Each weekend I would go up to help him to do this, because he couldn't afford paid labour, and together we worked hard to get it shipshape for the opening. Even Cy joined in, labouring like a good'un at the age of sixty-five. We were all desperately anxious that the enterprise should be a success, because up to now success for Geoff had seemed as elusive as an English Test victory. By the time opening day arrived, the place looked immaculate and the customers began to roll in.

While Geoff was running his garden centre, he met a lady gardener whom he venerated, partly because of her remarkably varied and interesting experience, partly because she was such a good grower and partly because she was such a gracious and generous-hearted person. She was Valerie Finnis, a renowned alpine grower and flower photographer. She is also well known as the founder of the Merlin Trust, which she set up in memory of her son, Merlin Scott who, whilst still an undergraduate, was killed in North Africa during the Second World War. Merlin was clearly a gifted amateur naturalist for he had found and identified every known species of British butterfly except one before he was twenty. The trust is also dedicated to her husband Sir David Scott, a diplomat and also a naturalist, who died just before his hundredth birthday. The Merlin Trust helps to fund gardeners and naturalists of all ages who wish to conduct natural history projects abroad and has so far funded 330 such expeditions. Valerie would supply Geoff with plants to sell and, each time she visited, he would take every opportunity to grill her mercilessly about her ideas and experiences. She says that she followed his career with admiration and found him one of her more amusing colleagues, so she would visit him as often as her busy schedule allowed.

Thinking Geoff was now on the road to fortune, I withdrew to my own family and the pursuit of my own career. After all, he now had a nice new house, a brand-new car and a new business, and what's more important, he seemed to be enjoying it. However, it is a supreme irony that the very attributes that were later to make Geoff a celebrity were now to drag him down again. He was completely dedicated to the provision of the best range of plants in the area and the best service that his customers could get anywhere. So he had to stock the garden centre with unusual and interesting plants, without considering that the vast majority of his customers would not have heard of them and would thus be reluctant to buy them. Go to any garden centre and you will see people buying laburnums and weeping willows in the tree section, tea roses and viburnum in the shrub section, and delphiniums and lupins in the herbaceous section. But Geoff didn't stock these. 'Too common for my customers,' he would say. 'I want them to come here for something different and interesting,' totally ignoring the fact such plants were what his customers *wanted* to buy. However, that desire to introduce others to new plants was one of the keys to his later success. His second mistake was to provide unlimited advice and guidance to his customers on how to get the best from their gardens, spending literally hours talking to customers and even visiting their gardens to advise them on the spot. He made no charge for this service and would even do it when people hadn't bought anything. Nevertheless, he was in his element when he was helping people to improve their gardens and little did he know that this was to be the training ground for a notable career.

Nor did anyone recognise the importance of an event in 1971.

While running the garden centre Geoff wrote an occasional article for local papers and gardening journals, as a result of which a man called John Parker came into the garden centre asking to see Geoff. He was the editor of *Garden News*, a highly reputable and well-known weekly gardening paper, and he suggested that Geoff should try his hand at writing an article for the paper and submit it to Geoff Amos, who was not only the technical editor for the paper but also a renowned garden journalist and broadcaster. Geoff later told Radio Leicester, 'I was pleased to be asked to do this because I had been good at English at school, I loved words and I felt sure I could make a good job of it. So I wrote the best piece of copy I could muster and then I spent three weeks polishing it and polishing it until I thought it was perfect.' He then sent it in to *Garden News* – only to receive a visit from Geoff Amos, with the copy in his hand. He told Geoff, 'This is useless. The gardening is immaculate but the piece is three times too long and not at all suitable for our readers. Rewrite it, cut it down by two thirds and read our paper so that you're sure the style fits.' Geoff knew and respected the work of Geoff Amos, so for once in his life, he listened, and he began to realise that quality is about satisfying the customer, not about providing what you think they should have. He rewrote it and resubmitted it, and it was accepted with some small plaudits and a suggestion that the paper would be interested to receive more. Geoff went on to write a freelance column on garden design, which didn't pay a lot but was a useful supplement to his diminishing profits.

John Parker was succeeded as editor in 1971 by Frank Ward, who describes his initial reaction to Geoff as 'instant aggravation'. This was because of Geoff's unfailing ability to deliver his copy just a few moments before the paper went to press. Frank said that if they had had a 'stop press' facility it would invariably have been occupied by a late-breaking garden design story. Hard-pressed Frank would often have to descend on Geoff at Kettering, vowing not to leave until he had the copy in his hand. During these vigils he would overhear Geoff's sales technique with his customers. When he questioned Geoff about the embarrassing, barely concealed insults he frequently heard,

Geoff advanced the theory that uncivil remarks gave customers a feeling of special relationship. Since the garden centre was not exactly a roaring success, this philosophy carries a degree of doubt.

Although such a fraught relationship must have been an irritation to Frank, Geoff had the ability to turn it into a firm friendship. Each of Frank's enquiries regarding the imminence of the copy, incorporating menacing and derogatory phrases, Geoff would answer with an excuse that strove to outdo the application in terms of its abusive tone. Thus began an epic exchange of insults, a duel of offence that at no time became anything more than an entertaining indulgence, and which ended only when Frank moved out of the editor's job in 1973.

In ever-increasing efforts to unsettle the unsettlable Geoff, Frank began to refer to him by an anagram of his surname, 'Thinloam'. It first appeared as the least insulting element in a specially compiled crossword packed with extremely abusive solutions that did nothing to improve the performance of this tardy writer. Thinloam became Geoff's name for the rest of his career and he responded as though he had been born with it.

Geoff's easy writing style became a great success with the readers of *Garden News* and as a result he was asked to write for *Practical Gardening*, its sister monthly journal. So he became busier and busier, and very slightly richer, which was just the way Geoff liked it.

Frank recalls that Geoff could always be relied upon to advance the frontiers of personal, public discomfort, as when he spilt coffee down the front of his trousers just before a joint business appointment in London. One of his most cringe-worthy moments was when they were attending a press conference together. 'This well-attended event,' he says, 'was temporarily suspended while the dowager lady gardening writer of a national daily made a late but extremely stately entrance. Taking her seat in the hushed hall, she sadly succumbed to an extremely loud outburst of wind. While everybody else extended the courtesy of disregard, or at least attempted to stifle their reaction, the merciless Thinloam stood and applauded.'

Then in August 1971 Frank received a telephone call from Anglia Television, inviting him to audition for a new series they were preparing called *Gardening Diary*. Frank's audition went very badly, and they asked if he knew of anybody else whom he felt might be suitable. Frank says that the name Thinloam immediately sprang into his mind. 'What a grand retribution for those countless production delays and rude, unrepentant responses. If he could suffer only half the trauma I had just experienced, justice might yet be served. Leaving Anglia with all Thinloam's details and the most glowing testimony to his suitability (plus, of course, reliability), I happily thrashed the company car back to base, eager to report this amazing opportunity to my target.'

So Geoff was, in turn, invited to audition. He was up against some well-known names, and he was rigid with fear, but when his interview started it all began to fall into place. He was asked to interview the presenter of Anglia's *Farming Diary* and, by a great stroke of luck, the presenter's wife had had a baby the night before, so he had been celebrating with his friends and was well lubricated, and loquacious. Geoff only had to ask a few questions and his subject was away. The interview was short, crisp and to the point but Geoff came away certain that he wouldn't get the job. He thought he had asked too few questions and allowed the interviewee to talk all the way through the piece. But when he reflected on this on the way home he thought that that was exactly the way an interview should be conducted. After all, the viewers don't want to hear the questions nearly as much as they want to hear the answers, so a good interview should be 90 per cent answers and 10 per cent questions.

Fortunately this was exactly the way the people at Anglia thought, and a few days later Geoff was offered the job. Colin Ewing, the series producer, says that Geoff was a breath of fresh air. They were aware of all the older professional gardeners who seemed to dominate the scene at that time and Anglia were looking for somebody younger who could appeal to the less mature audience they attracted. So when Geoff turned up in flared trousers and checked shirt, he looked like the man they were looking for. Frank Ward, of course, was in his own words 'gutted' but their mutual affronts continued unabated.

Geoff's good friend Adrian Bloom of the well-known nursery Bloom's of Bressingham had auditioned with Geoff and he was also offered a place in the programme, although, as he remembers it, Geoff did the lion's share of the presentation. Peter Seabrooke, now a well-known writer and television presenter, also made frequent appearances.

On the night the first programme was shown, I can remember a gathering of the Hamilton clan in the home of the matriarch and patriarch, Rosie and Cy. They had, naturally, been worried about Geoff's progress and the sense of relief that he was now achieving some success was palpable. Cy was a great maker of wine, which he made in a huge wooden shed at the bottom of his garden. Before the programme started he nipped out and returned with several bottles of his notoriously potent concoction. Our glasses were charged and we gathered eagerly around the television set. It is a strange experience to watch a member of your own family on television. It was not that we hadn't experienced it before, because brother Mark was a musician and had appeared once or twice in earlier years; but this was somehow more intimate because Geoff was appearing alone and in sharp close-up. The first programme was all about lawns and turf laying – not the most gripping of subjects but we, of course, were amazed at how good he was and there was much back-slapping and hand-shaking and naturally, the glasses were recharged. When the programme ended we excitedly discussed the glittering career that obviously lay before Geoff and there was much celebration and congratulation (and naturally the glasses were recharged again).

At first all the work Geoff presented was done in the studio, with filmed inserts, and the outside presentation was done by Adrian Bloom, but as the technology improved it became possible to do all the work outside and, as Colin Ewing says, Geoff was at his best when he was in his boots with a spade in his hand. When I look back at Geoff's performance in those early programmes and compare them with the highly professional presenter that Geoff became later, I realise how much he grew in stature. Nevertheless, the series received glowing reviews and was rated an enormous success, but after thirty-five programmes, over a period of two years, the programme, surprisingly, became a victim of the miner's strike of 1973–4, during which the number of television programmes was restricted – to save fuel. Television was only allowed between 6.00 p.m. and 10.30 p.m. – perhaps celestial retribution for Geoff being a socialist with strongly held views. *Gardening Diary* was dropped to make way for Anglia's highly acclaimed *Survival* series and Geoff returned to his writing job on *Garden News*. Rosie, however, basked in a glow of euphoria for months afterwards and never ceased to remind us all of his 'celebrity' status.

In contrast to his television success, gradually Geoff began to find that his monthly expenditure at the garden centre was beginning to exceed his income and, once again the letters from the bank manager began to arrive. This time they were joined by letters from creditors. As the pressure began to mount, he sought my help. He knew that I had done a bit of consultancy for a few small farmers, to supplement my own meagre income so he felt I might have some magic answer to his troubles. I went over to Kettering, sat down in his office and said, 'OK, let's start by looking at your budget and your cash-flow forecast.' He looked at me, crestfallen. 'Budget? Cash-flow forecast?' he said. 'OK,' said I, 'no budget or cash-flow forecast. All right, let's look at the books.' 'Books?' he said. 'Ah', said I, 'no books. Well, have you got any paperwork?' 'Oh yes,' said Geoff, 'I've got loads of that,' and he handed me two overstuffed lever-arch files, both marked 'unpaid' and another, much slimmer file marked 'paid'.

Once I had sorted it all out, it was clear to me that he was losing money at a rate of knots and some serious action had to be taken. I imposed a rule that all expenditure had to stop and no more stock was to be added to his already over-extensive range, and I set about making arrangements to pay his debts. Weekend after weekend I went over to try to sort out the mess, but in early 1973 one of his creditors threatened him with bankruptcy; Geoff paid an enormous bill that the bank wouldn't honour and it pulled the plug and called in the receivers.

This was perhaps the worst moment of Geoff's life. He had to sell his business, his house and his car and once more he found himself with nothing. During the bankruptcy proceedings he somehow managed to keep outwardly cheerful, but it was clearly just a front. The strain was too much for his marriage and, when the family was rehoused in a council house in Kettering, he left and simply disappeared. Even I didn't know where he was and I began to worry deeply about him. Eventually, after a few weeks, he rang me and we met for a beer to discuss his uncertain future. He and Colette were soon divorced and Geoff found himself alone and largely cut off from his family.

Although things looked pretty bleak for Geoff, there was some good news. He had been to see Peter Peskett, who had succeeded Frank Ward as editor of *Garden News,* to tell him that he had gone bust and his name would appear in the papers. This might not be good for *Garden News,* as he owed some of their biggest advertisers a great deal of money. He would understand if they didn't want to use him again. 'That's nothing to do with us,' said Peter, 'but what about you? What are you going to do now?' Geoff immediately reverted to type and said, 'Oh, I don't know. Something will turn up.' Peter says he saw this as too good a chance to be missed and he offered Geoff a staff job on the paper. He had no authority to do so and had discussed it with nobody, but he knew Geoff was going to be a valuable asset and he just backed his hunch.

Peter loved Geoff's contentious style, and he believes it helped to increase the circulation of the paper. 'If you want a paper that will sell,' he says, 'you need an opinionated writer who breaks the rules now and again – and that was Geoff.' But Peter doesn't believe that Geoff really appreciated the power that some of his pieces had, despite the fact that the paper received outraged letters from readers, from manufacturers of products he spoke disparagingly about and even from other gardening professionals. In any case, none of these bothered Geoff because they were offset by ten times the number applauding his views, and because he was buttressed by an earnest belief in the honesty and justice of what he wrote.

Peter says that he was envious of Geoff's natural talent and easy style. Later in his career, when Geoff began to work for the BBC, Peter would sometimes go to Barnsdale to watch the shooting of

Gardeners' World and sit next to John Kenyon, who was the director at the time and listen to John admiring his natural presentation style and think, 'What's the secret? How's it done?' Peter believes it was because Geoff simply didn't care about what people thought of him, but I could not disagree more. Geoff honed his talents to a very fine pitch and he was sensitive to criticism, if he felt it was deserved. I sometimes watched him being photographed and would see him set his face into an image he felt was his most attractive, like a model on a catwalk, though he would be horrified to think that I had plumbed this particular depth. He also watched his own programmes and carefully read all his printed copy, not out of vanity but because he wanted to find ways to make it better.

In 1973, while Geoff was working for *Garden News*, he became friendly with an attractive, intelligent and feisty woman called Glenn Barker, who was the news editor on the paper. Geoff, now a single man, was immediately attracted to her, but Glenn tells me she wasn't particularly interested and their relationship 'just happened'. Be that as it may, they began to see enough of each other for office rumours and speculations to start. Glenn lived in Peterborough but had always fostered an ambition to live in the country and, before their relationship was many months old she bought an old thatched house in a tiny village called Maxey, in Lincolnshire. Geoff moved in with her, thus confirming all the office speculation. Together they set about restoring the house to its former glory. Geoff was a competent carpenter and could turn his hand to most other jobs, so most of their spare time was spent in renovations and rebuilding the two-acre garden. With the help of some outside craftsmen, they slowly but surely began to build a comfortable home for themselves.

Nevertheless, despite the surface appearance of a friendly relationship, there was an undercurrent of unrest and disagreement. Glenn was a spirited woman who, unlike most of Geoff's women before her, could give every bit as good as she got and gradually their arguments became more frequent and more acrimonious. Geoff had always been liberal with his attentions to pretty women and Glenn certainly didn't like this and said so. Because they worked in the same office and Geoff's behaviour was quite transparent, the tension between them grew.

I would visit them frequently and I can well remember having dinner with them on one occasion and, although they were both charming and attentive hosts, I left with an uncomfortable feeling that the relationship was doomed to failure. I could sense a tension in the air and, whilst no hard words were exchanged in front of me, I knew that it just couldn't work. In fact I was so preoccupied with my concerns whilst driving home that, having reached the A1 and turned, as I thought for home, I suddenly saw a sign that read 'London – 30 miles'. I had turned south instead of north and now faced a journey of about sixty miles instead of twenty.

The end of the relationship came in 1977, when Glenn discovered that Geoff had had a short dalliance with a girl he had met while he was away at a horticultural show and, when he returned, Glenn insisted that he leave. She was, of course, right to feel cheated and annoyed and there can be no doubt that her association with Geoff caused her a lot of emotional turmoil; but, if the truth be known, Geoff's personal demon was a fear of being disliked, heightened by his succession of business failures in the past. This produced in him an emotional requirement to prove to himself his own attractiveness and appeal. So, whilst by no means a promiscuous man, he certainly carried out numerous flirtations – but it was the thrill of the chase rather than the conquest that interested Geoff.

After his break with Glenn, Geoff disappeared once more, clearly distressed at the thought that he had been unsuccessful yet again, and once again even I, his closest confidant, knew nothing of his where-abouts. What I did know, with great certainty, was that he was a survivor and that sooner or later he would surface again with his rueful smile restored to his face and his indomitable spirit looking for the next adventure.

It emerged later that during what we had presumed to be solitary confinement he had made friends with another man who was also on the ropes, having won and lost a highly successful career. Denis Orton, a cultivated, well-rounded person, had been marketing director of Letraset, a highly successful company that had one of the highest growth rates in the world, largely, no doubt, because of the efforts of Denis. Unfortunately he had become involved in a boardroom tussle, the result of which was the demise of Denis. His marriage was also shaky and he returned one day from Singapore, suitcases in hand, to his house in Wimbledon to find that his wife was asking for a divorce and that he had been dismissed from his job. Confused and disorientated, he simply walked back up his garden path and sought a bed with a friend in Lincolnshire. Confident that he could rebuild his career, he left his wife with everything – a large, opulent house, its valuable contents and, worst of all, the contents of their bank account and his pensions. After several failed attempts to get a new job, he ended up trying to sell life insurance for Hambros Bank on commission only. Of course he failed, as most salesman on that kind of arrangement do, but the bank had lent him money to 'tide him over', so he was locked in to the job. So he did what any self-respecting English gentleman would have done – he ran away to Sweden, where he knew a girl with whom he lived for the rest of his life. During the couple of years before he escaped, however, he would spend each evening in the Goat at Frognall with Geoff, where they drowned their sorrows and planned for the future. Denis moved to Rutland when Geoff did and he became a very welcome and valued member of the little community which grew up around us.

A few weeks after his disappearance Geoff came to visit me one Sunday and, during our conversation, he told me that he had been living in one room in an unfurnished cottage in Thorney in Lincolnshire. He had scrounged a camp bed and a sleeping bag and he cooked his meagre meals on a Primus stove. He told me that the only outdoor space he had was a small concrete yard outside his cottage and if he didn't get his hands back into a bit of soil soon he'd go mad. He saw some proper gardening as the only way to ease his troubled mind – it was either that or resorting to the bottle. Clearly something had to be done. I contacted one of my old friends, Jim Dickinson, a big diamond of a man who lived with his mum at Barnsdale Hall, a huge house near Oakham in Rutland, which his father had bought just after the war. Jim, like a lot of big men, gave an outward impression that he was not a man to be crossed, but inside he had the kindest of hearts and a great sense of humour. Jim used to walk into our local pub and announce to all the assembled company, 'Who wants a drink? I've got a pound!' When I explained Geoff's predicament he said, 'Yes, I've got a bit of land he can rent, and what's more it's got a cottage on it. It's not much but it'll do until he can find something better.' So Geoff went to see the cottage and the land, and decided that this was his salvation. He didn't know it at the time, but he was on his way at last.

CHAPTER 6

A Burgeoning Writer

I THINK EVEN JIM DICKINSON, GEOFF'S new landlord, would
have admitted that the cottage from which Geoff was to make
his new start was far from palatial. It had two tiny bedrooms, a
kitchen-cum-dining room, a living room and a small bathroom. The
roof of the bathroom had collapsed and the bath was full of rubble.
When Jim showed Geoff into the bathroom, he said, 'Well, Jim, you
might at least have cleaned the bath after you got out of it!' Geoff
bathed by the light of the moon, which shone through the hole in the
roof, taking great care not to disturb the owl which had nested just
inside the hole in the wall. He was inordinately proud of the owl,
claiming that he was the first human being to bathe with a wild bird of
prey. During the winter, when it wasn't possible to bathe in such frigid
conditions, he bathed in the kitchen sink. It was a large 'butler's' sink
and he would shift the crockery and the pans and sit in it, his
curtainless windows allowing a clear view to the outside world – not
that there was much world out there. 'Well,' he would say, 'if it's good
enough for Alf Garnett, it's good enough for me.' There was a lot of
wildlife living in the cottage – a toad in the hall (known, rather
predictably, as Toad of Toad Hall), a squirrel in the spare bedroom, a
family of house martins sharing the bathroom with the owl, and a
plentiful supply of rats and mice. The cottage was built against a huge
earth bank and surrounded by trees so it was also very damp. In fact,

Geoff had a fairly unusual feature that not many normal homes can boast – bracket fungus growing from the wall in the living room. He left that where it was as part of his philosophy of unity with nature. His first renovation job was to scrape the green slime from the kitchen walls and paint them, so that he at least had a base to work from.

For most people the prospect of living in a place like that would have filled them with despair, but Geoff had a tremendously buoyant personal chemistry and the cottage delighted him. He knew he didn't need the trappings of success and he was totally confident about what he did need. What he needed was land. He devoted all his spare time to the cultivation of that two and a half acres. Because he was now single, he completely neglected any housework, so the place got dirtier and dirtier, but he was as happy as a pig in whatever pigs are happy in. I used to tell him it was the only house I knew where you had to wipe your feet on the way *out*. (OK, it's an old joke but I can't tell you how apt it was.)

At first he cultivated this big garden for fun and for the deep satisfaction it gave him. It was what he'd always done and the feeling of relief that he was back with some soil was unmistakable. His clerical grey face returned to its normal shocking pink and he was back in business. After a short time he began to think about the practical uses to which he could put his garden. He toyed with the idea of growing fruit, vegetables and flowers on it to sell locally, but with a demanding job which often took him away from home this was clearly not a practical proposition. Then the idea began to form in his mind that he could combine his horticultural skills with his journalistic skills and use the land to support his writing. Why not turn it into a trial ground and demonstration area for *Garden News*? The trial ground would enable him to try out some of the theories he had about new methods and help to explode some of the multitudinous myths that abound in the gardening world. He could also use it for taking pictures, particularly those that would help people to turn his written ideas into reality. Some were used as the basis for line drawings and others were used as they were. It was in this way that he developed his 'step-by-step' approach to illustration, which was to become such a valuable feature in all his books.

First he had to persuade his editor, Peter Peskett, that this was the right thing to do, but he had no difficulty with that at all. Peter, a visionary and adventurous man, jumped at the idea and so the trial ground was born. *Garden News* gave him a modest budget, so he could now afford to run the trials, which gave rise to his sometimes contentious claims which he was not afraid to express quite forcefully, even in the face of shouts of protest from other people in the gardening media. More of that later.

Geoff's great mentor and friend at that time was Geoff Amos who, as related earlier, had really got Geoff started in writing. Geoff Amos is still writing for *Garden News* and occasionally broadcasting, though he is now a sparkling octogenarian with a fine Worcestershire burr and a wicked sense of humour. He lives on the Norfolk coast and when I visited him recently and remarked that it must be a bit bleak in the winter he told me that 'the wind blows straight from the Russian urinals'. He remembers Geoff, when he first joined *Garden News* as a staff writer, as a bit raw, needing quite a lot of guidance but falling over himself to learn. In the early days his articles were still too long and too wordy, which was not what *Garden News* readers wanted. So the two Geoffs sat together, with Geoff the Elder guiding and coaching Geoff the Younger until they both felt confident about his professionalism and skill. 'In fact,' Geoff Amos said, 'he quickly became a better writer than I was and he began to write more and more of the paper.' The paper had a very small staff of writers, so Geoff soon found himself in great demand. Geoff Amos says that, whilst his copy was good and getting better, as when he was freelance his ability to meet deadlines was always a worry to the editorial staff. They would have to push and push for material and there were occasions when, half an hour before the paper was due to go to press they would still be waiting for Geoff's copy. But Geoff would simply sit at his desk, with his battered typewriter and his two-fingered typing and do the necessary. 'And what's more,' said Geoff Amos, 'it was always good copy, which gave the lie to the idea that you write your best copy when not under pressure.' In fact, Geoff seemed to relish the crises and his secret smile while he was writing seemed to say, 'Don't panic, it'll be OK.' During the whole of his time at *Garden News* and subsequently writing for other journals and newspapers, he never missed a deadline, although it has to be said that he had some pretty close calls.

Among the duties that Geoff had as a writer at *Garden News* was to attend functions and shows, sometimes as an adviser and sometimes on a 'question time' panel. This brought him face to face with the Great British Public again, as he had been when he was running his garden centre, and he revelled in it. He made every occasion memorable, not only because of his substantial knowledge but also because of his charm and his offbeat sense of humour. Geoff Amos agrees with this point of view, but he adds that Geoff could sometimes be downright embarrassing. He told me the story of the time the team attended the Harrogate Show to man the *Garden News* stand and they were put up at the Old Swan Hotel. Now the Swan Hotel is quite the classiest hotel in a very classy town and, in those days at least, set standards for its guests, which it enforced politely but firmly. The team arranged to have dinner together and Geoff, as usual, turned up a little late, after all the others had taken their seats. When he came into the hushed dining room he was wearing the old sweater and jeans he had been wearing during the day. A horrified head waiter bustled over to him and said, 'I'm sorry, sir, but you will have to wear a tie to enter the dining room.' 'But I haven't got a tie,' said Geoff, 'I never wear a tie.' 'We can supply you with a tie,' said the head waiter, an offer which Geoff was hardly in a position to refuse, so he went back to his room to change. When he returned he was still wearing the jeans but he had removed his old sweater and was wearing a collarless T-shirt, with the tie hanging limply in the front. The head waiter was aghast but powerless, and the *Garden News* table suddenly became a lot merrier than it had been before.

Peter Peskett of *Garden News* confirms this view of Geoff as a scruffy dresser. He says that at public events everybody else on the team would present themselves in well-pressed suits and ties but

Geoff would arrive in his jeans and the inevitable checked shirt, sometimes partially covered with a baggy sweater.

Geoff Amos saw Geoff as the star of the show when they appeared at *Garden News* events because, he said, Geoff was a better communicator than he was a gardener at that time. He believes that, despite his horticultural training and experience, his time at *Garden News* taught him more gardening than he had ever known before, simply because he had to write about it. Facts had to be checked and advice had to be sound or else Geoff the Younger would find Geoff the Elder bearing down on him with his copy in his hand and some words of admonition on his tongue.

Garden News was part of the EMAP publishing group, which at the time consisted of about twelve titles. EMAP then was a much more intimate company than it is now, because it was much smaller and everybody knew everybody else. Roger Chown, who was outside events manager for the group, says that, to the staff, EMAP stood for 'Every Moment a Party', so it is not difficult to believe that Geoff fitted in very comfortably. Meetings were usually held in pubs and they would all have a pie and a pint together at lunchtime, so the atmosphere was relaxed and friendly.

Roger and Geoff came up with the idea that they should take *Garden News* out to the people, so they decided to travel around the country together doing a form of 'gardeners' question time', managing to get sponsorship from Fisons, who were manufacturers of growing media, fertilizers and chemicals for the horticultural market, and at the forefront of gardening innovation at the time. The gardeners' question time shows soon became very popular with the public, and *Garden News* received requests to do about fifteen of these every year. They always travelled together and the pair of them would take a van, loaded with all the equipment needed for the event, and set off on a tour, sharing the driving. Roger says that these trips were one long laugh from start to finish.

They would often have competitions with each other to add some spice to the evening and the one that Roger remembers most fondly was at a gardeners' question time at Westland Helicopters' social club in Yeovil in Somerset, when whoever laughed first during the evening was to buy all the drinks for the other. Roger felt he would have a distinct advantage because he was able to stand at the back, unseen by the audience, showing the films and working the public address system. Geoff Amos introduced the event and chaired the meeting, which started with a Fisons promotional film. Roger's first move was to run the film backwards, but Geoff's impassive face showed no sign of amusement.

When the lights came up, still unseen by the audience Roger stood on his chair and pulled faces, dropped his trousers, put his finger up his nose – everything he could devise to make Geoff laugh. But still his face was impassive. Then Geoff Amos started the questions and a little old lady put up her hand. She said, 'The leaves are dropping off my rubber plant. I wonder if the panel could help me.' Geoff immediately signalled that he would like to answer and said, 'Yes, madam, I think I can help but first I would like to know what variety of rubber plant you have. Is it a *durexica* or a *gossamerus*?' Well, Roger couldn't contain himself and there was a muffled shout of laughter from the back of the hall, which signalled that Geoff was about to have a free evening. Nobody in the hall laughed at all and the little old lady who had asked the question said, 'I don't know, I bought it at the market,' which caused Roger to fall off his chair.

On another occasion, when they had a fairly local event, Roger took his father along for an evening out and to meet Geoff. There had been some kind of failure in the publicity department and the event had not been properly advertised, so the audience consisted of only eighteen people, one of whom was Roger's father, who sat in the front row. During the evening they held the inevitable raffle for a range of Fisons products, some of which were of considerable value. Roger's father bought a number of tickets and he arranged them innocently on his knee but unbeknown to him, in a position where Geoff, who was drawing the raffle, could see them. Each time he drew a ticket he would look at the tickets on Roger's dad's knee and announce one of them as the winning number. Roger's dad was amazed to find that of the nine prizes available he won seven. Had the rest of the audience known what Geoff was doing I'm sure there would have been a hanging outside the hall.

Geoff at that stage of his life was seen as a buccaneer, who lived his life as he wanted and got the most he could from it. This sometimes led to some rancour amongst other members of staff, though not from the team that worked directly for him. This was fuelled, Roger believes, largely by envy. My own view is that it is no surprise at all that after the troubles he had been through he tried to enjoy what promised to be an improving position.

In 1976 the editorship of *Practical Gardening* became vacant and Geoff applied for the job. Geoff Amos feels that, considering the short time Geoff had spent in the business, this was a very cheeky move. *Practical Gardening* was in the same stable as *Garden News*, in fact in the same building, just across the corridor, but it was a very different publication. It was an up-market, glossy journal filled with colour photographs of a very high standard, and not at all what Geoff had been used to. So before the interview for the job he went to see the magazine's printers and badgered them for information on printing methods, requirements for photographs and the routines adopted by the existing editor. During the course of this conversation he did his best to remember all the technical terms so that he could appear knowledgeable at the interview. This shrewd piece of research obviously paid off because, much to the surprise of Geoff Amos and some of his colleagues, he was offered the post. Ray Edwards, who worked as a technical editor on *Practical Gardening* at the time, has the good grace to admit that he was not only surprised but furious, because he thought he was in line for the job. But his fury was short-lived, and Geoff and Ray became the best of friends and good colleagues.

When Geoff arrived at *Practical Gardening*, the staff was very small and obviously needed augmenting. His first appointment was Adrienne Wilde, who had come from the Botanic Gardens in Edinburgh. She had applied for a job with *Garden News* as a 'troubleshooter', which was really concerned with answering readers' queries, but Geoff Amos, who interviewed her, thought she was too good for the paper and should be working on something more exciting. Adrienne remembers how she was duly wheeled in front of Geoff, who was dressed in his old brown and orange anorak, which would eventually cause him to be voted 'the worst-dressed person on TV' by the *Manchester Evening News*. She says she had an extraordinary interview with Geoff, Ray Edwards and Geoff Amos. It was the most relaxed interview she had ever had, with Geoff telling her more about the number of proposals of marriage that had appeared in the post-bag than asking questions about her suitability for the job. This was typical of Geoff. He would have known instinctively whether or not she was right for the job and would have been bored by the prospect of having to verify what he already knew.

They then went out to lunch and Geoff asked her to write a feature for him, telling her that if it was good she had the job. In his cheerfully chauvinistic way, he told her, 'You do like greenhouses and you do like house plants, because that's what women like,' so she knew what she had to write about. Adrienne wrote an excellent piece and turned out to be worth her weight in gold. In fact she went on to become editor of *Practical Gardening* and is now editor of *Your Garden*, another glossy, high-profile magazine, so Geoff's judgement couldn't have been too far out.

About six months after employing Adrienne, Geoff employed another technical writer, Graham Rice, who was living in Ireland at the time of his application. His interview was similarly disorganised and scatty. Geoff picked up Graham from the station and took him to his trial ground, where they strolled round and chatted about plants and gardening, and then they went to the pub for a drink and some lunch. The only two serious questions Graham remembers were, 'Can you hold your drink?', which he later learned was asked to ensure that he could cope with boozy journalists' functions, and the second was, 'Are you prepared to get your hair cut?', because Graham had a ponytail at the time and Geoff, completely out of character, was concerned that this would frighten the old ladies who attended gardening events. Either times have changed or Bob Flowerdew has proved that Geoff was quite wrong.

Geoff and his team interviewed quite a few people for the job that Graham eventually got and Adrienne says that he used to pass doodles around the interviewing panel – perhaps a picture of an 'egghead' or a 'gnome' – which were designed to communicate Geoff's impression of the applicant.

Both Adrienne and Graham agree that Geoff's editorial style was 'relaxed' in the extreme. He provided guidance where necessary and if he didn't like a piece he would say so, but otherwise he simply let them get on with what they were doing. With this seeming lack of control he coaxed enormous productivity out of his staff. He and I would discuss the issue of managing staff from time to time, because I was, by this time, out of farming and concerned with training managers in industry to manage. His argument was that most managers over-manage and direct people to do things that *they* believe should be done whilst ignoring the fact that their subordinate probably knows more about the subject than they do. His style must have been effective, for under his editorship the magazine became a 'market leader', with a rising circulation.

Adrienne and Graham were roped in to help with the work at the trial ground. They both remember the '*Good Life*' air about the place, with Geoff growing all his own food and revelling in the joy of it. In particular Adrienne recalls making tea in Stable Cottage, Geoff's falling-down abode, and having to step gingerly over dead rabbits that had been brought in by his huge and tiger-like cat, and noticing shelves groaning under what she describes as 'jars and jars of manky old beans, beetroot and pickled onions'.

Gradually, however, whilst maintaining a good chunk of vegetable and fruit content to satisfy the '*Good Life*' readership, Geoff and his team steered the magazine more towards ornamental gardening and landscaping features. The haphazard style of editorship continued and the production of the magazine relied on the enthusiasm of an excellent team and Geoff's astounding productivity. The magazine would often be only half complete a week before publication, which is close to disaster for a monthly journal, and Geoff would ask Graham to write six features and Adrienne six, and he would go off to write twelve. And his features were always good – direct and to the point, never written in a high literary style which would win prizes, but that was not what Geoff calculated his readers wanted to read. Another of his talents when writing was to ignore the brief, which he and his team had agreed during the planning stage. He would decide that he had a better subject to write about and would do what he wanted, submitting the copy just before the magazine required it, thus leaving no time at all for adjustment and infuriating the rest of the staff, but shrugging it off with a cheeky smile. It was a harum-scarum kind of existence, but they all loved it. Both Adrienne and Graham feel that, whilst it was a bit 'scary', it was possibly the best journalistic practice you could get.

Adrienne recalls how Geoff got Cy and Rosie, our mother and father, involved in the work. Avoidance of nepotism was never one of Geoff's weaknesses. They would go to the house in a small village in Northamptonshire where they now lived and where Geoff had designed and built a beautiful garden for them, to take photographs and to press-gang Cy into using his carpentry skills to make items to illustrate the journal. It was Cy who made the first portable cold frame for very small gardens, which eventually became famous on *Gardeners' World* as 'the carry-cot frame'. Rosie would invite them all in for lunch and for numerous cups of tea, but not before she had supervised the removal of muddy boots and dirty jackets – she was very house-proud. She was especially careful with Geoff, who she knew seemed to have a childlike predisposition for getting himself covered in mud, making him sit on newspaper to avoid muddying her furniture. But then Geoff was always dirty when he was gardening. He gave a whole new meaning to the expression 'getting close to nature'.

Geoff seemed to have very little respect for anything which wasn't living or supporting life. Material things meant nothing to him, and he had a special contempt for the motor car. Peter Peskett of *Garden News* tells an endearing story about the awful state of Geoff's company car, which everybody else he worked with confirmed – not that I needed confirmation, having driven his car a few times. On this occasion Geoff was coming into work one day when the engine began to die and, however hard he pressed the accelerator, he couldn't get it to go above twenty miles per hour. So he crawled into work and took the car to the company garage with a request to fix it. When he picked it up that evening he asked what the problem had been. It was an orange stuck under the accelerator pedal!

Graham Rice recalls that Geoff rarely got a change of company car because he treated them so badly. He didn't believe it was a sensible use of his time to be lavishing care on his car when he could be out in his garden growing something worthwhile. There would be much anguish and wringing of hands when Geoff's car was put into the garage at *Practical Gardening* for servicing because, before they could attempt to valet it, they would have to muck out the passenger well, where Geoff would discard all his old sweet papers, sandwich packets and fish-and-chip wrappers. I can vouch for this because I was once stupid enough to tell Geoff that I had to go to the Hawker Siddeley plant in Surrey to see a client. 'Oh great,' said Geoff. 'I've got some plants to pick up in Surrey. You could save me a journey. Mind you, you'll have to take the Transit van, but you won't mind that, will you?' I protested loudly at the prospect of arriving at Hawker Siddeley in a Transit van, but Geoff was a charming and persuasive old devil and, after all, he was my brother. So I gave in. My first task, before setting off, was to muck out the passenger well, which was literally knee-deep in rubbish, at the bottom of which I found a polythene bag containing two rotting pig's trotters. But, with good heart and a smelly dustbin, I set off for the nursery in Surrey to pick up the plants and then for the factory. What he didn't tell me was that the 'plants' were in fact twelve-foot trees which stuck out of the back of the van like a huge mobile bush – and that was how I and the van arrived at Hawker Siddeley, to some very quizzical looks from the security staff. We didn't get the job, but that may have been as much to do with my state of nerves as to Geoff's trees.

It was evident from my discussions with Geoff's old colleagues that they enjoyed working for him and that he was a considerate employer. Adrienne recalls that the only time she had her expense claim rejected it was because it was too low. She was called into Geoff's office and gently carpeted for 'letting the side down', after which Geoff opened his desk draw and gave her a small sheaf of petrol receipts which he kept for such occasions. It is perhaps as well that he is now out of the reach of the *Practical Gardening* legal department. He had occasional lapses of consideration, however. Adrienne recalls how she was allocated one of the greenhouses on the trial ground and she painstakingly sowed and potted on some plants, but when Geoff saw them he decided he didn't like them, so he simply didn't water them, and they died. Not one of his most considerate actions.

One of Geoff's more exciting duties at *Practical Gardening* was to host trips abroad, which were 'special offers' advertised each year in the magazine. During these trips an itinerary of garden visits would be planned and Geoff would accompany his group to talk to them about each garden and generally take care of their needs. This wasn't always easy. On a trip to Canada, he had a call at 2.00 a.m. from a gentle, retired lady who rang him to ask for his help as she had a drunken Red Indian, in war paint and full regalia trying to break into her room. He managed to sort that out, with the help of the mounted police, who got their man, and the following morning he met one of his guests at breakfast. 'Good morning, Mrs Smith,' he said as cheerfully as he could after his disturbed night. 'How are you this morning?' 'Oh, I'm all right,' she said. 'It's my Ron. He had a terrible night. I rang you at two to see if you could get him an extra pillow, but you weren't there. He really does need three pillows, my Ron – ever since he cut his throat.' Geoff didn't enquire further but it explained why poor Ron always wore a scarf, even in the hottest weather.

During these years as a journalist Geoff made a number of invaluable contacts in the horticulture business. One of these was Tom Sharples, now marketing and technical manager at Suttons Seeds but then working for Dobies Seeds. He first met Geoff in 1976, before he became well known on television. They became good friends immediately. Tom's first impression was of a man in love with his subject and overflowing with enthusiasm. Geoff was particularly interested in Dobies' growing techniques because Dobies' trial ground was in north

Wales on the side of a mountain, which presented some unusual and interesting problems. They didn't always agree, because Geoff became a devotee of organic methods and Dobies used chemicals on their trial grounds, but they respected each other's views and never fell out. Tom's greatest lesson from Geoff came when he said, 'Never overestimate the knowledge of the average gardener' – in other words, don't get so close to the subject that you assume that everybody knows what you know. This simple view was perhaps the secret of Geoff's success and his accessibility and the thought has stayed with Tom ever since. If only the writers of computer software manuals could bring themselves to adopt the same approach.

The thing that Tom feels contributed most to their relationship was the fact that Geoff was always available, as long as he was home. As he was never protected by an over-zealous secretary, as many people in his position are, Tom could always talk directly to him – and he also always knew he'd get a straight answer. Perhaps there's a lesson for businessmen there. They both profited from their contacts because Geoff was always ready to admit that he didn't know everything.

Another of Geoff's friends in the writing business at the time was Alan Titchmarsh, who was deputy editor for *Amateur Gardening*, a rival magazine. Geoff admired and respected Alan's work, and Alan continued to be a great and trusted friend of Geoff's. Now Alan is one of the highest-profile gardeners in the business (and also voted the sexiest, I have read), but he wasn't as high-profile when he first met Geoff. They had exchanged greetings at seed trials and conferences but their first serious business conversation was when one day Alan was bemoaning the fact that having just started a family he was constantly short of money. 'Well,' said Geoff, 'why don't you write some stuff for me?' 'I can't,' said Alan. 'I work for *Amateur Gardening* and they'd have my guts for garters if they found out.' 'Write under a pseudonym,' said Geoff. So Alan became Tom Derwent and wrote prodigiously for Geoff for some time, until he too found his feet. He told this story at Geoff's memorial service in London, when he said that he adopted the pseudonym for security reasons – Social Security reasons. Somehow I think we can stop worrying about him now.

Also during these years Geoff refined his skills as a journalist. However, it can now be admitted that he was something of a cheat when it came to taking the pictures for *Practical Gardening*. He was always faced with the problem that photography had to be done well in advance of publication, which sometimes called for great ingenuity. For example, he once had his staff tying dozens of apples bought from the greengrocer on to apple trees with fishing line, so that it looked as though the trees were fruiting. That particular picture misfired to some extent because it was clear that, whilst the trees in the foreground had a good crop of fruit, those in the background had none. I can remember being pressed into service to go down to the greengrocer's one Saturday to buy lettuces, carrots, spinach and anything else we thought we could disguise as growing plants, in order to take a single picture of a deep bed. It looked highly productive and Geoff stood proudly in front, leaning on his hoe as though it was spring. The only error was to leave a huge bank of snow in the background, so the finished picture was hastily cropped.

Geoff was not infallible with his journalism. I was greatly amused to open my new copy of the magazine one day to find in the middle of a piece he had written a black and white picture of some weeds growing in his garden. It later transpired that he had too little copy to fill the space and, as usual, too little time to do much about it. So he had searched quickly for a picture and come up with this uninspiring example, underneath which was the glorious caption, 'Weeds are an abomination to the good gardener.' I would never let him forget it. At moments of great triumph for him, and there were many, I would return him to earth by whispering in his ear, 'Weeds are an abomination to the good gardener.' I also cherish a copy of the magazine dated February 1979, on the front cover of which is a picture of Jim Dickinson, Geoff's landlord and good friend, chitting potatoes into a tomato box. The tomato box has 'TURINE' printed on the side facing the camera, but unfortunately it has been cropped so that it reads 'URINE'. Well, we all make mistakes!

By and large, however, his writing was impeccable and the

circulation of *Practical Gardening* steadily grew, along with his reputation. His writing was fresh and unassuming and, even though he had considerable knowledge, he departed entirely from the serious and rather ponderous way in which the established writers wrote. Adrienne Wilde says that it was full of phrases like 'cheap and cheerful' and 'for a couple of bob', which had an immediate effect on his readers, and later, of course, his viewers. They were able to identify directly with that kind of language and felt impelled to go out and try out his ideas for themselves. His other departure was that unlike many gardening writers he would take a fresh look at everything he did and challenge accepted practice at every turn. Geoff had a theory that many old wives' tales and myths about gardening were perpetuated simply by repetition of information in one book that had been taken from another. So he would check his facts in practice wherever possible, which gave rise to some remarkable and interesting trials on new products, new plant varieties and new growing methods. Additionally, he would scour research reports and visit research stations to keep abreast of the rapid advances that horticulture was making and then think through how best he could present these advances in a simple, straightforward way so that the reader could use them in their own garden. Perhaps the best example of this is the deep-bed system, which Geoff didn't invent but he certainly popularised hugely, with the result that it has now become a widely used way to grow large quantities of vegetables in a small garden. He encouraged his two loyal staff writers to take a similar approach.

Mike Wyatt, who worked in Special Publications for EMAP, says that he felt that he knew Geoff even before he had met him, because of the way he always personalised his writing and brought a sense of tremendous enthusiasm to the page. He felt that this ability to get enthusiasm across was a very rare quality, which not many journalists or authors have – especially in gardening. This view is reinforced by Adrienne, who says that the greatest lesson she learned from Geoff was that it's the *passion* which counts, not the layout or even the pictures. If you can communicate that passion to your reader, you will maintain their interest. If you can't, get a proper job!

* * *

By the end of 1981, by which time Geoff was doing his regular programmes for BBC *Gardeners' World* (more of which later) and writing for several other publications, he had become less comfortable with the management of EMAP, who disapproved of his loose style of management, which led to a number of disagreements. So he decided that he would relinquish the editorship of *Practical Gardening* and work as a freelance writer for the magazine, as well as writing a column called 'The Last Word' which appeared on the back page of *Garden News*, in which Geoff would explore a topical subject and pronounce his opinion. Alan Titchmarsh, who saw Geoff as a laid-back, slightly anarchic character who didn't necessarily play everything by the rules, says he was amazed at how many issues Geoff found to be angry about on the back page of *Garden News*, where he would lay into those he saw as his opponents with a fierce and cutting tongue. Of course, whilst Geoff was passionate about the things in which he believed and the injustices that seem to abound in the world, he was almost never angry – but he knew his words would be more likely to be read and acted upon if he seemed that way.

The editor of *Garden News* was then Norman Wright, who endeared himself to Geoff by telling him that he knew nothing about gardening and was going to need some help. That kind of candour was always refreshing to Geoff, who told him that he could call on him any time he liked if he was in need of help. So their friendship grew, though Norman occasionally had cause to ask Geoff to tone down some of the remarks he made in his 'Last Word' column, particularly if he was denigrating a company which was about to place some major advertising. This was the only issue on which Geoff and Norman nearly fell out, because Geoff would never compromise his beliefs and principles and Norman ruefully admits that Geoff was so persuasive that he often took the risk and published a column in which Geoff attacked a company. This sometimes resulted in calls from companies who would complain about the piece and add, 'And what's more, he still owes me some money from that bloody garden centre he had in Kettering!' Each year Geoff would renegotiate his rates with Norman and they always did it at the Noel Arms in Whitwell, Geoff's local pub. They would have a couple of pints and some lunch and the talk of the money was always left until the final five minutes. Geoff had an uncanny knack of knowing just how far he could push the fee and it was always just a little above what Norman had in mind, so every year he would leave with a sinking feeling that Geoff had outwitted him again.

Geoff was succeeded at *Practical Gardening* by Mike Wyatt, who met Geoff at a Christmas party for the staff at EMAP just after he had resigned, when Mike's appointment was due to be announced. When Mike was editor, Geoff was the magazine's biggest contributor, not only writing for it but actually growing for it and providing photographs of the work he was doing. So he was looked upon as a very valuable and reliable resource.

Mike feels that part of Geoff's achievement was that he did more than anybody to advance the interest of women in gardening. It is certainly not true to say that gardening was a purely male preserve before Geoff came on the scene, but it was for the normal amateur rather a male-dominated activity, apart from the obvious stars like Gertrude Jekyll, Vita Sackville-West and the modern luminaries such as Beth Chatto, Valerie Finnis and the like. Now, of course, women are highly influential in gardening and Mike believes that Geoff played a prominent part in promoting this by recognising that women are equally proficient gardeners, demolishing the myth that they are useful only for wandering about in a flowery hat deadheading; he encouraged women to garden too, in his writing with his universally accessible style and later on television with his attractive personality. Mike points out that the old television gardeners such as Percy Thrower and Arthur Billett, good though they may have been, were hardly pin-ups, whereas Geoff had a certain magnetism, as evidenced by the multitude of love letters he would get from admiring fans.

Much as *Practical Gardening* valued him, that didn't always mean that Geoff made their lives easy. On one occasion he wrote a piece in which he made a derogatory remark about another writer. The writer wasn't named in the article, but the person concerned thought that he could be identified, so he demanded a retraction, threatening a libel suit. When the company caved in and printed an apology Geoff was outraged. He valued loyalty very highly and he saw this as a breach of trust between him and the company, but when Mike Wyatt explained the position to him and offered a few soothing words he soon forgot the affair.

Geoff Amos, who continued to work at *Garden News*, takes the view that Geoff was contentious and often invited trouble he didn't need. By this time Geoff was entering his organic and environmental phase and in his 'Last Word' column he would tear into the manufacturers of pesticides and herbicides as well as the extractors of peat and limestone for rockeries – or anybody else he felt was despoiling the countryside, cheating the public or mistaken in their gardening practices. Geoff Amos was always amazed at the way in which Geoff managed to be so confrontational about a brand-new subject every week, but he feels that he sometimes went too far and left himself in a position from which he couldn't retract. I believe that this was a manifestation of the passion of Geoff's belief in whatever he was writing about and he wouldn't have retracted if you'd offered him millions. Geoff's stance led to some quite difficult experiences with ICI, Fisons, *Gardening Which*, the Royal Horticultural Society and a number of others. But his support far outweighed his opposition and there were vast numbers of people who would turn to the back page of *Garden News* before they could bring themselves to look inside. Although he and Geoff Amos didn't always see eye to eye, Geoff steadfastly respected his views and never forgot that without Geoff Amos coming to Kettering and telling him how to get his writing act together he might never have started a career in the media and might have struggled all his life for fulfilment.

As Geoff's reputation grew, and particularly as a result of his television programmes, he became much in demand as a writer. One of his commitments came about through another of his greatest friends in gardening journalism: Adam Pasco, who is now the editor of the BBC's *Gardeners' World* magazine. When they met, he was a technical writer for *Garden Answers*, of which he eventually became editor. He, like Mike Wyatt, says that he felt he knew Geoff before he met him, but their real association began when Adam went up to Barnsdale to watch the filming of *Gardeners' World*. In 1986 *Garden Answers* was bought by EMAP and Adam moved to Peterborough to work with Mike Wyatt and the *Practical Gardening* team. He eventually became editor of *Garden News*, which brought him into weekly contact with Geoff, while he was writing 'The Last Word' column and, as Adam put it, 'sounding off' about environmental and consumer subjects, making sure the gardener got the best value for money.

In 1988 the BBC launched *Gardeners' World* magazine and they asked Geoff if he could recommend an editor. Geoff had no hesitation in suggesting they should talk to Adam, as a result of which he was offered the job. Adam speaks very warmly of Geoff's help and support during the start-up of the magazine. His editorship brought Adam and Geoff into much greater contact, since Geoff was presenting the *Gardeners' World* programme, which was heavily featured in the new magazine. Adam would spend a lot of time at Barnsdale, gleaning information and ideas from Geoff and directing the photography, which was done by Geoff's son Steve.

The first column Geoff wrote for *Gardeners' World* magazine, in March 1991, was about 'green gardening', which was designed to reinforce and promote Geoff's organic credentials. He then went on to cover the 'how to do it' ideas that he became so well known for – compost heaps, frames, deep beds, cloches, propagators, etc. – all supported by step-by-step photographs which could easily be followed by the raw amateur. Later this column became the 'Barnsdale Diary', which Geoff continued to write until the day he died. He was always at the forefront of new ideas, which his readers could easily introduce to their gardens: coir compost instead of peat, pelleted chicken manure, organic pest and disease controls – all things we now take so much for granted. The magazine was an instant success, the first issue selling out within two days – 150,000 copies. Now the magazine has a circulation of 380,000. Adam believes that Geoff played a large part in developing the success of the magazine and the television programme.

Adam also speaks very warmly of the generous support Geoff gave to all the people he dealt with, freely exchanging ideas and information, never hiding behind a secretary or an agent, even though he must have been frantically busy, and never giving the feeling that he was better than any other journalist simply because he presented the premier gardening programme.

Geoff's attitude sprung from a genuine belief that nobody, but nobody, was better than anybody else – a true socialist. They might not have been better educated, or richer, or have an upper-crust accent, they might have ridden with the hunt or they might be more intelligent than most, but nobody was intrinsically *better* than anybody else. They might have had bad breaks or disabilities or inherited a dubious set of genes or simply made some life-shattering mistakes, but they were all entitled to equal attention, generosity and care. In fact Geoff had nothing but contempt for the British class system. Perhaps one of the reasons for his popularity on television was that he would accord the same degree of interest, courtesy and respect to the Queen (whom he met once or twice) as he would to the humblest farm worker. The secret was that he earnestly believed that the humblest farm worker was no more humble than the Queen. This was why he stepped so easily into the role of 'the people's gardener'.

As well as his column in *Gardeners' World* magazine, Geoff wrote a weekly column for the *Daily Express* and a quarterly piece for *Country Living*, a weekly column for the *Radio Times*, a weekly piece for the *Mail on Sunday* and several one-off contributions for papers like the *Sunday Times*.

Both John Sebastian and Roger Watkins, who dealt with Geoff's column in the *Express*, say that he was the ultimate pro. If they needed more copy, or if they needed to cut some he was always amenable and efficient. No precious attitudes with Geoff, as they would get with some of their other columnists – he just got down to it and delivered the goods. Brian Donachie, then special events manager at the *Express*, speaks warmly about the fun they had later when they built the *Express* exhibition gardens at the *Gardeners' World* Live show at the National

Exhibition Centre in Birmingham. Laughter seemed to follow Geoff wherever he went – largely, I think, because of his irrepressible silliness and the fact that he so much enjoyed what he did; he saw jokes in everything. Even when they were struggling desperately to finish setting up the shows on time he would still have room for fun, which made him a great joy to work with. But Brian Donachie believes that the *Daily Express* missed a trick by failing to make full use of Geoff's potential. The problem was that the powers that be at the paper didn't personally observe the fact that he would stand for three hours at the NEC, signing autographs for queuing fans. They didn't see how deftly and charmingly he dealt with the winners of *Express* competitions who had won a day at Barnsdale with Geoff and they didn't experience the look of ecstasy on their faces when they left.

Nicholas Brett, the editor of the *Radio Times* from 1988 to 1996, also has very affectionate memories of Geoff's relationship with his paper – in fact he calls Geoff 'one of the nicest men who has ever lived'. Geoff started writing for the *Radio Times* shortly after Nick had become editor, in the spring of 1989. It was just after television and radio listings magazines had become deregulated, so a new form of competition was on the horizon. Nick was charged with the task of meeting the competition by turning a rather drab, black and white publication into a much more lively magazine that would attract a bigger readership. He first decided to print in colour and then turned his attention to getting some contributors. He made a list of all the subjects that were likely to attract a reader's attention – food, films, health, gardening, etc. – and he had no hesitation about putting Geoff's name against the gardening item. When approached, Geoff jumped at the chance. Nick says that he found him not only delightful and funny but also highly professional. If he asked for 500 words he got 500 words – not 499 or 501, but 500, on the nose. If he asked for it by tomorrow afternoon he got it by tomorrow afternoon, so he was an editor's dream, an easy ride. Geoff called Nick 'my city friend', often referring to him as such in the articles he wrote. This was done entirely for his own amusement and arose because Nick, an embryo gardener, rang him one day to say, 'Geoff, I've taken your advice about making compost but my compost heap is surrounded by bugs and flies and all kinds of creatures. What can I do about that?' Geoff just about fell off his chair laughing and told him that that was what it was all about and if he wanted compost he'd better learn to live with them.

The *Radio Times* used Geoff on the front cover of the magazine about four times a year. On one occasion Nick wanted to put across the theme of 'flower power', so he rang Geoff to ask him if he'd ever been a hippie. 'Well,' said Geoff, 'I'm certainly into flower power and peace and love and all that stuff, so yes, I guess I could be called an old hippie.' 'Great,' said Nick. 'Come down to the studio and we'll get a cover picture.' The photographers persuaded Geoff to dress in a bright yellow shirt, hung beads and flowers from almost every appendage and persuaded him to raise two fingers in the traditional hippie sign for peace. When I bought my *Radio Times* the following week my embarrassment at looking so much like my nutty brother almost caused me to ask for it in a plain envelope. Nick says that Geoff became what he called 'the older women's crumpet' – a kind of bucolic sex symbol. Nick was frequently asked for pictures, preferably signed and full length, wearing his jeans. Pictures which showed him wearing the leather holster which contained his secateurs were apparently even more popular. Geoff would have been surprised and slightly embarrassed by this, but I believe, secretly delighted.

Susy Smith from *Country Living* magazine says that Geoff became so popular through his lively and imaginative writing that they were obliged, by readers' demand, to increase his contribution from two pages each month to four. He was also asked to give talks at the Country Living Fair, which is held each year at the Business Design Centre in Islington. Susy says that the talks were always over-subscribed and she often had to console people who were weeping with disappointment because they had failed to get in to listen to him.

In addition to this enormously heavy burden of writing for news-papers and magazines, Geoff wrote twenty-two books during his career, the last seventeen years of which he was also working on the *Gardeners' World* television programme. How he found the time and the energy I am quite unable to tell you.

CHAPTER 7

A Family Affair

GEOFF'S FAMILY AFFAIRS WERE, FROM THE outset, to say the least, unconventional. I have already described his marriage to Colette and their early life at the Old Vicarage in Ware Park, a cold and slightly damp house, with an acute shortage of furniture and the normal accoutrements that go into a house, and thus rather uncomfortable. Nick remembers the cosy little house they moved to in Wharf Road, Wormley, close to Cy and Rosie in Broxbourne, as an idyllic place to live, with the woods and fields just a stone's throw away, providing the opportunity to do exactly what Geoff and I had done, in almost exactly the same place, when we were kids. Even so, Geoff's approach to being a father might be described as unusual.

One of Steve's earliest memories of life with Geoff was doing the *Guardian* crossword, aged about three. It was Geoff's idea of an early education. He would read out a cryptic clue to Steve and ask for the answer. Steve would dutifully ponder it and then admit to not being able to fathom the answer, at which Geoff would write it in and ask if he understood it. Steve would ponder again and finally admit that he didn't. So Geoff would move on to the next clue and the pondering process would be repeated. In fact Steve never solved a single clue, but that didn't seem to deter Geoff one iota. How he could expect a child of three to interpret the *Guardian* crossword goodness only knows, but it is strange that Steve has grown up to be the most avid reader of the three boys, with a great love of words and an enviable facility with language. Perhaps Geoff was right all along.

Geoff would read to his three sons regularly, believing that he could impart not only his own love of literature but also a sense of adventure and inquisitiveness through books. He went through the usual range of classics which every middle-class parent reads to their kids – *Alice's Adventures in Wonderland*, *The Wind in the Willows*, *Winnie the Pooh*, etc. – but he interspersed these with *Swallows and Amazons*, *The Last of the Mohicans*, *White Fang* and even some Dickens. *A Christmas Carol* was, of course, a great favourite at Christmas and Geoff would not only read the story but act all the character parts as well. I'm sure that it was partly this education, coupled with a natural zest for life, that made the three boys as lively and exuberant as they were, always looking for adventure, and getting up to the most outrageous pranks, just as their father had before them.

They would also spend a good deal of time at the rowing club, where Geoff spent much of his sparse leisure time. He got his children a boat that, true to Geoff's quixotic sense of humour, had a hole in the bottom. He would send them paddling out to the middle of the river whilst the boat gradually filled with water. As it eventually sank he would ask them to stand up and salute him, the Admiral, as they sank from view. They would then swim back to the club landing stage, take the rope which Geoff had thoughtfully tied to the boat and laboriously haul it back, bale it out and repeat the process, much to the bemusement of the people on the opposite bank. Geoff was quite convinced that this kind of behaviour contributed vastly to their development. Apart from giving them confidence in the water it also gave them a true appreciation of the surreal and unconventional.

One of Nick's earliest memories is of the punishment Geoff would administer for childish pranks. First would come the telling off, then they would be offered a choice of punishments – either 'the quick, painful death' or the 'the slow lingering death'. These were both tickling sessions, the first being intense and the second being less dramatic but lasting until the victim was exhausted with laughter. A torture that was not prompted by a prior prank was known as 'the knee'. This was administered in the car to the child sitting in the front seat, from which there was no escape. Geoff, whilst driving, would suddenly say, 'I think I feel the need for a knee coming on' and suddenly a hand would shoot out and grab the poor unfortunate just behind the knee, where the tickle was most intense.

Adventure was a feature of the boys' lives right from the start. Geoff would wander the countryside with them and, when they were too small to walk very far, he would put them into his old Boy Scout rucksack, tie up the top so that just their heads were poking out and, if the weather was cold, stick one of his old Scout berets on each head to keep them warm. He also joked incessantly with them, for example by burying them up to their necks in sand during seaside holidays and then refusing to release them as they watched the approaching tide. It is self-evident that he eventually relented as they are still alive and kicking and still causing mayhem wherever they go. Geoff had a theory that kids like to be frightened, as long as their basic security is not threatened, and I'm sure he was right. This led to the night-time ritual of chasing the boys to bed whilst doing his Quasimodo imitation, swinging his arms and baring his teeth, until they scrambled into bed with squeals of delighted terror.

Geoff would also torture his children mentally for short periods, not as a part of their education but just for his own fiendish pleasure. Steve remembers the day he came home in his capacious van, called them out of the house and lined them up in descending order. He called on Chris first, making him stand stiffly to attention, and said, 'Chris, you haven't got a bicycle. Here's a bicycle.' Then he reached into the van and drew out a brand-new bike. Chris was ecstatic and, wild with excitement, jumped on it and tore off down the lane. Next it was Nick. 'Nick,' he said, 'you haven't got a bicycle. Here's a bicycle.' Then he reached into the van and drew out another bike, which Nick jumped on and he tore after his brother. By this time Steve was taut with excitement and jumping from leg to leg. 'Stephen,' said Geoff, 'you've already got a bicycle, so here's a saddlebag for it', and he reached into the van and drew out a small saddlebag. Steve was crushed but, because of his quite strict upbringing, he knew that he was obliged to show gratitude and appreciation, so he thanked his dad with sinking heart, turning away to hide his disappointment, when Geoff called him back and said, reaching once more into the van, 'Oh, I nearly forgot, and here's a new bike to go with it.'

In fact Steve should have been better prepared for this than he was because he got his first bicycle in a similar way. On that occasion it was Christmas Day and, amid almost explosive excitement from the three boys they gathered around the Christmas tree and Geoff began to dish out the presents – he always played Santa Claus and he and Colette always ensured that their boys had one big present and a number of small ones. Of course they started with the small ones and Nick and Chris finally received their big presents, with shouts of delight. But there was no big present for Stephen when Geoff declared the present-giving session closed. Steve sank back in despair and defeat and began to play half-heartedly with his small presents, when Geoff said, 'Hang on, what's that at the back of the tree?' Pinned to one of the branches at the back was a small card which read, 'To Stephen, from Santa. Follow me.' Leading from the card was a piece of black thread, which Stephen began to follow. It went up the stairs, into the first bedroom, into the second bedroom, into the bathroom, back down the stairs and into the kitchen, outside round the garden, into the shed and finally into the cupboard under the stairs, where there stood a gleaming new bicycle, the first he had ever had. Cruel, some may say, but it has furnished Steve with a memory of his dad that is warm and happy and that he'll carry with him for ever. Steve now does similar things with his own children – and they love it.

But there were some strange paradoxes about Geoff that must have been confusing for his family. On the one hand he was full of childlike fun, pranks and grand gestures, but on the other he was a stern disciplinarian who would not accept weakness or failure in his children, despite (or perhaps because of) having had a fair share of failure himself. Sometimes even the smallest misdemeanour would attract a punishment quite disproportionate to its gravity.

For example, Steve couldn't eat spinach and Nick couldn't eat rhubarb. In each case they made them feel physically sick and still do to this day. But Geoff was a paid-up member of the 'You'll sit there until you eat it' brigade, perhaps resulting from his wartime upbringing when such an attitude was more important, but there was no pressing need for it when his children were young. There they would sit, sometimes from lunchtime to bedtime, listening to the other kids playing outside, building up a resentment that could have been easily avoided. The following day, of course, it was all forgotten and would not be mentioned again – until the next time spinach or rhubarb was on the menu. He would not allow bad manners of any sort and even banned talking and laughing at the dinner table when the boys got too boisterous. This, of course led to a bottling-up of their laughter, which was almost uncontrollable, and they would tempt each other into laughter by pulling faces or making funny noises, all of which generally ended up with another roasting from Geoff. I was surprised when Steve told me this, because our own father banned talking and laughing at the table and we experienced exactly the same pent-up hilarity that was extremely difficult to control. Geoff should have remembered.

Chris remembers being hauled over the coals for falling out of a moving car one day. They were only just pulling away so no harm was done, but his door was not properly closed and Chris, who always had an endearingly Stan Laurel approach to life, said in alarm, 'Dad, my door's not—' He was unable to finish the sentence before he fell out into the road and Geoff, far from administering sympathy, raged at him for being so stupid.

The only victory Steve remembers having over Geoff was the day he ate the spare Kit-Kat. Geoff had brought home a packet containing six bars, and there was one left over after they had each had one. Steve, when backs were turned, ate it. When Geoff discovered it had gone, he launched into one of his terrifying inquisitions, concentrating his accusations on Steve, who was it has to be said, usually the culprit. Steve was outraged at having to face the blame and subsequent punishment, even though he knew he had sinned, and with tears welling up in his eyes sobbed, 'You always blame me for everything and I didn't do it. It's so unfair. Why can't you have a go at one of the others for a change?' Geoff, seeing that the punishment didn't fit the crime, dropped the whole issue and turned to comfort Stephen, and the matter was forgotten. But when Steve was in his twenties and beyond chastisement he went to Geoff and, with a smile of triumph said, 'It *was* me who ate the spare Kit-Kat.' Geoff exploded and said, 'I bloody well knew it was you who took the Kit-Kat. I always knew it was you.' 'Yes,' said Steve, 'but I got away with it and I shall never let you forget.' And he didn't. Whenever Geoff was having a go at him for something Steve could always defuse the situation with the words, 'Don't forget. It was me who took the Kit-Kat and I got away with it!'

Whilst most times with his sons were happy and carefree, there is no doubt that Geoff put the fear of God into his kids from time to time, not by beating them but with the power of his scathing tongue. When you had a telling-off from Geoff, you really knew you'd had it, says Steve. He would much rather have had a slap on the back of the legs than a telling-off, because Geoff had the power to crush people when he was really angry, which thankfully was very rare.

And yet, in complete contrast, there were times when he was liberal and understanding, clearly remembering the tortures of his own growing-up – separation from our father during the war, shortage of money, the aching problems of young love and, of course, the discovery of our hormones before we were ready to deal with them and without any knowledge of their power. Steve has a good example of this. One day, aged about eight, he and his friend David had been playing up in the woods when they stumbled across somebody's den, in which was a copy of *Playboy* magazine – an exciting find indeed. There were pictures of naked ladies in all their glory, a thing neither of them had seen in such titillating detail before so, with great excitement, they tore it in half, each one intending to study it in more detail later. But as Steve entered the gate to the back garden he saw his father standing in the window. Quickly he stuffed the naughty magazine down his shorts but because it had been torn in half, the pages had become detached and he suddenly felt individual leaves sliding out from the bottom of his shorts and being distributed throughout the garden. As surreptitiously as he could he gathered the remaining pages and darted into the garden shed, where he quickly hid his booty and sauntered innocently back to the house. But there was no fooling Geoff. 'What have you just hidden in the shed, Stephen?' he asked sternly. 'Nothing,' said Steve, cold fear beginning to gather in the pit of his stomach. 'OK,' said Geoff, ' I'll just go and have a look.' With that he went out to the shed, returning moments later with the copy of *Playboy*. Steve stood trembling, but Geoff simply gave him the magazine and said, 'Look, Stephen, there's nothing to be ashamed of in the human body. We all like to look at lovely ladies, so go ahead.' And then he launched into his lesson about the birds and the bees. Oh no, thought Steve, please, please spare me this. Just smack me and send me to bed. Far better to face the disgrace than the sex education with his own father. 'You shouldn't be embarrassed about talking about it,' said Geoff. Oh dear God, thought Steve, how I wish you were.

Geoff was enormously generous with his money, when he had any, to the point of utter folly. All the boys remember the time he got paid, in cash, for his first big landscaping job, and, bursting through the door of their home at Wharf Road, flung the notes up in a great shower, some of it landing in places from which it was never recovered. But it was the grand gesture and that was important to Geoff. Later in his life, after he had made some more serious money he had more opportunity and he would spread his money about with gay abandon. An instance that was typical of his approach arose when he read the headlines in the local newspaper concerning a single mother and her two small children, who were about to be evicted from their council house because she was unable to pay £1,000 in rent arrears. Geoff fumed and fulminated about the insensitivity of the council and immediately sent a cheque for £1,000 with a brusque letter that said, 'Here is a cheque for the rent arrears for the woman you propose to throw out of her house. Don't do it!' A few days later he got the cheque back with a letter that said, 'Dear Mr Hamilton, Thank you for your generous gesture but we are returning your cheque for these reasons. Firstly she is using the house for the purposes of prostitution, secondly she is a drug addict, thirdly her children are about to be taken into care because she neither feeds nor clothes them adequately and fourthly, when the weather is cold, she burns the council's furniture for fuel.' 'Ah well,' said Geoff, with a small defeated smile, 'it's the thought that counts.'

Some time after this we heard that our much-loved cousin Roger, a builder by trade, had succumbed to the great Thatcher recession and had gone into liquidation. As soon as we heard this bad news, Geoff rang me and told me of his plans to invite Roger up to Barnsdale to convert his office and to build a photographic studio for Steve. My concern to keep Geoff on the financial straight and narrow, irritating but consistent, caused me immediately to question this decision, pointing out the substantial cost involved in both these projects. 'Look, boy,' he said, admonishingly, 'this is family we're talking about here.' Well, that was enough. I knew I would never persuade him to change his mind so I gracefully withdrew. As it turned out the infuriating old sod was right again. It was a very happy time for both Roger and Geoff, as it tided Roger over until he found another excellent job, Geoff got a fine new office and Steve got his studio.

He even made me an offer I had trouble refusing. One day we were talking on the phone and he asked me how my business was going. 'Bit of a cash-flow problem at the moment,' I said. 'One of our biggest clients has changed their payment period from one to three months, so I'm having a bit of a worrying time.' 'Well, you shouldn't worry about that,' said Geoff, 'it's only money.' 'Yes, Geoff,' I said, 'it may not worry you, but it worries me.' 'How much do you need?' he said. Now I knew he was about to offer me money, which I wouldn't take under any circumstances, because I knew he didn't have a lot himself at the time, so I pitched the figure much higher than he could afford. 'Oh, I don't know. A hundred thousand pounds should do it,' said I. Without a moment's pause he said, 'I'll give you a hundred thousand pounds.' And he meant it. OK, he didn't have it, but he'd have raised it somehow, and what's more he meant 'give', not 'lend'. I know full well that he would never have asked for that money back. I didn't take it, of course, but it was comforting to know it was there in case disaster struck.

But on the other side of the coin he was far from generous to anybody with his time. This was partly because he was always so busy, but this should not have prevented him from sharing his time more generously. His three boys felt this perhaps the most keenly, and, although he would always compensate with one of his famous 'grand gestures', there was a feeling that the money was not a substitute for the man. After he and Colette were divorced, for example, he would sometimes arrange to pick up the boys at the weekend and fail to arrive. The following week he would turn up full of apologies and excuses and would give them a grand treat (although Steve remembers that one weekend he could find no grand treat available, so he took them to see Clodagh Rogers, the singer – not the most inspiring outing for three small boys). Chris remembers a time, after he had set up home for himself in Hertfordshire, when Geoff arranged to visit him, because he had an event to attend locally. When he arrived at the house, Chris had gone down to the corner shop for something and he had clearly not gone for long as the door was open. But on his return Chris found a note from Geoff which said, 'Came in. You weren't here. Had a pee. Left. Dad.'

Nick feels that part of his reason for overloading his time to the extent he did, particularly in the later stages of his career, was that he didn't understand how popular he was. Geoff always had a naïve and insecure view of his popularity, so whatever he was offered he would take on. Likewise if the BBC asked him to do something (or, indeed, *not* to do something) he always conformed to what they wanted because he was fearful that if he didn't they would simply get somebody who would. For example, he was once asked by the *Daily Express* if he would be photographed handing out packets of free seeds they were giving away for publicity purposes. He agreed, on the condition that the BBC agreed, but they flatly refused because, they said, it was blatant advertising, with a direct horticultural connection. Yet the presenters who replaced Geoff now seem to be able to do as they wish. Nick believes they are just more astute than Geoff, aware of their value and thus their clout. Geoff simply didn't appreciate his own worth and connect that with the fact that the BBC would not have dropped him in a million years; and he could never bring himself to believe that with this popularity came the power to dictate his own terms. I feel that this was a pity, as Nick does, not only for Geoff but also for the BBC, because if he had been more forceful and confident about his pulling power they both would have benefited from more of his creative and innovative ideas. But on the other hand, perhaps the fact that he wasn't was what made him such a pleasant man to work with.

Although the boys regret the fact that he was able to give them little of his time, it didn't detract from their love and respect for him one iota. In fact both Steve and Chris, independently told me that they thought they had two perfect parents and didn't regret anything about their upbringing at all. With Geoff's strict discipline, offset by his almost constant bouts of silliness and fun, and Colette's compassion and care, they thought they had the best possible combination. Of course they missed Geoff after he left home, but they grew to recognise that it was not a very compatible marriage and what Geoff did was probably the only answer to a deeply difficult problem. When they grew older, Geoff saw even less of his boys but though they resented it at the time, they have a philosophical attitude about this, now that both the eldest boys have had their own marital problems and realise how difficult it would have been to constantly renew a relationship that had broken down.

Despite his sometimes unusual ideas about bringing up children, Geoff was a great traditionalist, loving to tell his children about the things that had happened during his own childhood and in the rest of the family. One day Steve was helping Geoff do some fencing at Barnsdale and Geoff said, 'Just put your spirit level on that post to make sure it's straight.' Steve replied, 'Near enough,' which prompted Geoff to put down his spade, go across to Steve and say, 'My old Dad always used to say, "Near enough isn't good enough," and he was right. Now is it straight?' Steve might not have liked it at the time, but he finds himself saying exactly the same to his own kids now. And he liked to keep family traditions going if he could. Steve remembers

Geoff insisting that he should warn his kids not to be a 'meddlesome Mattie' or, better still an 'interfering Isaacs' – both phrases that Rosie used about us and her mother had used about her. Our mother also used to give us slanderous nicknames. Mark, Geoff and I were known respectively as 'Jaw-me-dead', 'Fisticuff' and 'Gom', which I believe is Yiddish for 'stupid' (or maybe it's just one of our Grandmother's well-known inventions which became adopted into the family language). I think Geoff applied these individually to his own children where possible.

To their regret the boys do not remember many holidays, largely because they didn't have many. They were always too short of money or Geoff was constantly working. There were occasional holidays by the sea, but they were few and far between. What they do remember is Geoff taking them to the woods to teach them some of the things we had learned as Boy Scouts, usually of very little use. For example, Geoff advised them that if they ever needed to hide from a pursuing enemy they should hide not in undergrowth or bracken, but in a tree, because people very rarely look up when pursuing a quarry. It only occurred to them later in life that the chances of being pursued by an enemy in the woods were, thankfully, fairly remote. It was mainly determined bank managers, tax persons or creditors who would pursue them and in those circumstances a tree would do little to hide them. But he also taught them how to make bows and arrows, Indian moccasins, etc., as well as how to survive and what you could eat in the woods and what you couldn't, which was very exciting for three excitable kids and sparked in all of them a thirst for more knowledge of this kind, which gradually evolved into Steve and Chris's love of nature, music and art and Nick's love of all things that grow.

Perhaps their greatest contact with Geoff when they were young was during the time he was at the garden centre, when they would spend a lot of their time helping him with whatever tasks of which they were capable. This was undoubtedly where Nick was bitten by the horticulture bug. Chris, on the other hand, says that Geoff saw him, one day, watering a plant over the leaves and he was advised, gently, that it was better to water the soil around the base of the plant.

This, he claims, turned him away from gardening for ever. Ah well, the best laid plans …

When the garden centre was put into the hands of the receivers and eventually put on to the market, and his marriage was in trouble, Geoff, as I have said, simply disappeared, largely, I think, from a sense of shame and because he felt that his only escape from his failures was to leave. Colette, in fact, feels in hindsight that the marriage was doomed anyway as they were incompatible from the start and that, even if there had been no financial difficulties, their marriage would probably not have survived. They had different aspirations for marriage, which would never have fitted together. Geoff was an outgoing, fun-loving, irresponsible kind of person and Colette was a quiet, home-loving, affectionate person who just wanted to live quietly with her family. She generously agreed that it is not sensible to try to change somebody's personality. She now feels that what happened was probably for the best, albeit that it took her a long time to recover from the heartbreaking decisions that had to be made.

Steve says that he didn't feel a great sense of loss when Geoff left home, a fact that took him a long time to come to terms with and to understand. He now realises that, although he and his brothers delighted in Geoff's sense of fun and excitement, he was actually with them infrequently before he left, so the sense of loss was diminished. He was always either working long hours to try to recover his doomed financial position or at the rowing club, where he sought relief from the stress of the business, so his time at home was limited. Nick, he of a placid nature, just got on with it, missing the company of his dad but secure in the company of his mother and brothers. It was Chris who felt his father's departure most keenly and this feeling developed into resentment, fuelled by the feeling that Geoff had deserted them and brought unhappiness into the house. They never fell out and Chris quite clearly loved and respected his father and was never really in doubt of Geoff's love for him. But it is true that, in the early days, Geoff's emotional turmoil, though hidden successfully from the world, led him to be short and tactless with his boys, which disturbed them deeply. The power of Geoff's personality and his facility with words always made him the victor in any discussion or disagreement and Chris, perhaps the most gentle and peace-loving of them all found this difficult to handle, even in later years. I have to admit that I felt this myself on many occasions. I loved Geoff dearly, but there were times when I would come away from a discussion with him feeling bruised by his inability to see and accommodate my point of view.

The way Geoff showed his love for his children after he had recovered his own equilibrium and become financially secure was by always being there for them, helping them all out financially and continuing to bale them out when things got tough, and ensuring that he could provide a good future for them – another example of his generosity. He set up a nursery at Barnsdale for Nick to manage and a photography business for Steve to manage. Chris had gone his own way, pursuing his artistic bent, but Geoff would hold conversations on the telephone with him that would often last more than an hour, discussing politics, current affairs, art, music and of course, Chris and Katherine, his wife. Chris has paid me the great compliment of pursuing these kind of discussions with me now, because he misses his intense, and even sometimes inane conversations with his dad. Mind you, Geoff was sparing with his praise to his kids, except when telling *me* about them. He would, for example, bring me his latest book, hot from the publisher, and the first thing he would say would be, 'Look at those pictures. That's what will sell the book. Good old Steve.' Or he'd walk me round the nursery, pick up a plant pot and say 'How's that for a healthy plant? Not a bad grower is he, old Nick?' I think he felt that effusive praise to them would devalue it and it is certainly true that the three boys all felt pretty good when he did give it.

The nursery began because Nick, who had been working at a commercial nursery in Birmingham, found he disliked it intensely, so, rather than waking up each Monday morning and dreading going in to work, he did the sensible thing for a man with no ties and resigned. He then went to live with Geoff at Barnsdale for a couple of months and began to look for other jobs. But during this time Nick worked on Geoff, who had always harboured a notion that he would like to start a family business, a nursery at Barnsdale. So Geoff paid a hefty price for another five acres adjoining Barnsdale, found Nick a tiny house in Oakham and the nursery was launched. In its early days it made little money because they were not able to promote the nursery in the way it needed. When Nick began the mail-order side of his business, he placed an advertisement in the gardening journals for 'Plants raised at Barnsdale'. This led to a storm of protest from other commercial growers who wrote to the BBC complaining about his advertising. The BBC did not ask for the advertisement to be removed, but Geoff felt it would be prudent to do so.

For all Geoff's support for his children, it was a strange facet of his personality that he found it difficult to demonstrate his undoubted love for them. I regret that I suffer from exactly the same problem and I have not the remotest idea why. Geoff was not the kind of person to be embarrassed by anything; poor reviews, gaffes on TV, irate letters from viewers and readers – none of these bothered him in the slightest. Yet he seemed to be acutely embarrassed by outward displays of love and emotion, especially towards his kids. As an example of this, Steve remembers the time when our father, Cy, died.

In the late seventies we began to be concerned about the state of Cy's health. He developed slight chest pains and a pain down his arm, which was diagnosed as heart disease. Apart from the drugs he was given there appeared to be little more that could be done for him, although this news didn't seem to daunt him one iota. He was still jovial, argumentative and intent on enjoying life to the full, just as he had always been, but it became more and more noticeable that any unusual exertion would cause him to become breathless and some-times result in the most alarming palpitations. Then, on 3 April 1981, we got the much-feared telephone call from Rosie telling us that Dad had suffered a massive heart attack and died. We were all devastated by the loss of a man we loved so much and who had given us such rich experiences but Geoff was utterly distraught. He and I clung to each other and wept like children while Mark stepped into the breach and, with uncharacteristically calm efficiency, made all the necessary arrangements. Cy had worked unceasingly and unpaid with Geoff, in an effort to ensure his success, and, during that time especially, their bond of companionship and mutual respect had grown tremendously. So it was probably Geoff who suffered most over the loss of Cy and it was a long time before he recovered from his dejection and distress and became whole again.

Cy was a natural born grandfather and all Geoff's boys loved him dearly. So Geoff drove round to tell them, put them all on the back seat of the car and drove them out to the countryside, where he stopped the car and said that he had some bad news for them. When he told them that their grandfather had died the three boys were devastated – but not nearly as much as Geoff. He didn't turn round during the whole time he was talking and Steve is sure he was weeping, but he would never have wanted to let the boys see that. He put them all on the back seat of the car because he knew he wouldn't be able to contain his emotions.

Nick remembers this trait too. Geoff's discomfort with outward displays of emotion sometimes made it difficult for him to deal with a public who clearly loved him. Sometimes, when he was seen in the nursery or in one of the 'duplicate' gardens that he built just outside Barnsdale, close to the nursery, he would be recognised and people would rush across to give him a kiss or a hug, which would greatly embarrass him. If they simply greeted him or wanted some advice he would be his usual cheerful, charming self, but give him a weeping fan and he just didn't know how to handle it.

Geoff and Steve worked closely together because Steve, as an accomplished garden photographer, took all the pictures for Geoff's books and many of his articles, but their similar personalities were to clash constantly. Steve was very 'laid back' about his approach to the job and frequently kept Geoff waiting to start work; he made several bad financial decisions in the running of his business, ran up huge debts on his credit card; he wore the kind of clothes and had a haircut that Geoff saw as unacceptable – all of which disappointed and exasperated Geoff, despite the fact that Steve was behaving in exactly the same way as Geoff had behaved when he was young. So there would be stormy meetings and tense photographic sessions, the consequences of which, however, were always superb pictures, which

Steve felt were justification for what Geoff saw as unacceptable. With the tension building, Steve decided that their relationship would never improve until he had confronted Geoff with his feelings and found some kind of compromise. They were due to shoot the cover picture for Geoff's *Cottage Gardens* book and the pair of them stayed in a hotel close to the chosen location. That evening, sitting in the hotel restaurant, Steve decided to put his case. As he began to explain his feelings, he says, Geoff got angrier and angrier, getting up several times to leave, but Steve managed to persuade Geoff to hear him out and eventually they talked it through until they could see each other's point of view. Steve said that it was the best day's work he ever did. Not only did it clear the air and induce them to adjust their approach to each other, but it gave Steve a chance to explain to Geoff that, despite all that had gone before he still loved and respected him. This was a timely reconciliation because after the *Cottage Gardens* series came *Paradise Gardens* and then Geoff died, and it was a comfort to Steve that their relationship was mended before that sad event.

Nick was an entirely different kettle of fish. He and Geoff also worked closely together but Nick was, and is, much less emotional, with a tendency to work methodically towards his goals without fuss or fluster. Although he is particularly creative in the way he plans, builds and maintains his gardens, Nick is totally unlike Geoff in his business activities. Where Geoff was a loose cannon, managing by emotion rather than method, Nick is a systematic, resolute, determined achiever, careful with his money and maintaining tight and accurate control over his business. He is also, by his own admission, as stubborn as a herd of mules and his solution to dealing with Geoff's more difficult suggestions was simply to ignore them and go his own way – which usually turned out to be more prudent and profitable. He was more amused than annoyed by Geoff's inconsistencies. He would often seek Geoff's approval for an item of expenditure at the nursery, only to be told by him, when the bill arrived, that they didn't have the money. 'But you told me it was OK,' Nick would say, to which Geoff would respond, 'Oh, you don't want to listen to what I say. You know I'm no good with money.' Nick would just smile at him, think what a funny old bugger he had for a father and go back to what he was doing before.

Chris did not work with Geoff, so he didn't experience his inconsistencies quite so closely. Geoff used to think him a hopeless, quite irrecoverable, but intensely lovable nutcase, but again he was quite wrong. I think this view was just based on fatherly concern, for in fact Chris has gone on to build a successful career and a satisfying life, which would have made Geoff very proud, had he lived long enough to see it.

Another of the paradoxes tangled up in Geoff's complex personality was his attitude to celebrity. On the outside he would maintain an air of disdain for his fame and distinction, claiming that it was much overstated and overrated. But the truth is that he actually revelled in it. Whilst he was a private person and would not have liked his home to be invaded by his fans, when he was off his beloved home ground he delighted in the fact that he had found a way to please and instruct so many people. Charm and conversation came easily to Geoff and he had that happy knack of making you feel that he was interested in what *you* had to say and that *you* were the most important person he had met that day. This was totally sincere and arose from his genuine lack of any kind of prejudice or stereotyping. If you were prepared to talk to him he was prepared to listen and if he could help you to improve your gardening prowess he was always ready to answer questions and discuss the pros and cons. He was undoubtedly proud of his success, as is evidenced by an incident in WH Smith, where he had gone to buy some stationery. When he paid by cheque, he was asked for a cheque card. 'I haven't got a cheque card,' said Geoff. 'Well, I can't accept a cheque unless you have some form of identification,' said the assistant, at which Geoff strode to the bookshelves, picked out one of his own books with his picture on the front cover and said, 'Will this do?' He told me that story with the utmost glee – but who could deny him his right to a touch of self-satisfaction? On the other hand, as Nick says, he would not have liked pop-star celebrity. He always kept his celebrity status understated and under control, which was the way he liked it – but like it he certainly did.

His son Chris is immensely proud of the fact that Geoff never compromised his principles, be they about politics, friendships, colleagues, gardening or anything else. He was entirely consistent about doing things in the way he truly believed they should be done, even though this led him, inevitably, to cross swords with industrial giants, gardening colleagues and occasionally producers who didn't agree with his ideas and methods.

He would rant and rave against producers when they wanted to send him to a stately home to behave graciously. He would say, in exasperated tones, that his audience was made up of modest people in modest homes with fifty square metres of modest clay and builder's rubble at the back and they just wanted to know what to do with it. It is noticeable that in all the programmes where he was sent to the country seat of some member of the landed gentry, from whom he freely admitted that some good ideas could be obtained, he always returned with something that could be duplicated on a smaller scale in a council house garden.

One of Geoff's idiosyncrasies was that he rather prided himself on being one of the old school. Perhaps he was born a couple of hundred years too late, for he revelled in the simplicity and romance of the old country way of life and yearned to return to it, never considering all the hardships entailed. So he loved the time he spent with George Flatt, an old Suffolk farm worker who lived a simple, self-sufficient country life, quietly tending his garden and exuding peace and serenity, and Hannah Hutchinson, who lived in exactly the same way. He met both of them whilst making his *Cottage Gardens* series and although they had different backgrounds – George's was hard and Hannah's was more privileged – they both gardened in traditional ways, spurned all the ostentatious trappings of modern-day life and, though elderly, were bursting with energy and enthusiasm. Geoff loved and admired them deeply, as he did Millie and Horace Hunt, whom he met during the filming of *Paradise Gardens* and who had the same values and joyful enthusiasm.

Geoff would castigate people who seemed to be obsessed with

material things. I would have to bring him down to earth by saying, 'Yes, I agree. I know people who live in big Victorian farmhouses with ten acres of garden who go out and pay cash for new Land Rovers and new BMWs for their wives and new computers and all sorts of other things.' He would, of course, recognise himself and shamefacedly smile at me and say, 'Ah yes, but that's different.' He also hated any technology that wasn't gardening-based, and he didn't want to become involved with it, but his job obliged him to, though he desperately tried to hide the fact. On one occasion he covered his fax machine with a large cardboard box and cut a slit at either end, so that he could feed paper through at one end and receive a fax at the other without having to acknowledge its presence.

It was Geoff's rabid socialism (and he was a *Guardian* reader to boot) that probably was the foundation of his desire to share his gardening knowledge with the man or woman in the street. He would discuss his views with anybody who would listen to him, his family, his camera crews and particularly me, in the pub. He was scathing about public schools because they opened their doors only to the privileged. He was against hunting, which he saw as the sport of the rich, and he once had a most acrimonious exchange with the Master of the Cottesmore Hunt, who had allowed horses and hounds to trample his emerging garden. In fairness they did offer him two tickets for the Hunt Ball in recompense but he returned them with a terse note. He believed that all pensioners should get all public services for nothing – water, electricity, gas, television, health care, the lot. 'They've paid their dues and made their contribution. Now it's time for us to look after them,' he would say. When I asked him how he proposed to finance it, he would suggest that we should redistribute the nation's wealth. Asked how he would do this, he said, 'Just take it from the rich and give it to the poor,' to which I replied, 'Well, why don't you set an example and make a start?' This was a bit unfair, given that he was actually an extremely generous man, but who better to be unfair to than my old sparring partner? Now that I look back, I realise that I also have this idealised and probably unattainable view of a country without poverty and suffering and with good manners and social values, but we had fallen into the habit of putting contentious views to each other in order to provoke an argument – and very stimulating and enjoyable they were too.

Geoff felt strongly that those fortunate enough to be born equipped with the intelligence, energy and health to be able to earn a good living should be quite prepared to take care of those unable to do so, not through charity but through good government. This was why he never sought to avoid paying his taxes; nor, as evidenced by his earlier experiences, would he ever draw the dole. This brought him one difficult moment when his son Chris, who was between jobs, was drawing unemployment benefit whilst staying with Geoff. When he got an offer of a job in Kent, he moved down some time before he was due to start, to get settled, but his giro was delivered to Barnsdale. Geoff sent it on but Chris was unable to cash it there, so he signed the back and nominated Geoff to draw it in Oakham. Geoff was appalled. 'I can't do that,' he said. 'They'll think I'm unemployed!' But there was no alternative, so he crept down to the post office and explained to the teller that he was most embarrassed because everybody would think he was unemployed. 'No, don't worry about that,' she said. 'They'll think you're drawing your pension!' Collapse of stout party.

The complexity of Geoff's character is sometimes difficult for people to understand. Though a stern disciplinarian at times, he could also be wildly irresponsible and wayward; though an inwardly reserved man he was outwardly confident and ebullient; though a deep thinker and philosopher he delighted in the fun of life.

Multi-faceted though his character was, it was this delight, his silliness, which is the abiding memory for many – and of which examples abound. Sue, his secretary, who became Nick's wife, recalls that they had adjoining offices, with a kind of open hatch between them and she would often find herself being bombarded with screwed-up balls of paper because Geoff needed a diversion. He would also whistle into his dictaphone whilst dictating a serious piece, or punctuate it with completely silly lines, because he liked the thought of Sue typing away, only to stumble on an outrageous comment, which she didn't know whether or not to include. An alternative was to just say parts of words and leave her to guess the rest. Nick tells of them being out together in Oakham when, seeing some of his friends across the road, Nick said, 'Just hang on a minute. I want to go to talk to those guys.' 'OK,' said Geoff 'I'll come with you,' and with that he took Nick's hand, to see him across the road. His friends were more than a little surprised and Nick was most embarrassed which, of course, was precisely Geoff's reason for doing it.

Geoff's tendency towards silliness is one of the legacies for which all the boys are most grateful, for they have all inherited it – a kind of Pythonesque quality. For example, when Chris had finished the bust of his father to be erected in the memorial garden at Barnsdale, they seriously toyed with the idea of putting a pressure mat under the bench which faces the bust, so that when people sat down either Geoff's bust would speak to them or his eyes would flash. I'm glad to say they decided against either, even though Geoff would have been helpless with laughter had they done it.

In fact, Geoff's own wishes for his funeral were either that his coffin should be so built that the bottom would fall out as it was being carried up the aisle or alternatively, that I should get into it and begin to bang on the side during the eulogy. His favourite idea was to arrange for the grave to be dug too small to take the coffin, so that the vicar would have to jump up and down on it to get it to go down. He threatened to write all these things into his will, but of course he didn't and we were grateful to him for that.

The emotional turbulence in Geoff's life ended when he met Lynda Irving, who gently steered him into quieter waters. They met through a typically bizarre set of circumstances, which are perhaps worth the telling. In 1979, a group of us were standing around the ashes of the fire after the 5 November fireworks display at our local, the Noel Arms in Whitwell. There were Geoff and I, Dan the Languages Master and Fay his wife, Mick the Thatcher, Brian the Insurance, Carol the Gardener, who worked for Geoff and later married me, Moira the Teacher, Willy Brown the Helicopter Mechanic and one or two others – a motley crew indeed. Suddenly somebody began to sing and, almost magically, harmonies sprang up all around, soprano, alto, tenor, bass, tone deaf – the whole lot. Before we realised it we had a choir. We only sang Christmas carols because they were the only words we knew, but at the end of each carol we looked at each other with amazed satisfaction, because it didn't sound bad at all. Dan suggested we should do it more often, so the following weekend we met at Mick's house in Maltings Yard in the picturesque village of Exton, close to Barnsdale, and so the Exton Singers were born. We each spontaneously brought a bottle of wine to our first practice and as the evening drew on the singing got worse but sounded better. In the sober light of day we decided that the singing should be a wine-free zone and that the drinking should take place afterwards.

Before long we were joined by some rather better musicians, including Paul Latchford, who had been musically trained and who took on the arduous task of teaching us to sing. As we were desperately short of good sopranos, a few weeks later Dan, who was head of languages at Oakham School, brought along a young French teacher who had an angelic soprano voice and a personality to match. This was Lynda. She and Geoff were instantly attracted and sang together right up to his death.

However, Geoff had met his match and his courtship was far from a walkover. Lynda was very suspicious of Geoff when they first met because she had recently been divorced, or 'dumped' as she now laughingly puts it, and she had also heard a little of Geoff's reputation for being cavalier. In fact, she regularly saw another male friend, which caused Geoff to fume and rage and denigrate a man who was actually a very kind and charming person. Lynda also had two boys, Jeremy and William, who were of paramount importance to her, and she determined to be very careful not to expose them to a relationship they might not enjoy. So Lynda made Geoff work very hard for her favours and, if ever I had occasion to drive past her house in Balmoral Road (or Immoral Road, as Geoff would call it), more often than not I could be sure that Geoff's car would be parked outside. But if it wasn't, I knew I could expect a call for a consolation pint in the evening because she was out with her other friend.

Lynda had been born in a small village in Leicestershire, surrounded by a close and supportive extended family. Her father, a country man, was an obsessive gardener. So obsessive, in fact, that he would wait up until twelve every night in the winter so that he could stoke the solid fuel boiler that heated his greenhouse and then get up at six so that he could do it again. He grew tomatoes and cucumbers in his greenhouse but he also grew flowering plants, fruit, cut flowers and vegetables, which he would sell at the hosiery factory at which he worked, in the next village. He would win most of the classes at the local horticultural show, though his fury knew no bounds when his son, who had recently left home and set up his own garden, won the carrot class. Her father taught Lynda a lot, so she was not overawed by Geoff's knowledge which, as those who ever crossed swords with him will know, he was able to put across quite forcefully.

Geoff claimed to have an ambivalent attitude to commitment or settling down, because of his past experiences, and Lynda felt that was fine because she felt the same. However, I believe he would have married her the day they met had he been given the chance. He said later that he saw Lynda as a challenge and he was quite determined to win her. Geoff, when set upon a course of action, was very hard to deflect; but, though they kept meeting at singing practices, perform-ances and parties, with the occasional night out together, Lynda is also a determined character, though in a quieter and less flamboyant way, and she was resolute about not falling into the same trap again.

She kept Geoff waiting, doing her own 'proving trials' just as Geoff recommended, for five years – about the time it takes to turn a garden organic and to build up sufficient strength to keep the pests away, so perhaps it was a significant time. I know with certainty that this was a period of great but sweet frustration for Geoff. They eventually bowed to the inevitable and were married on 16 December 1985. The wedding was as small and discreet as it could possibly be, held in the Register Office in Oakham, with me as the 'best man' or witness and no other guests at all. But immediately afterwards there was the mother and father of all parties up at Geoff's house at Barnsdale. To me their relationship felt right, unlike many of the doomed relationships Geoff had had after his divorce, and I instinctively knew that this was a good marriage that would make Geoff happy for the rest of his life. I slept easy in my bed that night, though I have to admit to some slight dehydration the following morning.

Lynda's mother had always been anxious that she shouldn't marry a farmer because she would have to live a life surrounded by mud and soil so, after she had graduated from university, she married a solicitor. However, when eventually she ended up with Geoff, for whom she would sweep away mud and be constantly covered in soil, it can't be said that Lynda's mother was disappointed because Geoff was on the telly, which made him OK. He was also very polite and solicitous to her, as he was with Lynda's endless cohorts of in-laws and out-laws, and entertained them at Barnsdale whenever his mountainous schedule permitted him some leisure time, so he met with the approval of the family generally.

I think both Geoff and Lynda were concerned about how to handle Geoff's relationship with Lynda's children, who at the time were young and vulnerable and possibly bruised by the break-up of their parents' marriage (although now large, attractive and irritatingly successful). So Geoff could have been wary and tentative in his approach. But he wasn't. He just treated them as he did his friends, with a cheery 'Hello, chaps' when he met them, doling out gardening jobs to them, just as he did with his own children (although, as with Geoff's son Steve, when the jobs were distributed it was hard to find Jeremy). They would discuss politics and current affairs with him and, because they were intelligent and articulate, Geoff often found himself on the wrong side of the argument, much to my secret glee. Gradually, through the way Geoff accorded them the status they deserved, respecting and never patronising them or commiserating about their family problems, they formed a strong and loving bond which, I'm delighted to say, I shared in from time to time and value very highly indeed.

Lynda was a fair match for Geoff in the gardening field, although she learned much more after their marriage, and is now a very accomplished gardener herself. She has a comprehensive knowledge of Latin plant names, through noting them as she weeded, watered or edged lawns, and helped by her facility with languages. She and Geoff would walk round the gardens at Barnsdale each evening and he would explain what plants were and what conditions they liked, and Lynda, an inquisitive character, would question him constantly about why things were done in the way they were, often causing Geoff to scratch his head and rethink his methods. They would also go on extensive plant-hunting expeditions, consulting the *Plantfinder* to devise a route round interesting nurseries, staying in bed-and-breakfast accommodation, with Lynda accumulating knowledge in her extraordinarily retentive mind on the way. Nevertheless Geoff would still tell her that as a gardener she made a good French teacher, although, if you see her garden now this is clearly a dreadful calumny.

Although Geoff claimed that he only married Lynda for her sofa (she did have a very nice sofa), she actually became his citadel, his place of safety and his refuge. Whilst he retained, or indeed, increased his fun-loving approach to life, he lost the hint of waywardness that had always been a feature of his personality. Whilst our political arguments in the pub didn't stop, they became more reasonable and less aggressive. It was as though he had found what he had always been seeking and was content to bask in its comfort. It became clear that Geoff had come home at last. He was like a dog with two tails. He once described his life with Lynda, in his usual florid and dramatic way, as 'unremitting ecstasy' and I really believe that that was the way he felt. He reduced the times he went out looking for fun and adventure, and when he did it was almost always with Lynda at his side.

He was so content that he became almost antisocial, avoiding parties and other shindigs, where he would previously have been the first to arrive and the last to leave, preferring to spend his precious and sparse leisure time at home with Lynda in some quiet pursuit. He would often seek her advice on ideas for *Gardeners' World*. Sometimes he would ring Lynda on the internal telephone from his office in his big barn across the yard with an urgent request to come over. Lynda would do so, sometimes having to don her wet weather clothing and her wellington boots to protect against the driving rain or snow, to be confronted by Geoff sitting at his word processor saying, 'Lynda, can I say this?' A measure of his confidence in her was that when I would protest at this, in Lynda's presence, Geoff would grin at me and say 'That's what I got her for!' Not that Lynda would ever presume to suggest alterations to the technical or political content of what Geoff wrote. She was far too diplomatic for that, knowing that if Geoff felt passionate about a subject he would have the courage of his convictions and pursue it with the utmost vigour, letting nobody stand in his way. But, because of Geoff's predisposition to jump in with both feet and make dramatically radical claims, Lynda did act as 'devil's advocate' and put the other side of the story. Perhaps because he was a journalist himself, he tended to believe everything he read in the newspapers, so if, for instance, he read about BSE or the proposal to sink the Brent Spar oil platform or a chemical company spilling pollutant into a river he would leap to his word processor and dash off an angry piece. This was when Lynda's calming, more rational approach was invaluable, but whilst it sometimes changed his copy it never changed his general argumentative approach.

Just after Geoff died, Lynda received a letter from Ray Hough, one of his television directors, who said that a great part of what made the man great was the woman he married and I would endorse that sentiment entirely. She never tried to change him or make him do anything he was unhappy about – she just let him live his life as a free spirit; they each had their allotted tasks and each supported the other to the full.

Lynda, who was still teaching when they married, found it harder and harder to go to school as she got more involved in the work at Barnsdale and in July 1991 she resigned as a senior French teacher to take up a more elevated position as weeder-in-chief, watering manager, head cook, bottle washer and grammar consultant to Geoff. Actually, Lynda found her consultancy role the least arduous of them all because Geoff had the ability to sit at his word processor and just write, with the finished product needing very little editing or amendment, but he liked to feel that it had her approval and, if I know Geoff, her admiration.

The truth is, though, that they didn't get much time together when they were at home. Geoff was always involved in designing and building gardens for a television shoot or in the shooting itself; or, with press and publishing deadlines always pressing, he would be hidden away in his office, sometimes until the small hours of the morning, writing for one of his many enterprises. The kitchen at Barnsdale was also constantly full of people – TV crews, newspaper men, other growers, other presenters, his staff and, of course hordes of kids – Steve's, Nick's, Lynda's, mine, and all with friends in tow. Lynda coped with all this with supreme equanimity partly because of her training as a teacher and partly because she was used to it, having been surrounded by her family as she grew up and living in a home with an ever open door. The times they were most frequently together were actually away from Barnsdale, and both Geoff and Lynda would love these private moments together. Geoff enjoyed driving his big Land-Rover Discovery and with Lynda by his side they would listen to the afternoon play on Radio 4 or to some music, or they would simply chat to each other about life and the future and what a fortunate couple they were. They would stop for pub lunches and stay in small hotels, finding good restaurants for an evening meal, filling his car with plants the following day or meeting the interesting people he would shortly have to interview for television.

Because Geoff was working all summer he and Lynda were unable to take holidays at the times people normally took them and had to take theirs in the early spring, autumn or winter. Although they took a few holidays in France and Spain, Geoff, always a great adventurer, was more inclined to take exotic holidays in the sun. So they went to Kenya, where Moira, one of our singing buddies, now lived, to Goa, where Lynda was attacked and knocked from her bicycle, to be rescued by Geoff and some passers-by, to Texas where, rather tamely, they were not attacked at all, to New England and to New Zealand. Geoff had done some filming in New Zealand for a month a short time before and he was so enraptured with the country that he wanted to show it to Lynda. An expensive indulgence of rapture, but that was Geoff.

Geoff's ability to manipulate words and to give every situation a funny interpretation made him very stimulating for Lynda. He also had some bizarre little habits that would amuse Lynda greatly. For example, although he hated the conventions of etiquette, he would always walk on the outside of the pavement when he was with Lynda, explaining, 'This is to guard your crinoline from mud splashes from passing carriages.' I laughed when she told me this because I know exactly why he did it and it wasn't because of that. He did it because Rosie, our mother, would have torn him limb from limb if he had been impolite to a lady, and he felt her eyes always upon him.

A sadness overtook us all in 1995 when on 30 August Rosie died of cancer. She was eighty-four and a fighter to the very last, but this wasn't the local council or her MP, whom she could fight with one hand tied behind her back (and frequently did) – this was the Grim Reaper, to whom we shall all succumb eventually. Geoff and Lynda and Carol and I took turns to sit beside her when she was taken into hospital and it was my sad shift when she breathed her last. Just before she did, however, she opened her eyes and as she looked at me I saw a faint, mischievous twinkle. She said, very faintly, 'You're a funny-looking bugger, you know.' It wasn't a jibe and certainly wasn't meant to be cruel – it was her last, spirited little joke, which she knew I wouldn't be able to return. Good old Rosie. Geoff laughed a lot when I told him.

That sadness aside, Geoff was acutely aware of his privileges and would often tell his family that he had everything he had ever wanted: enough money not to have to worry about it, a job that was his daily delight, a lovely house to live in, and the ability to share it all with his family and his wife, whom he loved with a passion that even exceeded his passion for his garden.

CHAPTER 8

The Barnsdale Story

APART FROM HIS MARRIAGE TO LYNDA, there is no doubt that Geoff's salvation was Barnsdale, which brought with it the professional fulfilment that had eluded him for so long as well as personal joy. But the Barnsdale that became Geoff's happiest home and the location for the greater part of his television career was not the first Barnsdale but the second.

Barnsdale began on the two-acre plot that had acted as the *Garden News* trial ground, from which Geoff conducted experiments on different growing methods, used it for photography for the paper and derived his inspiration to write. This was the land on the Barnsdale Hall estate that Geoff rented from Jim Dickinson, as well as Stable Cottage, where he lived for a short time.

As Geoff made friends very easily, before long Stable Cottage was visited by a motley crew of the most wonderful people – Dick Clarke, a potter and artist, who set up a small pottery in one of the loose boxes in the stable yard and was always accompanied by his joyous, bubbly girlfriend Anna; Jim's brother Bill, an antique dealer who would strip pine in the yard outside the cottage; David Vibert, a cabinet maker and carpenter; Johnny Lewin, a builder of motorway bridges; a multitude of gardeners; and a whole population of other interesting but offbeat characters, including, I suppose, me. We were all unkempt, unconventional and stuffed to the gunwales with love and peace. Although his cottage was less than a 'des res' I had not seen Geoff happier for years. It was as though he could see into the future and he knew that this was the start of something really good. His cares seemed to slip from his shoulders and his lack of possessions and status seemed to have removed all his earlier pressures and to fit snugly around him.

One day Geoff brought his youngest son Chris, then about fourteen, down to see Dick Clarke in his pottery. He explained that he had expressed an interest in pottery and asked if Dick could show him a trick or two. Dick, ever obliging, agreed and that was the start of a friendship that lasts to this day. Chris is now a potter and, when he is in Rutland, it is seldom he doesn't drop in to see Dick (who now owns and runs a thriving art gallery in Oakham), to show him some of his latest work and to wag a chin or two. That was the kind of community it was. It was a very supportive little society who would look out for each other, share their joys and, without intrusion, help each other along wherever possible, to advance the quality of their lives – the perfect socialist state.

Often, on summer weekend evenings, Geoff would gather his friends around him, cook a meal that, with hindsight, we should have tested for botulism, and talk, sing and laugh until dawn. Wonderfully inventive plots for fun were hatched, the world of politics was set to rights and firm, everlasting friendships were formed. It was a life of some privation but a life which needed only one thing for it to be sublimely happy – friendship. I am not sure that, after being trapped by celebrity and responsibilities, Geoff ever had such a good time again – until he met Lynda.

In 1979, a neat, cosy little cottage called Top Cottage became vacant and Geoff was able to move up there. Also owned by the Dickinson family, it was right next to the land he rented, and it was only a hundred yards from Stable Cottage, so Geoff was able to keep in close touch with all his friends, but in much more comfortable surroundings.

The garden around Top Cottage, which was adjacent to his trial ground, was contrastingly rampant with brambles and nettles and scrub. Geoff determined to put that right as soon as possible, but his first priority had to be to get the house to his liking. It was a much easier job than it had been at Stable Cottage; nevertheless he was shameless about enlisting the support of his good-hearted friends and it was quite common to see the place littered with people sand-papering and scraping and painting with exuberant enthusiasm. How he managed it I will never know, but manage it he did, and without payment of any kind, except a few beers, a lot of encouragement and cheerful, joyous friendship.

These friends were rewarded by some quite phenomenal parties, the best of which marked the occasion of one of our joint birthdays. Geoff was at last beginning to make some money and so was I, so we pooled our resources and hired a marquee, which was erected on Jim Dickinson's land, a short walk from Top Cottage. We com-missioned a very accomplished local jazz band, led by Knocker Cooper, and we laid on enough booze to drown the British Army. Unfortunately the marquee directly overlooked the main road so, before the party had barely begun we found the population of Rutland turning up as well. So big Jim Dickinson guarded the door. Provided they had brought something to drink they were admitted, but woe betide anybody who was trying to bum a free drink – you don't argue with big Jim. It was a warm, balmy evening in mid-August, so there was a great deal of romance in the air and many a new friendship began on that night. The party went on all night, and at five thirty in the morning many a bleary-eyed man could be seen trudging his way home desperately trying to think of excuses. It was this that gave Geoff and me the idea for our new business. It was to be called 'Excuses Unlimited' and we would issue each member with a plastic card, which he could use when unable to conjure up a plausible excuse. So if he had been out with his secretary until four in the morning, was totally inebriated and covered in lipstick he would simply ring up for an excuse, which we, with our extensive experience, could provide at the drop of a hat. We never actually started the business, but it was an amusing idea.

★　★　★

Then, one day in 1979, came a meeting that was to change Geoff's life. One of his great friends in journalism was Graham Rose, the brilliant *Sunday Times* gardening correspondent, a most unusual extrovert, gently kept under control by his lovely wife. He took his friendships very seriously, and he conspired with Geoff to arrange a 'chance' meeting with John Kenyon, the BBC's gardening and farming executive producer, who had mentioned that he might be looking for a new presenter for *Gardeners' World*. So Geoff 'just happened' to be driving close to Graham's home in Somerset one day and decided to drop in. Graham was with John recording a programme for the BBC and, when they stopped for a break, who should John find sitting in Graham's kitchen but what he described as 'a scruffy young man' who announced himself as the editor of *Practical Gardening*. Geoff, of course, began to steer the conversation round to *Gardeners' World* and John mentioned that he was looking for a back-up for Arthur Billett, who was at the time the lead presenter on what was, and still is, the BBC's flagship gardening programme, filmed at the time mainly from Clacks Farm in Worcestershire, Arthur's home.

John felt that the programme had, to date, appealed largely to the older gardener and he wanted to broaden its appeal so that it would embrace the interests of younger people, without losing the established audience. He was also aware that Arthur, who John actually admired greatly, was getting on in years and, since he had a weekly slot to fill, he felt it was important to provide a back-up in case he became indisposed.

Changing presenters would involve changing locations as well since John didn't see it as a practical proposition for the new presenter to be based at somebody else's garden. So Geoff, eager to exploit any opportunity to further his career, suggested to John that he should visit Barnsdale to see the *Practical Gardening* trial ground. Poor old John, sitting, glass of wine in hand, amongst convivial company and warm enthusiasm from Graham Rose and his delightful wife, could hardly disagree and, almost before he realised what he was doing, had agreed a date for a visit. John later agreed that this sounded quite an attractive proposition, since Geoff was already involved in gardening journalism, he had a new site that was in need of development and also they got on rather well together – they liked each other from the start, which is always a help.

When Geoff got back to Barnsdale, the clarion call went out for reinforcements to help to get the trial ground into the best possible shape and the storm troopers from the Stable Cottage community marched shoulder-to-shoulder up the lane, shouldering hoes, spades and forks to meet the challenge. It was a rare sight to see such an assortment of bottoms in the air, backs bent and legs akimbo as people weeded, dug and tidied to prepare for the all-important visit – the potter, the carpenter, the antique dealer, the motorway builder, the second-hand car salesman, the teacher – all but Uncle Tom Cobley, barnstorming to help their neighbour.

John Kenyon made his visit to the trial ground and Geoff auditioned for *Gardeners' World*. Also auditioning at the time was Alan Titchmarsh, who believes that Geoff won the race because John might have thought that Alan's garden in Hampshire would be too warm. John confirms that his thinking was that *Gardeners' World* was a nationwide programme and thus the timing of sowing, planting, etc. had to be as universal as he could get it, which meant a Midlands location. I think it was more a matter a location closer to the BBC's studio at Pebble Mill, Birmingham, the weekly budget in those days being no more than £500, and I have a faint suspicion that John felt that Geoff would suit the times more effectively. Well, everything comes to he who waits and I am quite sure that Alan has no regrets now. Alan and Geoff were always the best of buddies, but they didn't agree on everything. For instance, Alan would joke about Geoff's attempts to persuade people to use old coat hangers and cling-film to make cloches and Chinese takeaway containers for seed trays. (I disagree with him: I see the sense in showing people with no money how to feed their family for nowt and I would defend that stand to the death. I think Geoff led a lot of people into gardening by showing its less daunting face and that has got to be good. Those who are not in a position to buy two tons of paving and three quarters of a ton of decking may well be thanking Geoff for his down-to-earth approach.)

★ ★ ★

Once Geoff began working on *Gardeners' World*, he suggested to John that the little garden surrounding Top Cottage, which at the time was head-high in brambles, docks and thistles, could be made into a very fine garden, which would make good television. At first John was stunned by what he saw but, on reflection, he realised that this was the kind of environment that a lot of gardeners had to start with, so it might be an ideal introduction. In addition to that he wanted to change the format of the earlier programmes, which had only shown Arthur Billett and Peter Seabrooke's polished perfection, to demonstrate that the ordinary gardener need not be daunted by an unruly plot and that it was possible to tame it. He was also keen to show that even the best gardeners made mistakes. So he told Geoff that he would shoot some programmes at Top Cottage (which, with the trial ground, was called 'Barnsdale' for the purposes of the programme) provided Geoff was prepared to show it how it was – warts and all. The programme was also to be presented as highly practical, with the front men involved in actually *doing* the gardening. Previously, largely because of the limitations of the equipment – huge cameras, miles of cables and lights which had to be manhandled all over the piece – it had consisted of a bit of doing, a bit of looking and a lot of chat, but not a lot of planting, sowing and pruning, etc. So the transformation of the garden became a regular part of *Gardeners' World*. The aim, right from the start, was to make direct contact with the viewer, by offering a straightforward, pragmatic approach that didn't cost the earth and that could be achieved using the kind of skills and tools that most people would possess. In the early days Barnsdale didn't feature very often – the BBC would be there every six weeks or so – but gradually the intervals shortened until Barnsdale became the home garden. (I'll say more about *Gardeners' World* later).

The transformation of the garden also led to Geoff writing a BBC book called *Gardeners' World Cottage Garden*. I remember Geoff resorting to some dirty tricks over this. He wanted a picture of himself, leaning on a hoe outside the house for the front cover but because the garden was very young there was less colour in it than he would have liked. So he got me to go round the garden and dig up anything that was in flower at the time and plant it in the spot where he was going to stand for the picture. The cover of the book shows him with a beatific smile on his face, surrounded by the most magnificent floral display, but what his readers didn't know was that, an hour later the flowers were all heavily wilting and close to death.

Geoff realised that he could not continue to seek the favours of his friends and would need some paid help. Once again fate smiled on him, seemingly trying to right the wrongs she had done to him in the past. He was standing in the local one evening, pondering the problem of how to get a reliable but cheap gardener when he struck up a conversation with a pleasant young man called Rod Biggs. He had spoken to Rod before, but only superficially, at parties or in company with other people, and had never talked to him about his aspirations. He discovered that he was unemployed and he didn't like it, but jobs were very hard to find at the time. Without knowing any details about him, except that he was not related to the more notorious R. Biggs, Geoff immediately suggested that Rod should come up and work at Barnsdale. Geoff always acted instinctively and he was seldom wrong about the people he employed, although his instincts about other things had not always led him in the right direction.

So the following Monday Rod started work with Geoff and so began a relationship that was not only to give Rod a more satisfying and rewarding life but was also to lead to his meeting his future wife, Amanda. Amanda was employed part time by Geoff as a secretary, fighting a never-ending battle with Geoff's chaotic paperwork. She was and, I'm glad to say, still is, a lovely, happy, intelligent girl with a quiet manner and a bubbly sense of humour, and Rod was, I think, bowled over. It was all very romantic and we followed it like a soap opera – one of the many pleasant events that were given life at Barnsdale.

Rod had admitted to Geoff that he had no knowledge of horticulture and had never done any gardening in his life; but it wasn't knowledge Geoff was looking for in this case, it was enthusiasm and Rod certainly had plenty of that. He worked hard and steadily, stopping only for his sandwiches and one of his notorious roll-ups, sitting under the hedge looking out over the shimmering expanse of Rutland water. It was an idyllic existence for Rod and he loved it. He lived in one of the two tiny, single-bedroomed gatehouses that flanked the gates to the Earl of Gainsborough's estate, about half a mile from Barnsdale. It was what estate agents would have described as a 'bijou residence' and it fitted Rod like a glove.

Shortly after Rod had been employed, Geoff took on Carol Woods, a local girl who also knew nothing about gardening, to help, mainly but by no means exclusively, in the greenhouses that were erected. She moved into the gatehouse opposite Rod, where they sat there like a pair of bookends, helping each other with the two-handed jobs of life. There is a photograph published at this time that I value highly. It is a picture of 'Little Carol' (as she was known by everybody), tipping some rubbish into a compost bin, the top of which she can hardly reach. The caption says 'A young girl lends a willing hand piling up the compost for Dad.' She was no more than forty at the time. Geoff eventually financed Carol so that she could attend a two-year course on general horticulture at Brooksby, the local agricultural college near Leicester, and it is perhaps a testament to his skill at passing on his own knowledge that she became Student of the Year and passed with flying colours. Incidentally, she was surprised and delighted that Geoff found the time to go to the 'passing out parade' at Brooksby to see her receive her award – but she had underestimated his dedication to the well-being of his colleagues. Carol became Geoff's Girl Friday, working long hours and growing plants that far exceeded the quality of those he could buy in. I got to know her very well and eventually in May 1994 we were married, partly because I also had a big garden that needed looking after and partly to ensure that she continued to work for Geoff, because she had become indispensable. In weaker moments I have to admit that there were other reasons as well – in fact it was another fabulously happy outcome from the Barnsdale stable. Her gardening skills have blossomed and flourished and she is now a very talented gardener, particularly in the greenhouse and with the flower borders. She has also developed her man management skills to a high degree, so I do the heavy work and I am closely supervised by Carol, who reminds me, whenever I step out of line, that she was Student of the Year.

One day in 1983, Rod came into work with the news that a group of our friends, who lived in a large farmhouse called the Grange, were going to have to look for new accommodation because the owner of the property, Lord Campden (the son and heir of the Earl of Gainsborough, who owned the estate), was about to put it on the market. The Grange, which had five acres of land attached to it, was close to the two gatehouses where Rod and Carol lived and about half a mile from Top Cottage. By this time Geoff's commitment to the BBC was expanding, he was earning more money and he was outgrowing the gardens at Barnsdale, so his thoughts immediately turned to the possibility of buying it. In fact he was secretly overcome with excitement about the possibility and, whilst he telephoned me to tell me about it, he kept the news very much to himself, not even telling Rod or Carol. He did this for two reasons: firstly he didn't want to appear to be profiting from the misfortunes of his friends and secondly he was anxious to get his offer in before the news had become public property and Lord Campden's agents were inundated with offers.

Hardly able to contain his excitement, he waited until nightfall, so that none of his friends would know of his intentions, and then crept up to the farmhouse with a shaded torch like a member of the French Resistance. He didn't blacken his face for camouflage, although I'm sure it must have crossed his mind. His first sight was the dark outline of a solid, stone-built, four-square house with a light showing dimly in one of the downstairs windows. He inched his way quietly up to it and looked in. There were his friends, all sitting around on the floor, a noticeable paucity of furniture, psychedelic paintings on the wall, candles in old bottles, glasses of wine standing on the floor and an atmosphere of great comradeship and fun. His first thought was that he couldn't be a party to breaking up this happy bunch, but this was quickly dismissed, partly because he knew that if he didn't do it somebody else would, but mainly because he knew he had had his first glimpse of the place that was to become his home and his happiness, and it had to be his.

He stole on into the yard and found a great stone barn with huge wagon doors and a row of outbuildings alongside. He crept inside the barn and, flashing his torch around, he saw the fine stonework of the walls and a high vaulted roof; it was perfect for his needs. A row of loose boxes at right angles to the barn were surmounted by a long hayloft that ran the whole length of the building. With excitement mounting, he made his way cautiously into the field attached to the house and found it bounded on one side by a towering avenue of trees and on the others by high hawthorn hedges. He could not, of course, know that night what the soil was like but his exuberant optimism told him it would be OK. In any case, he thought that in time he could get it right, whatever the starting point.

Having phoned me to tell me what he'd found, he slept fitfully that night and the following morning drove up to see Lord Campden to find out the asking price. Fifteen years ago £100,000 was a great deal of money, particularly for a man who had virtually nothing. He actually claimed during an interview with Radio Leicester that he had £8, but I have to say that I think he was exaggerating, as was Geoff's wont. It is my suspicion that he didn't even have £8 but was the unconcerned possessor of a sizeable overdraft. Nevertheless he expressed his interest to Lord Campden and drove down to the bank to see the manager to negotiate a mortgage. The manager was reluctant, to say the least. He knew the state of Geoff's finances and was cautious about lending such a large sum to somebody who had hardly started a career in what had always been a highly competitive and unstable industry. He asked for assurances about his future from the BBC and he insisted that Geoff raised the deposit of £10,000 before he would entertain it.

Geoff immediately got on the phone to John Kenyon, his director, to beg for a letter confirming the security of his future. This, of course, was a thing that would have been completely against the code of the BBC. Writing a letter like that would have been tantamount to a contract, with all kinds of legal implications, but loyal old John never gave it a second thought. Completely unauthorised and risking his own career with the BBC, he wrote to the bank, on BBC letterhead, telling them about the way the BBC viewed Geoff's future and his prospects. Sir Laurence Olivier or Richard Burton couldn't have got a better testimonial. John really laid it on with a trowel and in so doing armed Geoff with exactly the ammunition he needed.

Geoff's next hurdle was the deposit, but when some good friends heard about Geoff's need they immediately came up with the offer of a loan. It was a gesture so magnanimous that Geoff could hardly believe it. It is almost certain that without it his career would not have been nearly as bright as it became and he could never have found the happiness he eventually did. He knew he owed them a lot and he never forgot it.

So, a very short time after his first approach, he was back in the bank manager's office with the BBC letter in one hand, the deposit in the other and a hymn of gratitude to John and his friends singing in his heart. I'm certain the manager was surprised and not a little concerned but now that Geoff had met his requirements he was more or less obliged to offer Geoff the loan.

The speed with which Geoff left the bank and drove to Lord Campden's agents should have got him disqualified for life. After all the legal documents were drawn up, Geoff became the owner of the farmhouse, which was to be the new Barnsdale. The name was moved to the property, to avoid confusing his viewers, and the following spring it became the home of *Gardeners' World* until Geoff's death.

Geoff hadn't told the bank when he got the loan that he had been bankrupt and, two years later, in some unexplained way, they found out. They told him that he would have to find a backer or they would foreclose. He rang me in some desperation and asked for advice. I suggested that his first course of action should be to offer my name as a guarantor, and see if they would accept me. Much to our joint surprises they did, even though I didn't have £100,000 either, although I did own a house and a business, both of which I was probably putting at risk. I suspect that they knew by now how popular Geoff was, saw how much money he was now making and realised that publicity about the matter would damage not only Geoff but also the bank, and they clutched at the straw I offered, to appease head office. Anyway, Geoff was off the hook and we all breathed a heavy sigh of relief.

I have to admit that I was really concerned about Geoff taking on this property when he first mooted the idea to me. Our father had died by this time, so I was the only close family member to advise him, and I can now come clean and admit that I advised him not to do it. What a senseless decision that would have been, and how glad and grateful I am that he didn't take my advice – not that he was in much danger of doing that. He rarely took my advice; after all, he was thirty-five minutes older and that made all the difference between wisdom and stupidity.

Before Geoff could move in, it was clear that all the present incumbents had to move out, but he was liberal about this, allowing them time to get settled elsewhere. Meanwhile he had a problem. The last programme of the *Gardeners' World* year had just ended and he was faced with the task of getting something ready for the beginning of the following year. All he had was a five-acre flat field of coarse, tussocky grass on a bed of heavy clay. I would visit him from time to time to indulge my patronising 'I told you so' attitude, but he was in his element and he just grinned at me and assured me, as he had done so many times before, that everything would be all right.

During the time between exchanging contracts for Barnsdale and Geoff being able to move in, every plant that was movable from Top Cottage was lifted by Rod and potted into a container by Carol. They then moved hundreds of these containers up to the new Barnsdale in their cars and stood them in the yard, the job being made more difficult by the fact that the whole thing was filmed for *Gardeners' World*. The place looked like a garden centre and their cars looked like agricultural vehicles, inside and out, but these plants were going to provide Geoff with the start he needed. The land had to be mole ploughed to improve the drainage – a once-and-for-all job – and then ploughed with a conventional plough to turn the grass underneath the soil. By the time this was finished it looked less like a garden than anything I'd seen and my fears for Geoff's ability to start on time began to mount. He, however, was totally undaunted and filled with enthusiasm for his new project.

He seemed to me to be taking a while to get started after he moved on to the land, but I later discovered that this was because he was spending his time thinking and planning how the garden should be designed. He told me that his aspiration was to build one of the classic gardens of England and that the up-front design time was all-important. So he spent much time just walking his land, mulling over ideas and putting them down on paper. He knew that he would have to divide the land up into small gardens to provide material for the BBC, but he wanted a central feature, not only for the television programme but also to provide him with a satisfying garden close to the house.

In the end he chose to design a fairly formal garden, inspired by the formality of the gardens at the Palace of Versailles. A long, straight stretch of lawn would lead up to a statue or an urn which could be planted with colourful plants each year, and the lawn would be bounded on each side by deep borders closely planted with shrubs and herbaceous plants, chosen to provide some colour or foliage all the year round. To connect the gardens in the rest of the garden he planned a long curving pergola which would be planted with laburnum, clematis, rambling roses and other climbing plants, to give the garden stroller a sweet-scented exit from the part of the garden that came to be known as 'Versailles'.

His first job was to give the garden some height by planting trees, but because the cameras were due to roll soon these had to be big, to give the impression of at least some maturity. Geoff found a specialist nursery that could supply big trees, which duly arrived on an enormous low-loading trailer. It was quite a sight to see the great root balls being carefully lowered by a crane into deep holes, which had been dug by a mechanical excavator, which then refilled them with tons of soil. The BBC filmed the whole process, even though the job was done outside the normal season for *Gardeners' World*, because it was too exciting a sight to deny the viewers. I can report that they all lived and are still alive and well at Barnsdale (the trees that is, not the viewers).

Because Geoff's budget was very small and the publicity value to the tree nursery was high, the nursery agreed to do the job for about £200, a fraction of the real cost. But how to get the publicity in the face of the rigid BBC rules about advertising? Well, John Kenyon, the producer, decided to risk his all again and said to the driver of the low loader on which the trees arrived, 'Look, if you just happened to leave your truck door open, it's just possible that one of my cameramen might make a mistake and, by pure chance, film the name of the nursery, which I believe might be painted on the truck door.' And that's what happened. But John was carpeted when he returned to his office after the screening of the film and I don't think he ever risked such a 'mistake' again.

After the vast borders had been spread with pea-gravel to lighten the soil, double dug and thoroughly mucked, there began the task of planting the multitude of plants that had been brought from the old Barnsdale. These were supplemented by a number of unusual and extraordinarily beautiful plants that Geoff had long dreamed of having and which he knew would interest his viewers.

Then it only remained to lay the lawn, after which he was faced with the knotty problem of whether to buy a statue or an urn for the feature designed to draw the eye to the end of the lawn. In the end he chose an urn, because, although he had a great appreciation for fine statuary, he knew that it would have to be very fine indeed to blend with the statuary that God had already provided. A Rodin or a Hepworth seemed to be outside his range, so an urn it had to be. At the time he was seriously considering releasing me from my obligation to provide him with a suit every time he needed to attend an important meeting (although it had to be very important indeed to persuade Geoff into a suit – especially one of mine) by buying a suit of his own. He couldn't afford both, but there was no contest: the urn won hands down and he bought a very handsome beast indeed. I continued to provide Geoff with an off-the-peg tailoring service for many years to come.

The development of the rest of the gardens at Barnsdale was dictated largely by the requirements of the BBC, although Geoff was by now making most of the suggestions about what should be done. More of those adventures later. Meanwhile there was a large area of land vacant and this was fenced off to provide grazing for Amanda's horse, Mancha. Mancha would have been more appropriately called Muncha, because she would frequently break out of her paddock and stand in the middle of the vegetable garden – munching. Rod would fly into apoplectic rages and grab her mane in a futile attempt to drag her back to the paddock. This would often result in the undignified sight of him being dragged over flower borders and lawns by a rampant, out-of-control beast. Far from this causing trouble for Rod, Geoff, Carol and even Amanda would be grateful for yet another Barnsdale opportunity for paroxysms of laughter.

The chickens were another of Geoff's romantic adventures, which caused more trouble than they were worth. Though they began life in a pen, Geoff felt guilty about their imprisonment and eventually let them have the run of the gardens. As a result most of the out-takes from the BBC filming would feature pictures of chickens wandering, unconcerned, into the picture. This may have been all right in normal circumstances, but the tamest of these birds had been involved in an accident and broken its leg. Nursed back to health by Carol, an incurable animal lover (who, before disinfecting a greenhouse would spend two hours collecting all the spiders, woodlice, earwigs and other bugs and placing them out of harm's way), the chicken, which had developed a strange gait, would goose-step in and out of the picture, reducing Geoff and the camera crew to helpless fits of giggles.

Geoff also spent a lot of his time on the house, helped by Carol, who stripped wallpaper, sanded doors, plastered and painted for all she was worth. I had never seen such application from Geoff, who worked all the hours God sent to get his garden and his house into order before the BBC descended and consumed all his time. But by the time they did come the psychedelic paint was gone, the fine York stone paving in the hall was spotless, the kitchen floor was newly tiled and the kitchen housed a noble pine table around which the BBC crews would sit and drink coffee, plan their work and laugh.

Geoff's work for the BBC continued unabated for the twelve and a half years he lived at Barnsdale, with *Gardeners' World* in the summer and six-part series such as *The Ornamental Kitchen Garden*, *Cottage Gardens*, *The Living Garden* and *Paradise Gardens* being made during the spring and summer but going out during the winter. Geoff also continued to write prodigiously – weekly columns for *Garden News*, *Practical Gardening* and *Radio Times* as well as a book to go with every series.

With this heavy workload, Geoff realised that he needed further help. So in November 1989 he advertised in *Horticulture Week* for a kitchen gardener. He looked for a kitchen gardener because he knew it would be difficult to find anybody with the creative flair he needed for his ornamental garden and vegetable gardens do not, of course require a great deal of creative ability. What he got, however, turned out to be far better than he had expected.

Of the several applicants he interviewed the one he liked the most was a quiet young Scot called Ian Spence. He had just the kind of background that Geoff needed and showed the brand of application and determination that seems to be a trait of a certain kind of Scotsman. Ian found the interview with Geoff just as laid back and relaxed as Adrienne Wilde and Graham Rice had found theirs a few years before. He was nervous, of course, because he had watched Geoff on television frequently and he realised what a high-profile job it could turn out to be. But Geoff immediately put him at his ease and showed him round the garden – not without leaving poor Ian with his best shoes and trousers caked in mud. A few days later, he wrote to offer him the job. Ian started on 8 January 1990, and moved into some accommodation which Geoff had found for him, with some kind and friendly farmers just a couple of hundred yards from Barnsdale.

In the winter there was no activity with the BBC, but as soon as spring came along Ian was plunged into the world of the media, helping to prepare for programmes and often appearing in them, giving Geoff some help with a two-handed job. He never actually got a speaking part, but he was a terrific spear-carrier. By this time significant advances in technology had been made, and the BBC's lumbering scanners had disappeared and with them the crew of riggers. So if there was any work to do like erecting towers for overhead shots Ian was asked to do it. He became a mini-technician by the time television at Barnsdale ended and thoroughly enjoyed the work.

The demands of television often required set pieces to be prepared earlier than normal. This required all the ingenuity of an expert gardener and Geoff found that Ian was just the man for the job. He became something of a wizard at persuading plants to believe that it was later in the season than it actually was. He also, much against his natural instincts but with Geoff's well-cultivated guidance, became a first-rate cheat. He once had to arrange a demonstration of the effect of growing carrots on stony ground but, in the absence of any stony ground Geoff persuaded him to gather stones from all over the garden and dig them into the ground. I would often ask Geoff what justification he had for adopting this 'Bill Sykes' attitude and teaching his protégé such evil tricks but he just rubbed his hands and cackled his pseudo-Bill Sykes laugh.

Ian had not worked for long at Barnsdale before Geoff, realising his immense potential, promoted him to head gardener. As such he directed the work of Carol, who was responsible for the management of the greenhouses, and a young lady called Lorraine Shone, who was invaluable in the gardens generally. Her father was a gardener for one of the local 'big-wigs' and he had taught her enough horticulture to make her very knowledgeable, so she came pre-packed and oven-ready. Because he worked with two such capable people Ian did not have to exert too much control, but he was certainly a source of a great deal of advice and wisdom.

In 1984, after Geoff had moved to the new Barnsdale, Amanda, his part-time secretary, had left him to seek a full-time job (although her horse stayed) and her place was taken by Betty Franklyn, who was the mother of Geoff's friend Mick the Thatcher. Betty was a wonderfully capable woman, the type to roll up her sleeves and get stuck into the gardening whenever extra help was needed. She would work in the office in the morning and in the garden in the afternoon, weeding, watering and helping Carol in the greenhouses. But she regretfully left after five months because she needed to earn more money, to buy herself a house. She was replaced by Sue, another country girl, of good farming stock. Because of Geoff's good experience with Betty, Sue was conditioned right from the start. Geoff told her at her interview that her work would not only include the normal secretarial duties but would also involve some gardening, when the work pressures demanded. Sue, a country girl raised on a farm, saw no incongruity in this at all and readily agreed, so she was often pressed into service when some emergency weeding or planting was required for the programme. During the course of this work she would observe the methods used by Geoff, Ian and Carol, memorise plant names while she weeded round them and soak up the organic methods that Geoff was by then using exclusively at Barnsdale. As a result she became a very accomplished gardener herself and now that she is married to Nick they run Barnsdale Gardens hand in hand.

The workload at Barnsdale continued to grow. Once the nursery was launched in 1990, Nick was busy running it and, whilst he would help out in the gardens when needed, he was no longer able to provide the continuity of work Geoff needed. Geoff had so far done all the design and landscaping work, but decided that he needed some help in this area also, so in May 1990 he advertised, again in *Horticulture Week*, for a 'young landscaper'. He received a reply from a young man called Adam Frost, who had been well trained and was working in the landscaping business, and who immediately captured his interest, so he invited him up for interview. Geoff was flabbergasted to discover that Adam was the son of Martin Frost, who had worked for Geoff in his first landscaping business in Broxbourne. This fact alone removed in Geoff's mind the need to recognise any other competition or, indeed, even to interview him very thoroughly. Geoff had unfortunately caused his father, Martin, a good and loyal worker, to lose his job when he went bankrupt, and now he had an opportunity to make amends – which he grasped with alacrity. Not that this bizarre coincidence should take anything away from Adam's own credentials. He certainly made no attempt whatever to use his father's relationship to his own advantage and Geoff would not have given him the job had he not been impressed and satisfied that he would make an outstanding contribution to the team – and this judgement was to be proved right.

Paradoxically, although Geoff had employed Adam to ease his workload, he took on the writing of his weekly column for the *Daily Express* in order to pay Adam's wages. The spectre of driving himself into poverty again seemed to haunt him and his newly discovered sense of responsibility appeared to drive him to find a way to cover his expenses whenever he took on a new commitment. Not that the *Daily Express* was all that demanding. I can remember visiting him in his office one day to be greeted by the words, 'There you are, boy, a column for the *Express* done in two hours. That's £400 for two hours' work, or £8,000 a week. More than you earn that, so it can't be bad!' I then had to patiently point out that if he had done no other paid work that week he was actually looking at £400 a week, which wouldn't keep Barnsdale alive. But he only gave me that infuriating grin again and told me not to be so preoccupied with money. Me! The man had the cheek of the devil.

Nick was asked many times by nursery customers if they could go in to see the gardens and each time he had to refuse. The gardens were Geoff's private patch and he would not have wanted them invaded by a curious public; but, on the other hand, he didn't want to deprive them of the opportunity to see what was going on inside. So he decided to build a duplicate set of gardens just outside the back entrance to Barnsdale, on a piece of land close to the nursery, so that visitors to the nursery could see what lay behind the high hedges surrounding Geoff's private paradise. Adam was set to work building these.

Adam also helped Nick to set up the nursery, which had only just started. There were container areas to build, polytunnels to erect, greenhouses to set up – he even had to build some toilets for the use of customers. But toilet building was not Adam's first love. It was the landscaping that he really enjoyed and soon he was beginning to make design suggestions to Geoff, which impressed him so much that he decided to send him on a garden design course, to see if he could develop what was clearly a latent ability. After much searching they decided that he should go to David Stevens, an eminent garden designer, much admired by Geoff, who had met him on several occasions. During the one-year course, theory was interspersed with design assignments and Adam produced a number of designs that were eventually built at Barnsdale. He designed and built the Plantsman's Garden, the Reclaim Garden, parts of the Gentleman's Cottage Garden and the Town Paradise Garden.

Adam had his first experience of building a show garden early in his career with Geoff. Geoff was in at the beginning of Gardeners' World Live in 1993, a huge and highly successful garden event held each year at the National Exhibition Centre (NEC) near Birmingham. He wasn't involved in the organisation – God help anybody who asked Geoff to get involved in organisation – but he would appear on question time panels and give talks, and he also designed and built the exhibition gardens there for the *Daily Express*. The first garden was a cottage garden, designed by Dan Pearson, one of the country's foremost designers, at the very first Gardeners' World Live exhibition. The following year they built a combination of the Gentleman's Cottage Garden and the Artisan's Garden, both of which had featured on earlier television programmes. This was designed by Geoff and built by Adam and it won a silver medal from the RHS and the BBC's Feature Garden Award, a crystal bowl which now stands proudly on Lynda's sideboard. Next came a Mediterranean Garden, but the *pièce de resistance* was the Reclaim Garden, the following year, which was designed and built by Adam and later rebuilt at Barnsdale. It won a silver gilt medal and the BBC's Best Design in Show award. After the presentation Geoff put his arm round Adam's shoulder and said, 'You did us proud, boy. Well done,' and he thrust £1,000 in cash into his hand.

Adam also appeared on television from time to time, as Ian did, in 'walk-on' parts – helping to plant big trees, lining the pool or some other task which required two pairs of hands. Geoff was very cautious about allowing his staff to take speaking roles in these shots because he had worked out exactly how each shot should go and how long it should take and he didn't want that plan disrupted. He wasn't unkind or possessive, but he was professional and meticulous about the standards he achieved. Adam also gained experience at Barnsdale from the regular necessity to mix with so-called 'celebrities' such as Ken Hom, the Chinese cook, Lionel Blair, the dancer, and Ruby Wax, the comedienne, with whom Geoff did a *Children in Need* appearance, equipping him to work easily and naturally with people who he had never dreamed would enter his social circle.

Barnsdale was always full of people – camera crews, journalists, television gardeners, amateur gardeners, curious interlopers and, most of all, friends. The place was to Geoff's friends as the honey pot was to Winnie the Pooh. It was always a lovely place to visit, full of welcome, beauty, tranquillity and produce. It was seldom that the people who came didn't go away with a bag full of fruit and vegetables, a plant or a small tree. The queue for bedding plants, tender perennials and the like eventually became so long that even generous-hearted Geoff would have to limit what he gave away.

Laughter was the most common commodity at Barnsdale and I found it extraordinarily stimulating to become involved in it from time to time. There were endless tricks and not a few treats as well. I well remember the party that was held in the great barn at Barnsdale for the retirement of John Endal, the electrical wizard who, with astounding artifice and invention had kept the lights and the cameras rolling with bits of string and rolls of insulation tape. There was a sumptuous feast, supplemented by rivers of booze, and the highlight of the evening was when a light aircraft flew over, trailing a banner with the words 'Happy retirement John'. The boys had all clubbed together and the plane was organised by Jean Laughton, the inexhaustible production lady. As the plane flew by, many a tear was shed, even by the large and hairy riggers who reckoned they could deal with anything. Well, they couldn't deal with the loss of old John and they weren't ashamed to show it.

The television crews had to be delivered of a seemingly limitless stream of tea and coffee, which was invariably taken in the house, and these breaks from work were an endless source of hilarity. The jokes that were played would fill another book but, in any case, I must gloss discreetly over them here in order not to risk prosecution under the Obscene Publications Act.

When Lynda came to live at Barnsdale in 1985, an air of huge contentment spread over Barnsdale. The only thing that changed was Geoff. He had always been an optimist, even in the dark days, and he had always been energetic and hard working, though these qualities didn't always yield the returns he was looking for. But now an element of responsibility began to creep in. He started to do all the things I had been pleading with him to do in the past – he took out life insurance, he got himself a pension scheme, he signed up for private medical care and, joy of joys, he even bought himself a suit. As I have said, he was almost deranged with happiness and had everything he could possibly wish for. His only reservation was that he would have preferred to have to do less work to maintain the garden – but that simply wasn't true. If his work had in some way been curtailed he would have found something else to replace it. He had always believed in the dignity of hard work and his life would have been poorer without it.

CHAPTER 9

Friends and Fun

GEOFF SEEMED TO ATTRACT FRIENDS LIKE moths to a lamp. Many of his friendships developed with people he met through his work, but of course he had social, as opposed to professional, relationships too. Pubs formed the foundation and often the start of many of these. He was an exceptionally gregarious character and plunged himself whole-heartedly into our alcohol-based society. He did this not so much for the sake of the booze as for the bonhomie; in fact before he met Lynda he visited his local most evenings, not because he wanted a drink but as he once said to me, 'in case I'm missing anything'. In the early days most of Geoff's friends met in the Fox and Hounds in the village of Exton, close to Barnsdale, before the Noel Arms in Whitwell became our regular local.

Geoff's relaxed style made it easy for him to make friends, though some came from the most unlikely quarters. One evening, for example, we were standing at the bar when an attractive young lady came in and, in the most fearfully 'finished' cut-glass accent, said in a loud voice, 'I say, has anybody seen Amanda Bass?' Geoff and I, in unison said, 'Not *the* Amanda Bass?' Of course neither of us (nor anybody else for that matter) knew Amanda Bass from Margaret Thatcher, but we suggested that the young lady join us for a drink, which she did, I suspect to take the heat out of her reddening face. Chantal, for that was her name, became a lifelong friend after that and, although now living in Oxfordshire, still visits – but she has given up looking for Amanda Bass.

The Fox and Hounds had been taken over by our good friend William Brown, whom we had known for some years, and he was a frequent visitor to Stable Cottage in his days as a farmer. He was an extremely unconventional landlord, as many landlords tended to be before threats to their licences became so commonplace. His customers could drink until they felt like going home, but if William tired of them, he would simply give them the keys to the front door, ask them to lock up when they left and please leave the money for their drinks on the bar. Nobody abused the system and I believe the Home Office should seriously consider introducing it. If William recognised a financial basket case, as Geoff was when he first went there, the drinks would often be on the landlord and even meals were provided for needy customers. He was also, however, a competent man who seemed to be able to turn his hand to anything. Not only did he single-handedly renovate what had been a fairly forbidding pub and make it into a place of welcome, but he also cooked some great gourmet meals for his restaurant, which became very well known and popular.

It was when Geoff and I were standing at the bar one day, like bookends, talking to each other, that we struck up a conversation with Dan Howison and his wife Fay. Our first impression was 'French master and arty lady – not very exciting', but it took only fifteen minutes of conversation for us both to realise how wrong we were.

Dan, born in Rangoon of an upright family who had spent most of their lives in Burma, educated at Oxford, senior master in a notable public school, could have been expected to be rather inaccessible, but he was just the reverse. Witty, generous and down-to-earth, he was the ideal companion and the author of many of the zany schemes and hilarious parties that were to follow. It would be impertinent of me to call Dan eccentric, but just let me say that I formed a certain view of him when I first had the notable treat of laying eyes on his gardening trousers. Dan's gardening trousers were a triumph of trouser engineering, consisting entirely of multicoloured patches, each one added lovingly by Dan himself as a new hole appeared. They were not his first pair of gardening trousers, they were his *only* pair – the Methuselah of gardening trousers – the original Joseph and His Amazing Technicolor Gardening Trousers.

Fay, though not as rumbustious, was also funny and inventive, with a wicked sense of the bizarre. Our first indication of this came on the night when we were both invited back to their lovely old converted schoolhouse to have a final drink, sitting around the great pine table in their huge kitchen. We noticed that on the wall there were lines marking the heights not only of their children, with names and dates beside them but also of the children's pets, including their pony, which must have been trundled into the kitchen for the purpose. It also included the heights of all their friends, who were asked to add them when they first visited. When Carol, now my wife, first visited there was great amusement because she is only four feet ten inches tall, so her mark was only just above the pony, but Dan saved the day by making another mark, higher than all the others, which he solemnly labelled 'Carol standing on a chair'.

Michael Franklyn, who has been mentioned before and who was known to his friends as Mick the Thatcher, also figured large on our list of friends. Mick lived in a cottage in Malting's Yard, close to Fay and Dan, with his sparkling, dark-haired wife Sue. Mick was, and still is, an inveterate romantic who had spent his life doing old-time country jobs, just because he needed to immerse himself in the romance of doing them. He met Sue when he was working as a bargee on the Midland canals. Realising that he would be unable to earn enough as a bargee, he returned to the job he had been trained for, thatching; the bargee job was a temporary expedient to make enough money to start thatching again, because he'd inadvertently set fire to his straw and couldn't afford to replace it. With this kind of history he was an instant attraction to Geoff, who was every bit as romantic and unrealistic about life. Both had a naïve but immensely attractive view that life was not about realism and science – it was about music and art and gardens and joy. Mick was a very talented musician, a great raconteur and wit, and he could imitate any accent he cared to take on.

With these friends, and many more, together with the multitude of people who visited Stable Cottage, then Top Cottage and then Barnsdale, Geoff had an embarrassment of riches. He revelled in their humour, their kindness and their skills. It was with these people that he and I sang, conversed, drank – rather too much from time to time – and laughed until we could laugh no more. Don't let anybody tell you that it's boring to live in the country. I could tell you many a tale that will counter that argument.

One day we were standing in the pub bemoaning the fact that, since Rutland had now become engulfed by Leicestershire and Rutland Water had been built, the pub had become filled with fishermen from Halifax and Huddersfield. Whitwell was beginning to lose its identity and we should do something to regain it. Somebody said that what other villages did was to twin with another, similar village on the Continent, but this was quickly discarded as being too feeble for our fine village of thirty-nine souls (plus thirty-four ducks, which belonged to the vicar). Then Pat Beese, a tutor at a local college and clearly a man of immense intellect and insight, said, 'Why do we have to twin with a small village? What's to stop us twinning with Paris?' This was enthusiastically accepted and we immediately set up 'Le Comité de Jumelage' which, being translated, means 'the Twinning Committee'.

We decided to write an appropriate letter to Jacques Chirac, the Mayor of Paris, notifying him of our intentions, so Dan, the only fluent French speaker amongst us, translated our efforts into passable French. Dan designed a special letterhead announcing 'Le Comité de Jumelage, Whitwell-Sur-L'Eau, Premier Port de Pêche des Midlands', to impart the appropriate air of dignity to the enterprise. We felt it our duty to *notify* rather than ask because, after all, we had won the Battle of Waterloo. The letter eloquently made the case that there were distinct similarities between Whitwell and Paris – 'You have the Seine, we have Rutland Water. You have wonderful restaurants, we have the Noel Arms. You have a rather bigger population than us [the population

Planting the large semi-mature trees in the early days at Barnsdale, to give the garden height and a sense of adolescence, if not age

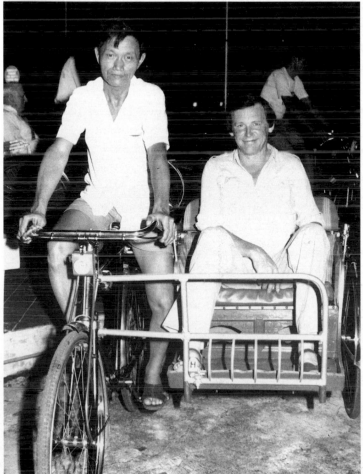

Geoff is transported in lordly style, during a visit to Singapore for *Practical Gardening* magazine

Allie, our dear old Gram, celebrates her eightieth birthday, surrounded by her great-grandchildren

Geoff's pride and joy, his three children, Steve (left), Nick (centre) and Chris (right)

Cy working hard to erect a fence at Barnsdale while Geoff larks about in the background

Geoff and Tony adopt their pompous MP look for the photographer at a wedding

EXCLUSIVE EXTRACTS **PART TWO OF** *THE HUMAN ANIMAL*

DESMOND MORRIS ON SEX

THE BEST ALL-CHANNEL MAGAZINE

RadioTimes

LONDON
BBC SOUTH EAST
ITV CARLTON/LWT

30 JULY - 5 AUGUST 1994 65p

9 770961 887033

30 >

Dig it!

Back to the 60s...
Geoff Hamilton on the roots of
the gardening revolution

Agreeing, somewhat reluctantly, to front the BBC's 'Flower Power' feature in *Radio Times*, Geoff was coaxed out of his jeans and into a yellow silk shirt and beads (*Mark Harrison/ Radio Times*)

Gay Search frequently co-presented with Geoff on *Gardeners' World* (*Stephen Hamilton*)

Paradise Regained.
Geoff's life was at last
complete with the arrival
of his first granddaughter

Family gatherings often
took place at Barnsdale,
and Geoff's barbecues
were wonderful in the
delightful gardens, but
Geoff could never resist
playing the fool

Geoff and Lynda travelled the world together, always choosing exotic locations because Geoff's commitments would only allow him to travel in winter

One of the few dignified poses ever recorded: Geoff after receiving an honorary MSc from Writtle College, his alma mater

Gardening

WHICH?

DECEMBER 1999

the century's best
gardeners,
bedding,
tools and **ideas**

favourite
plants

designs for a
new millennium

Gardening Which? was one of a multitude of journals, magazines and newspapers to which Geoff was asked to contribute (*Gardening Which?*)

Lynda was immensely proud to be asked to open the new hall of residence at Writtle College, dedicated to Geoff and called 'Hamilton'

Professor David Bellamy and Lynda dedicate Winskill Stones to Geoff's memory. Donations by Geoff's many admirers enabled Plantlife to complete the purchase of this inspiring wildlife area as a preservation site (*Farmers Weekly*)

Some of Geoff's family and friends gather at Seaton Meadows, an ancient water meadow, also dedicated to Geoff by Plantlife (*Rutland Times and Stamford Mercury*)

of Paris was 2.3 million] but at least all ours speak English. So we would like to twin with your city; would this be all right?' We felt the phrase 'Would this be all right?' was a masterstroke – so typically English it would be hard to refuse. We also notified him of a deadline, beyond which we would deem ourselves to be officially twinned.

Sam Healey, the landlord, offered to finance a marquee in the car park if we could get enough people to come. Regrettably we didn't print any tickets; we just went ahead, but good old Sam stuck to his promise. In the event, because word had spread around the county, six hundred people turned up to what became a very memorable night. Everybody came in some kind of French costume – we had tarts, madams, pimps, matelots, gendarmes, the lot. We even had William Brown as the Pope, a little incongruously on the door, but nobody seemed surprised.

Dan decided that, for the promotion of good Franco-British relations, it would be useful to publish a short phrase book that would be handed out, free of charge, to all visitors to the event. On the front cover was an explanation of its purpose, ending with the suggestion that any French visitors would find it easier to establish a rapport with the natives if they prefaced their observations with the traditional Rutland greeting 'Éyoupe miaule douque' (Eyoop me old duck). Useful phrases and their translations followed, including:

AU COMPTOIR	AT THE BAR
.58682612 *litres de Vielle Brasserie, s'il vous plaît*	A pint of Old Brewery please
Un grand Professeurs	One large Teachers
Mon ami payera	My friend will pay
Derrières en l'air	Bottoms up

DANS LES MESSIEURS	IN THE GENTS
Kilroy était ici	Kilroy was here
Excusez moi monsieur, je viens d'uriner dans votre poche	I am very sorry sir, but I have just pissed in your pocket

GENERAL	GENERAL
Coup de grâce	Lawnmower
Hors de combat	Camp follower

The evening started with a parade through the village, led by a Renault car with the roof open, through which the only token Frenchman we could find – Robert Bagur, a French master from Oakham School – waved graciously to the crowds. This was followed by the band, comprising trumpet, violin, drum and banjo, it being difficult to raise a more suitable band from a population of seventy-seven. All the six hundred people followed behind, in colourful array, the unbroken procession winding its way through the entire hundred-yard length of the village, directed by the gendarme (me), towards the ceremony of what was euphemistically called the 'inaugurination' of the outside pissoir by the surrogate Mayor of Paris, our noble landlord. A plaque was mounted in due style and then the celebrations began. It turned out to be the most extraordinary night, with a great deal of riotous revelry.

The *Sunday People*, a newspaper now sadly defunct, somehow got to hear of our intentions and sent a reporter and photographer to cover the story. We were then able to see ourselves the following Sunday, in glorious disarray, on a double-page spread, doing things that no civilised community would dream of doing. They also did some research into our legal position and discovered that there was no rule to say that a village, town or city had to seek the *permission* of its counterpart in order to be twinned. There is now such a rule, I believe!

To mark the event permanently we had a sign made saying 'Twinned with Paris' to mount underneath the village sign and I'm glad to say that it's still there.

We eventually got a letter from Jacques Chirac explaining that, whilst he didn't wish to cause an international incident he had to draw our attention to the fact that Paris was already twinned – with Rome, '*par traîté diplomatique*', as he rather pompously put it. Never did have much of a sense of humour, old Jacques. The letter was beyond our deadline for objection so we wrote back to notify him of the fact that we were now well and truly twinned, whether they liked it or not, so *dur fromage* – hard cheese. I often wonder why the French don't seem to like us as much as they should.

Geoff had some difficulty the following day. The party finished just as dawn was breaking and that day he had been assigned by *Practical Gardening* to take a group of people on a series of garden tours and sightseeing trips in Canada. Somewhat the worse for wear he had time to grab a couple of hours' sleep, then throw on a clean shirt, grab his bag and rush off to Heathrow. In his anxiety to get there on time and in a somewhat befuddled state, he forgot to remove the moustache he had worn for the fancy dress. He got some very funny looks at the check-in desk and realised just in time to remove it before he had to meet his first guest.

It was two years later before we thought about doing anything similar. Twinning with Paris was a hard event to follow and nothing really stirred our imaginations until William Brown suggested re-establishing the British Empire. We had all reflected longingly on the days of the Raj, sending gunboats up the Zambezi and deporting convicts to the Antipodes, so we felt that the establishment of an outpost of the British Empire in Whitwell would be good for the morale of the nation as a whole. Fired with enthusiasm, we began to turn the mighty mill of administration again. First we wrote to Lord Carrington, then the Foreign Secretary, to seek permission. Since the letter to Jacques Chirac had worked so well, we employed the same formula, lamenting the loss of the British Empire and proposing that Her Majesty's Government should formally recognise Whitwell as a colonial outpost, ending the letter with the phrase 'Would this be all right?'

Empire Night, as it came to be known, was as riotous as the twinning had been. Again we employed the band, the faithful violinist, trumpeter, drummer and banjo player all turning out smartly dressed in a variety of colonial uniforms. They were closely followed by Queen Victoria (my wife, Carol) flanked by one attendant sumptuously dressed in full Scottish regalia and another as an Indian servant, in full livery (Dan Howison and his daughter Lucy). Also present were a dancing bear (Pat Beese), a stuffed baby elephant that had been acquired from some dubious source by William Brown (he had tried to hire a herd of elephants from a local circus, but our event fell in the circus season, so this was impossible) a mounted policeman (me), and an ancient Indian Guru (Geoff). Geoff's disguise was so good that he sat for about twenty minutes talking to Rosie and Cy, our mother and father, before they realised who he was. Everybody else was in fancy dress and I have never seen so many pith helmets, safari jackets and be-shorted knobbly knees in one place before.

The climax came when the Union Jack was raised, 'Land of Hope and Glory' was played on an old wind-up gramophone and we all stood to attention and saluted. I can tell you, silly though it may sound, that I felt really moved and many an eye was piped.

Surprisingly, we never received a reply from Lord Carrington, who I feel sure must regret this unseemly lapse to this day, but the inhabitants of Whitwell still regard themselves as the last and staunchest outpost of the British Empire.

Geoff and I enjoyed many a fabulous party held by the Howisons from time to time. At one, we were given, late in the evening, party poppers, which are designed to cover the target in a coloured string-like substance. Fay pointed hers at Dan, pulled the string and the cap hit him hard in the eye. Dan, in some considerable pain and not a little annoyed, retired to his bed, but Geoff set to work on a message to cheer him up again. It ran:

> Here lies the body of one-eyed Dan,
> A very much abused man.
> His wife after only one small highball,
> Shot the poor bugger in the eyeball.

The message was duly dispatched to Dan, who laughed so much that he miraculously recovered both his sight and his temper and returned to the party, in case he was missing anything. With curative powers like that, perhaps Geoff should have entered the medical profession.

Our preoccupation with words also led us into some very funny conversations when we repaired to the pub after our Sunday singing sessions. Funny names for dogs was a particular favourite and we laughed most at the use of very commonplace examples – Graham, Trevor, Darren and Brian for dogs and Edith, Muriel, Sharon and Tracey for bitches. We had one hilarious evening devoted to an exposé of 'What you called your willy when you were little'. Try it – it will give you an hour of rib-aching laughter. Anagrams of our names were another amusement. Geoff was General Toffo Hyphen Times, his middle name being Stephen, Dan Howison was Noel O'S**t-in-Wardrobe, Fay was Showy Fiona, Carol was, quite genteelly, Lora Cowsod and I was Nathan Y. Monolith. As a result of my anagram I began to receive catalogues from Damart, who specialise in long johns and other thermal underwear, addressed to 'Mr N.Y. Monolith'. I know they came from Fay and Dan, but they have steadfastly denied it all these years. It seems nobody can be trusted these days.

Geoff was responsible for sparking off an assault on a company called LifeCell, who had announced a limerick competition in one of the trade papers. The limerick had to describe why LifeCell would make a good Christmas present. He put together a team consisting of Dan and Fay, himself and me to try to win the first prize, which was a case of champagne. LifeCell is a gardening irrigation tube that is designed to ooze water constantly to maintain a damp environment for plants – not the most inspiring subject for a group of highly developed literary minds. However, we put our heads together and came up with several examples, all of which we submitted. A selection will serve to give the flavour:

> When Santa homes in from infinity
> With LifeCell for all your vicinity,
> The Christmas tree fairy
> Had better be wary
> If she wants to retain her virginity.

A present you cannot refuse
Is LifeCell, the tube in the news.
It will water your beans
Or your grass or your greens
It can even ooze booze if you choose.

We won the first four prizes, all of which were duly consumed at a memorable croquet party in the summer.

'Fremoni' figured large in our vocabulary and became the label for any slip of the tongue or pen we ran across. The word fremoni arose from the longest misprint in history. It came from one of our local papers, the *Peterborough Standard*. The piece in question set out to report a ceremony held to mark the winding down of the Crowland Silver Jubilee Committee, held in the local library. It read:

> The jubilee fund, described by chairman Frank Parnell as 'one of the finest efforts in Lincolnshire', fremony in the library.
> The jubilee fund described by chairman Frank Parnell as 'one remony atremony aremony at the library.
> The jubremony at the library.
> Tremony at remony at the library
> Thremoni at tremony at the liremony at the libraremony at the library . . .

And so it went on for a three-inch column, before it broke into a curious football report. It was framed and became one of our icons. Each Christmas we would gather at Dan and Fay's house for the ritual reading of the fremoni, after which we would sing the most outstanding fremonis of the year to the tune of 'Earli in de Morning'. These were committed mainly by Fay, who had an unfailing propensity for putting her mouth where her foot should have been. Hers included: at a dinner party after somebody had said they were visiting Oxford, 'Why don't you go and look up my sister?'; talking of our old and absent friend Denis, 'Is he still sticking it out in Sweden?'; and,

190

speaking of Jeremy Thorpe, the MP who had been recently 'outed', 'Poor Jeremy. He's such a nice, kind man. And any of his friends would bend over backwards to help him.' Another memorable one was by Carol: on a journey when bladders were beginning to feel the strain, 'I'm doing it in my handbag.' (She was actually lighting a cigarette in a high wind.)

Singing was also a great source of pleasure and devilment. The Exton Singers shared some good times together, like the winter's night when the wind was whistling around the houses and all in Rutland were stoking up their fires, and we had a power failure that affected the whole of the county. I was sitting at home enjoying the peace of no television and reading by candlelight when I got a telephone call from Fay to suggest that as she and her husband had an old piano at their beautiful old converted schoolhouse in Exton, near Barnsdale, with ancient candleholders attached, we should hold our weekly practice there that night. During our break Fay, brought in a huge cauldron of soup, which we heated on the sitting-room fire.

We would take our practice very seriously because, under Paul Latchford's tutelage, we really wanted to learn how to sing properly. But after our practice we would retire to the pub when, in addition to our often-banal conversation we would sing, very quietly because Sam, our venerable landlord was not our greatest fan. Indeed, one evening when we thought our performance was going extremely well, he came across and asked, 'If I gave you a pound, would you go away?' We steadfastly refused and the uncommon strains of 'In a Monastery Garden', 'My Love's an Arbutus' and 'The Lark in the Clear Air' stole over the pub.

We would often be asked to appear at charity events and once we were asked to do two sessions at a Victorian evening being held for a charity. Dan suggested that as the major preoccupation of the Victorians was death, it would be an eminently suitable subject for our programme – an idea that was acknowledged with a ghoulish enthusiasm. The list included songs like 'The Lost Chord', 'The Long Day Closeth', 'Close Thine Eyes' and one, the words of which were composed specially for the event by Dan, called 'On to the Morgue'. Dan, a wonderfully humorous and inventive man, also composed two priceless sessions for the interval between our songs. The first was simply a list of expressions for death, read alternately by him and a fellow choir member, both dressed in black suits, tall hats and crêpe. It is actually extremely funny to listen to two deadly serious people reading, in sonorous voices, 'To shuffle off one's mortal coil', 'To fall off the edge of the plate', 'To pop one's clogs', etc. The second session was a list of stock from a bankrupt undertaker, as it would have been read by the bailiff – 'Twelve uninscribed headstones – granite. Six uninscribed headstones – marble, black. One inscribed headstone – would suit man called Ron Jones. Six tons green gravel, etc.' Although we lightened the programme with a couple of barber-shop numbers, still retaining the death theme, we were surprised at how much people enjoyed laughing at their own mortality.

This book is not long enough to give space to all the curious episodes and experiences we had, but suffice it to say that this was a time of Geoff's life that was constantly filled with laughter and good friendship. We were lucky enough to gather together a collection of people who, in Fay's words, 'saw the world through the same window' – a rare and sublime facet of life, if you're lucky enough to stumble across it, as Geoff was. The time of these friendships was a golden period of Geoff's life, which lasted until his death, getting more bountiful and fulfilling as it did.

As well as his social friends, of course, Geoff had many, many professional friends, some of whom I have described earlier and will appear in the chapters that follow. Sadly, though, the book simply isn't big enough to include them all and I know I have left out some for whom he had a particular admiration and affection, and who influenced his life and his gardening greatly – Beth Chatto, John Kelly, Derek Cox and many others. I hope they will forgive me.

One or two of Geoff's professional relationships were not always as smooth as they were with the people who surrounded him in Rutland. Geoff was an outspoken and passionate person and he was never afraid to put his point of view, forcefully if need be. If he really believed in something he would press his point home so that people simply had to listen and, where Geoff felt it to be necessary, he would find a way to coax, flatter, embarrass or force them into action. However, the vast majority of people found him to be generous-hearted and easy to work with, as we shall see, and many of them expressed not only admiration for Geoff but a deep affection which they claim will never disappear.

It was not only the friends I've described who filled Geoff's life with interest and joy; so too did all his viewers and readers, who shared his love of gardening and genuinely loved his presentation to them, week by week. He was constantly stopped in the street, on aeroplanes or even in far-off lands by people who had seen him and loved his gentle, humorous style. He was greeted in Canada, Kenya, New Zealand, Sri Lanka, India and many other places where one would never have believed he could be seen, but he was and people universally loved him.

CHAPTER 10

A Real Gardener's
Gardeners' World

THE FIRST *GARDENERS' WORLD* PROGRAMME THAT
included Geoff, very much the junior partner on the team,
went out at 6.55 p.m. on 21 March 1980, with Clay Jones
and Geoffrey Smith taking the leading roles, both being well-
established and experienced gardeners with a good track record of
television behind them. Geoff began by getting stuck into the wild
garden that surrounded Top Cottage, while Clay Jones and Geoffrey
Smith covered the planting of cordon apples, preparing for a succession of vegetables and turfing a lawn, which constituted the bulk of
the programme.

In those early days of Geoff's *Gardeners' World* career an outside
broadcast was a major undertaking, usually using two huge
pantechnicon-type vans which would lumber down the little lane like
two Trojan horses. One was a scanner, from which the programme
would be directed and the other carried the elaborate cameras and
the mass of equipment required for the job. Accompanying the vehicles
would be a crew of cameramen, sound engineers, electricians, director/
producer and assistant as well as a gang of riggers whose job was to
set up all the miles of cables and the equipment and push the great,

ungainly cameras backwards and forwards. This meant that the ground at Barnsdale had to be criss-crossed with paved paths so that the cameras could track smoothly over the land. It was a major undertaking to lay the paving, which Geoff and I sweated over for some time.

Because the outside broadcast vehicles were so expensive and much in demand for other events, programmes were usually made in pairs: it made sense to shoot two weeks'-worth of material while the crew were on location. So Geoff was used for the programme that went out the following week, but after that he didn't reappear until 16 May; and then there was another gap until he appeared again on 8 August. The programme made a number of visits to other gardens, often using contributors other than Geoff – to Beth Chatto's magical gardens near Colchester, to Dyffryn House near Cardiff, to Dr Sewell Cooper's highly successful organic garden at Arkley Manor, a garden that hadn't been dug for twenty years – surely a record, and many more. Gradually Barnsdale was visited more and more, until it was used for about half the programmes and Clacks Farm (the home of Arthur Billett, the programme's lead presenter) for the other half. However, by October 1981 Arthur Billett had decided to retire (Peter Seabrooke, the other lead presenter, having withdrawn at the end of the previous series in 1979), and then Barnsdale became the focal point for the programme.

As his experience and confidence grew, Geoff began to take on more and more of the work and an influx of letters to the BBC speaking in glowing terms about his style began to prove his value. Additionally John Kenyon, the producer/director, valued Geoff's technical expertise. Clay Jones, who became the anchorman, was by profession a seedsman and, whilst his knowledge in this area was unassailable, he admitted that his knowledge of general horticultural practice was not as extensive as Geoff's. They got on extremely well together and Clay would happily accept guidance from this young upstart. He was a warm and generous-hearted Welshman who was comfortable in his role as a presenter and his relationship with Geoff was never competitive. They remained good companions until Clay died, when I have seldom seen Geoff so affected by the loss of a friend. He gave the eulogy at Clay's funeral in Wales and he told me that it was the most difficult piece of presentation he had ever done. Experienced as he was by then, he felt in danger of breaking down with every word he spoke.

Geoffrey Smith gradually did less and less presentation on *Gardeners' World*, because he wanted to work on a new series on specialist subjects and to concentrate more of his time in his much-loved Yorkshire. It was during the last *Gardeners' World* programme that Geoffrey Smith presented that Geoff met Roy Lancaster, perhaps the most knowledgeable British plantsman and plant explorer living.

Roy is one of the warmest, friendly and unaffected people I've ever met and it's small wonder that Geoff got on so well with him. Geoff, of course, knew of Roy's reputation as a plant collector and knew that he had done some television work, though never with the BBC. Roy's first impression of Geoff was that he was confident and very welcoming, which pleased Roy since it was his first encounter with the BBC. They worked well together and at the end of the session Geoff thanked Roy and said that he hoped they could work together again. In fact it was the start of a long and fruitful working relationship as well as another firm friend to add to Geoff's already extensive list.

Roy says that he learned a lot from Geoff about presentation style because he was so relaxed and friendly. Roy had a tendency to allow his colossal passion for plants to carry him along in a great wave of enthusiasm, which Geoff felt would alienate viewers, because they couldn't identify with it. He would watch Roy from the scanner, parked some way from the site of the shot, and just quietly and tactfully mention to John Kenyon, the director, that he might be going slightly over the top. John, never a man to let tact encumber his directorial style, would bellow down the mike, 'Roy, Geoff says you're going over the top!' It is a tribute to Roy's professionalism that he recognised this was probably right, simply took it on board, and slowed down to a more conversational delivery, more interesting and accessible to those who perhaps didn't share his passion. In his delivery he took his lead from Geoff.

Geoff, Roy feels, was the supreme professional, who would talk about the garden as though he was talking to his family. He loved sharing his ideas and explaining his enthusiasms and it came naturally to him. 'He was like that,' says Roy, 'with whoever he talked to, whether it was a child, an old person, a young person, rich or poor – he didn't see any reason to treat them differently, even the Queen. He hadn't *learned* that skill, he was born with it and if anybody came to him for advice he would be pleased to help them.'

But the boot was, from time to time, on the other foot. As Geoff would have been the first to admit, Roy's knowledge of plants was greater than Geoff's. The first time Geoff got a variety name wrong, Roy was very reticent about pointing it out. Here, after all, was the guru, surrounded and supported by popular acclaim. How to tell him he was wrong? So Roy, quite diffidently, pointed out to John Kenyon that he thought Geoff might have got the variety name wrong. John, unencumbered by Roy's reticence, immediately bellowed into Geoff's earpiece, 'Roy says you've got that wrong!' Geoff made a little quip about 'old smart-arse' but then reshot the piece, using Roy's advice. At the end of the session, when Roy apologised for putting him right, Geoff said, 'What on earth are you apologising for? I don't know everything and if you think I'm wrong you have to tell me. You're the plantsman and if you let me make a mistake *without* telling me I'll have your guts for garters.' From that time onwards, their working relationship was easy, friendly and productive and they both enjoyed the warmth of their friendship immensely.

Roy said that whenever he speaks to groups of gardeners Geoff's name constantly comes up. He thinks there will never be another Geoff and that there must still be millions of gardeners who, having completed a job in the garden think, 'What would Geoff have thought of that?' That reflects exactly the way I feel myself. I constantly feel Geoff looking over my shoulder and good humouredly making sure I've made a good job of whatever I've done.

John Kenyon had a great respect for the highly professional nature of Geoff's presentation. He recalls one occasion when they were filming him making an artificial stone trough out of hypertufa, a mixture of coir and concrete, the generator broke down and they were left without power. It was lunchtime on the final day's shooting and the scanner van, together with all the equipment, had to return that evening, so there was some degree of panic amongst the crew and the producer. Hypertufa troughs are difficult to make and shooting such a sequence can take a long time, with shots having to be reshot every time there is a small glitch. But when Geoff got started it took him six minutes and fourteen seconds to make the trough and he did it all in one shot. At the end of the session the entire crew, in unison, stood and applauded. He had developed his technique into an exact science, knowing instinctively precisely what the cameraman wanted to do, and he planned the way he did things so that he would stand in exactly the right place to ensure that nothing obscured the shot and so present his piece to camera to maximum advantage.

John believes this hails back to one of Geoff's very early programmes, when he was still learning the ropes. He was training a weeping willow by tying the branches down, using long pieces of string. During this clownish event he got into such a terrible tangle that he had the camera crew rolling on the ground clutching their stomachs. Geoff took a joke against himself very well, but he hated to have his professionalism impugned, and John believes he just made up his mind that that kind of pantomime was never going to happen again. The experience taught him that if he was going to do a piece he had better have worked out *exactly* what he was going to do and how he was going to present it before he got anywhere near the camera.

John was a martinet as far as authenticity and accuracy were concerned. He didn't believe in disparaging methods simply because they didn't fit in with Geoff's views and he felt strongly that nobody should be contradicted or upset unless there was a very good reason for doing so. On the other hand, he didn't want a bland programme either. They had a few arguments – for instance, he wasn't always happy with Geoff's portrayal of the facts in his organic campaign – but he acknowledged the fact that 'when Geoff got a bee in his bonnet it buzzed very loud' and if Geoff had a strong statement to make about any aspect of his work he was given his head and allowed to say it. 'He was the expert, it was his programme, so in the end, if he wanted to do something he did it – but I made quite sure he knew my views before we went ahead.' They remained the very best of friends.

John had something of a tussle with Geoff when trying to persuade him to show the mistakes he made as well as his successes, but eventually he prevailed. They were filming a piece about some seeds germinating under black polythene, which they hadn't previously inspected, for fear of disturbing them. When Geoff and Clay Jones pulled back the polythene, their faces full of expectation, they discovered that it was nothing but an enormous sea of weeds, without a single plant showing above the forest of foliage. Geoff was very resistant to this shot going out, but by this time John had it on tape, and as he put it, 'I was in charge' – so it was duly transmitted to three million viewers. They were deluged with responses, all praising the fact that Geoff was prepared to show his failures as well as his successes, so from then on doing so became the norm.

These kinds of successes cannot be put down exclusively to either John's clever and imaginative direction or to Geoff's easy communication style. Making the programme was a team effort and a bit of the credit has to go to everybody. Geoff, and every other member of the team, had a very soft spot for one person without whom nothing would have got off the ground at all. That was the calm, completely unflappable Jean Laughton. She was called a production assistant and if you asked her to describe her job she would put herself down as a kind of administrative dogsbody – but she was far from that. It was Jean who arranged all the travel, the hotels, the equipment and the props, as well as looking after the continuity (a taxing job when filming over two days, particularly if the weather varies dramatically from day to day) and even keeping the unruly riggers in order. Her only lapse was to conspire with John to plant a house brick into the peat of a growbag just before Geoff planted it up, expecting to find a nice friable mixture. Such little things cause immense hilarity in a tense situation and it was twenty minutes before Geoff had recovered his composure enough to do the shot again – this time without the brick.

* * *

In June 1981, John was joined by a young, exuberant new producer called Denis Gartside, who would free John up for some of his other work. John was also producing the BBC farming programmes, as well as various offshoots from *Gardeners' World*, such as the *Shades of Spring*, *Shades of Summer* and *Shades of Autumn* programmes, which were shot at the appropriate time but reserved for screening in the winter. Denis was striking, to say the least. Nearly six feet five inches tall, with wild hair, long, long jeans and always either bare feet or sandals, he was unusual in the extreme. But he was good. In fact, he was very good, and he and Geoff hit it off immediately. Carol, who you will remember, is only four feet ten inches tall, had some difficulty with Denis, but only because she would constantly be speaking into his kneecaps.

Denis was as enthusiastic as John about the need to demonstrate practical aspects of real gardening; he eloquently puts it, 'I really did want to show that proper gardeners ended up with crap down their fingernails and plants covered in pests. So we set out to show the normal gardener how to deal with the normal gardening projects and normal gardening problems.'

One of the early meetings between Denis and Geoff was, coincidentally, one of the few times I ever went to see Geoff making a programme. I knew what pressures Geoff was working under, so I made it a rule to keep out of the way unless he specifically asked me to be there – which he did on this occasion. The programme was being made from a well-known herb nursery in Northamptonshire, and the owner was due to be interviewed and to take a leading part in the programme. Geoff and I met Denis together, both craning our necks to see the face of this enormous man, and I was invited to watch the proceedings. All went well in the morning, with Geoff interviewing the owner and talking about how to grow the herbs and the uses to which they could be put. All good, interesting stuff and Denis was well pleased. When the lunch break came, however, we all repaired to the pub for a quick snack, but the owner of the nursery, unnoticed by any of us, quietly got himself completely plastered.

When the afternoon session came he couldn't string two words together and kept falling over – not quite so satisfactory. I could hear Denis shouting from the scanner that they should get him off, so one of the production assistants politely suggested that the presentation would be better done with only one person. 'Yes,' said the owner, 'I quite agree. I can manage perfectly well on my own.' This was not at all what had been envisaged, so two hefty riggers were called in to carry him off to his house. This would have been fine and Geoff could have carried the second half of the programme quite easily had it not been suddenly interrupted by the sound of screaming engines and clanging bells as two fire engines came roaring up the drive. The owner, in his befuddled state, had set his house on fire! Geoff, of course, blamed me and saw me ever after as a jinx, but I don't think he really meant it.

Denis and Geoff went abroad a few times to shoot special programmes. On one memorable occasion they were working in Amsterdam and, of course, the conversation had turned to drugs and their ready availability. Geoff, whilst wandering through a glasshouse, had found and picked up a peat block which was curiously shaped like a cigar. So when they returned to this conversation he got it out of his pocket and said to one of the crew, 'There you are. If you really want to know what it will do, try one of these,' at which the poor chap put it in his mouth and lit it. I will draw a veil over his remarks after the coughing and spluttering had finished but let it be known that he was not best pleased. This was why Geoff was so popular – because whilst he was a consummate professional and demanded the highest standards, he was never a prima donna and always up for a laugh – and let me tell you there were many made against him, all of which were taken in good part – as long as they didn't interfere with the making of the programme. Trips abroad were to become much more adventurous later.

Denis remembers the last programme presented by Percy Thrower, the original and masterly presenter of *Gardeners' World*, before his retirement, in which Geoff played a minor role. Percy always appeared in his jacket and his first action, for which he became famous and much loved, was to remove his jacket and hang it on a hook on the potting-shed door. Geoff, the young upstart, pushing his luck with the maestro, replaced the metal hook with a rubber one, and as a result when Percy hung up his jacket it fell to the floor. Thinking he had missed the hook, Percy reshot the piece, only to find it happening again – and again and again. It was several takes later before he realised what was happening, but when he did he threw back his head and laughed till he cried.

The first *Gardeners' World* at the new Barnsdale went out after the winter break in January 1984. It featured Geoff moving the plants from Top Cottage to the 'new' Barnsdale, described earlier, and planting some of them in their new positions, with the help of Roy Lancaster, Anne Mayo and Clay Jones, for which some pretty rapid preparation work had been done so as to have somewhere to plant them. A greenhouse had been erected, so it was possible to film another programme about sowing vegetables, and choosing bare-rooted and container-grown shrubs, but at this stage it required all the inventiveness of the presenters and the production team to keep the material for the programme going. Perhaps the most dramatic programme in the first days of the new Barnsdale featured the planting of the semi-mature trees and the establishment of 'Versailles', both of which have been mentioned earlier.

However, although all this was liberally interspersed with broadcasts from other gardens and other specialists, it was soon realised that with the programme focusing so much on the building of a five-acre garden it would not be possible to retain the interest of viewers who had fifty square metres of land at the back of their house. Both John Kenyon and Geoff were acutely aware of the fact that such viewers represented about 80 per cent of their audience; he was adamant that *Gardeners' World* should not to be allowed to roam into the realms of the airy-fairy and that their needs should be served.

To this end it was decided to divide up Barnsdale, project by project, into a series of small, 'estate-sized' plots, each of which would be built, maintained and demonstrated, warts and all, as the project progressed.

The first of these was called, appropriately enough, 'Starting from Scratch', which was designed as a short item, to be followed through in successive *Gardeners' World* programmes. It was devised for two reasons. Firstly it would cover the fact that the new Barnsdale was, as yet, totally undeveloped, and secondly it would set out to show people with small plots, usually attached to new houses, how to deal with what may have seemed a daunting problem. Here again, some subterfuge was used because loads of builders' rubble and old pipes and tiles were dug in to simulate what the new gardener was likely to have found. Then it went on to show how a bare, uncultivated, hostile plot could be turned into a flourishing garden, which would cease to be hostile and would provide lasting pleasure for years to come. If only we could do that with people!

This garden was built and screened in tandem with the establishment of the bigger ornamental garden. Together they attracted the interest and enthusiasm of a wide range of viewers and the ratings began imperceptibly to rise. This practice of building small gardens, each with its own unique style and which the viewers could easily identify with, became the established method of operation for the programme and a fascinating learning experience.

One of Geoff's best ideas in the early stages of *Gardeners' World* was that the programme should have a running theme that could be established and then revisited during every programme that came from Barnsdale. The first of these began in 1984, when Geoff was given a budget of £104 a year for a garden in which to demonstrate how a family of three could have an ornamental garden and become self-sufficient in fruit and vegetables (described in more detail in Chapter 11). This concept was the start of a very interesting phase for the programme, because it gave it a strong cohesion and kept viewers switching on week after week.

At that stage in Geoff's career there were none of the dedicated series for which he was to become famous a little later, but one day John Kenyon attended a lunch with the controller of BBC2, together with a number of other producers. They were asked if they could come up with ideas for programmes that could be made reasonably cheaply but would attract good viewing figures. 'What about a programme from Barnsdale about house plants?' John asked. The controller pricked up his ears and said, 'OK, you can have a thousand pounds a programme.' 'Two thousand pounds,' said John. 'I'll write you a brief synopsis and if you don't agree to at least fifteen hundred pounds a programme I don't want to do it.'

John then phoned Geoff and put the idea to him and Geoff, still short of money (though not as short as he had been), agreed. John suggested that they should take the attention away from Geoff's ugly mug by using a celebrity and they both immediately thought of Susan Hampshire, who had a well-known interest in gardening and is, in fact, a very accomplished gardener herself. John points out that many programmes are given life in this way. 'Far from it being an incredibly innovative idea that came out of the ether and was driven forward by the drive and initiative of Hamilton and Kenyon, it actually arose simply from the controller asking for a cheap and cheerful programme.'

So in 1985 Susan Hampshire was invited to join the programme and gladly accepted. She and Geoff instantly recognised that they shared common qualities: not only a love of plants and gardening but also an interest in conservation – Susan is a director of the Conservation Foundation and has a particular interest in the preservation of our tree population. The series was called 'Going to Pot'.

A special studio was built in the barn at Barnsdale, looking like a house interior. Susan, who is dyslexic, was amazing with her facility to memorise her lines – a real trouper. She only needed somebody to read the script to her once and it was there, lodged firmly in her brain and delivered with the charm and affection that seems to come quite naturally to her. Susan became very friendly with my wife Carol, who supplied most of the plants from her greenhouse at Barnsdale, and for her it was an unforgettable and delightful experience.

John, however, found it much more worrying. He says that when Geoff and Susan got together they seemed to do nothing but 'corpse', which is the actors' term for giggling. When the pair of them got the giggles it was terribly difficult to get them down to earth again. When time was running out, John would be tearing his hair out in the scanner while both Geoff and Susan were unable to get control of themselves. This epidemic would quickly spread to the crew and a furious John would storm down from the scanner to try to save the few vital minutes left that were about to be lost. However, the series was made – although knowing Geoff as I did, I recognised a tell-tale twitch at the corners of his mouth – and, judging by the excellent viewing figures, it was a roaring success.

Geoff worked with a number of co-presenters on *Gardeners' World*: as well as Clay Jones and Anne Mayo, who worked with him from the beginning of his career, his co-presenters included Margaret Waddy, who came to the programme in 1985, and one of his favourite men, John Kelly, a quiet but unobtrusively expert Irishman, now sadly dead. Many other specialists were invited to appear on the programme and this made it endlessly varied and interesting viewing.

In January 1987, Geoff was joined by Anne Swithinbank, who had been working as a glasshouse supervisor at Wisley Gardens. She had appeared in a programme called *Gardeners' Calendar*, shot at Wisley by Granada Television, and the BBC, always hungry for new talent, and obviously impressed by her performance and her knowledge, asked her if she would like to do a piece for *Gardeners' World*. However, by that time a precondition of anybody appearing on the programme was that Geoff should interview them first. He always adopted a much sterner approach to people he didn't know than he did to those he did, because he was very much aware of the fact that a poor presenter would damage his and the programme's reputations as much as it damaged the presenter. Anne was scared witless by Geoff. Having heard so much about him and watched his programmes, she regarded him as *the* gardening guru. She also knew that he didn't suffer fools gladly and if you were going to become one of Geoff's colleagues you had to earn your spurs. But she must have impressed him more than somewhat because it wasn't long before the discussion turned to what she would be doing on the programme.

Their working relationship and their friendship burgeoned, budded and bloomed as well as anything else at Barnsdale. Geoff used to call her 'Flossie', for no reason other than his own amusement, although behind her back he and the rest of the crew would refer to her as 'the Milkmaid', because she was pretty and vulnerable and had a kind of nineteenth-century agricultural appeal. Nevertheless, she could work as hard as any of them, would pay minute attention to detail and quickly grew in confidence. Often Anne would have an idea for a piece to add to the programme, equip herself with all the plants and tools to do it, sometimes travelling hundreds of miles to do so, only to find when she got to Barnsdale that Geoff and the producer had cooked up an entirely different idea. She would then have to do something she hadn't thought through, adopting Geoff's ideas and methods. She was uncomfortable with this and it occasionally led to some dissent between Anne and the producer at the time, but matters were always smoothed out. Anne believes that the work with Geoff advanced her own career enormously and, although not appearing on a regular television programme at present, she is still broadcasting on *Gardeners' Question Time* and writing prolifically.

In 1988, Denis moved on to pastures new and Mark Kershaw, another experienced BBC documentary maker, joined John as series producer. He says he initially felt in awe of Geoff, although Geoff was by no means the sort of man who would set out to inspire awe, but Mark had come from a horticultural background himself, had watched *Gardeners' World* since he was a boy and had built a considerable respect for Geoff. However, Geoff soon put him at his ease and a good productive relationship began to develop.

Pippa Greenwood, the bubbly, self-effacing pest and disease expert, was brought in to augment the team in 1988. Pippa, who was working as a plant pathologist at Wisley, was approached by Mark Kershaw at the Chelsea Flower Show, where she had been asked to do a piece for television called *Going for Gold*. Mark asked her if she would like to do some work for the BBC and, with some anxiety about what she was letting herself in for, she cautiously agreed. She began by working with Alan Titchmarsh, who was at the time presenting the daytime television gardening programme *Pebble Mill*, but in 1989 Pippa was asked to join Geoff in a programme from Barnsdale.

After some difficulty in finding the place (although well signposted now, because it is open to the public, at the time it was carefully hidden and inaccessible) she arrived at Barnsdale with great trepidation. She knew *Gardeners' World* was the leading gardening programme and she had never done anything like it before. Pippa, surprisingly for a person prominent in the media, was brought up in a television-free zone – her enlightened parents believing curiously in conversation and having no television set, except for a short-term hire to watch the moon-landings in July 1969. So she had never seen *Gardeners' World*, never seen Geoff and had no idea of what kind of a chap he was. But, as always, he welcomed her warmly and they were soon strolling round Barnsdale discussing her contribution to the programme. In her anxiety Pippa had left everything she needed behind, like secateurs, etc., and, though ravenously keen to do it, she was panicstricken and wished she was back on familiar territory. Geoff calmed her down, lent her some secateurs, joked with her, ribbed her in the kind and cheeky way that only Geoff could, and it was not long before they were into the shooting of her first contribution to *Gardeners' World*.

Mark Kershaw had wisely arranged for Anne Swithinbank, a friend and colleague of Pippa's, to interview her, so the shoot went well and everybody was well pleased. Except Pippa! She says that she had found the experience so stressful that, on her way back to her home in Hampshire, she broke down and cried several times. As a seasoned professional, she can look back and laugh at it now, but that baptism of fire took its toll and it made its mark on her for all time.

Geoff and Pippa worked together regularly after that and it was to prove a rich relationship for both of them. Geoff never gave her gratuitous advice, but he was always on hand to help if help were needed and, above all, was greatly appreciative of a good performance. Perhaps most importantly, he helped Pippa through the maze of politics that always surround a big organisation like the BBC. At one time she was asked (or rather 'told') to wear a particular set of clothes that she really hated. She felt they were baggy and unattractive but, being the new girl on the block, she felt obliged to toe the line. Geoff, however, sensed her discomfort immediately and said, 'You don't like those clothes, do you?' Pippa admitted that she didn't, so Geoff said,

'Well, stand up for yourself, girl. If you don't like them, don't wear them. Just let them try that sort of thing on me!' So she did, the BBC caved in and Pippa was happy again.

She is also observant and canny and she watched the tricks that Geoff used for good presentation and took them on board for use in future programmes. Even now Pippa has a photograph of Geoff in her office and when in need of inspiration or having to deal with a personal problem she turns to Geoff and asks his advice.

Up until 1989, the programmes continued to be made, two per week, using the two lumbering vehicles, the teeming hordes of riggers (or so it seemed to Lynda as they tramped through the kitchen) and the elaborate cameras that had to be pushed around the gardens by a team of people. And then the new technology came along. The Birmingham Outside Broadcast Unit was closed and it seemed that, within a matter of moments, the cameras had shrunk to a size where they could be handheld and so the need for all the riggers disappeared. Geoff regretted this to some extent, because with the riggers went a lot of the banter and the fun. But the programmes became a lot easier to make and a good deal more variety was introduced because it was now possible to do multilocation filming – to make one rather than two programmes from a single location.

Single-camera filming opened up all kinds of new possibilities, the first one being a six-part series called *The First-time Gardener*, which was shot in Birmingham and co-presented by Gay Search. Gay had first met Geoff at a press conference on a riverboat on the Thames and they hit it off pretty well from the word go. Gay was writing a gardening column for *Woman* magazine (although when first asked she was reticent because of her perceived lack of knowledge, so *Woman* offered her some expert help in the form of a young Ilkley lad called Alan Titchmarsh). Geoff and Gay became buddies because they had similar senses of humour, a similar view of the world and, most importantly to Geoff, they both loathed Margaret Thatcher.

It was shot at a Barratt Home in Bournville in Birmingham because, although it was tempting to shoot it at Barnsdale, Geoff wanted to get a real taste of what it would be like for the buyer of a brand-new estate house who aspired to a beautiful garden. It turned out to be a tough assignment. In his book, which accompanied the programme, Geoff describes the utter chaos that faced them one cold, wet day in December when he and Gay Search went to see the site. The house was only half-completed and the garden was just an enormous heap of rubble. On further investigation they discovered that the dull thudding sound that had puzzled them was, in fact, a group of explosives experts blasting a solid block of reinforced concrete, fifteen feet thick, that had been the base of a factory that had stood on the site. That was to be the site for the new garden.

To make matters worse, while they were contemplating the challenge there came the deafening roar of a hundred yards of Inter City express passing within twenty feet of the patio doors. As Geoff said, hardly a rural idyll. Geoff spent a long time with Alison Hainey, the designer, planning exactly how to deal with what at first sight appeared to be a disaster. In the event, because the garden was so small it was not possible to cram in all the design features they wanted to show, so these were covered during visits to other small gardens that had been designed by members of the British Association of Landscape Industries, the cream of landscape gardeners. Despite a very unpromising start, with a lot of hard work, a group of dazzling designs and a scintillating double act from Geoff and Gay the programme was a huge success.

It was followed in 1989 by another six-part series, made primarily at Barnsdale and also screened during the winter, called *First-Time Planting*. This set out to remedy all the heartache that visitors to garden centres or nurseries have when they come home with a car boot full of plants and a breast full of enthusiasm, only to be devastated when their new acquisitions gradually fade away. It dealt not only with *how* to plant so that plants will thrive, but also with which varieties are most suitable for sun, shade, cold, wet, acid or alkaline soils – every condition one is likely to meet, in fact. It also made good use of Gay's deft touch with design and colour, she being loath to leave this aspect entirely to Geoff, who was known as a bit of a Philistine who 'likes a bit of colour'. Both programmes were accompanied by books, the first written solely by Geoff and the second by Geoff and Gay together.

In 1989, there were moves to reorganise programming at the BBC and John Kenyon decided to take early retirement, so Geoff and he were reluctantly parted. Geoff was one of his greatest and dearest friends. They had, after all, spent a lot of time together. They had worked together, eaten together, stayed in the same hotels, drank together and played together, and during that time they had had an awful lot of fun – just because they liked each other so much. When John left, there was definitely a vacuum at Barnsdale and Geoff seemed to feel that he had lost a good friend and mentor. In fact this was never to be the case. John continued to talk to Geoff about the work he was doing and to visit Barnsdale frequently, and he still continues to do so.

The 1989 reorganisation included drafting in a senior man called Cyril Gates, part of whose brief was to invigorate *Gardeners' World* and to set a new policy and direction for the programme. The whole television industry was going through a dramatic change at the time and the battle for the ratings was beginning in earnest. What this meant was a move towards less of the practical, 'hands-on' gardening that Geoff excelled in and more of a move towards entertainment. Geoff was deeply unhappy about this and spoke bitterly to me about the politics that were beginning to engulf the BBC and his earnest desire to stay out of them. He was convinced that the real gardeners amongst his viewers wanted horticulture and not frothy entertainment, which in any case he was uncomfortable about providing. It was perhaps the most unhappy period of his career with the BBC and he even talked to me of trying his luck with Channel 4. There was also a feeling at Pebble Mill at the time that programmes should not be too 'presenter led' and I'm afraid Geoff, a highly experienced and knowledgeable gardener, resented the idea of young researchers, straight from college, coming round to tell him what he should be doing. However, his loyalty to his old masters got the better of him and eventually, by careful negotiation, the differences were ironed out and the programme continued with Geoff as its lead presenter. His discomfort was somewhat alleviated by the fact that Cyril Gates was eventually promoted to a different job in Manchester. He also determined that, at the next contract negotiation, he would stick out for more money.

It was Mark Kershaw, who by now had taken over from John Kenyon as producer/director who had to face up to the force of Geoff's personality and persuasiveness at this stage, but in the event this turned out not to be a problem at all. The first programme they did together was made at the Glasgow Garden festival and, during the flight up together they had a good opportunity to talk over their respective problems and reach some sound compromises.

Incidentally, it was during this flight that the most extraordinary coincidence occurred, which Geoff and I laughed at for years afterwards. He had explained, whilst he was chatting to Mark, that he had an identical twin brother and that he was always concerned about the effect that his celebrity had on him, knowing that he was continually mistaken for him and had to explain our relationship. He could never believe that I was delighted and proud of my famous brother's achievements and the thought of any kind of envy never crossed my mind; as long as I could retain my supreme confidence that I was a better gardener than he was, I was happy. Soon after Geoff had explained all this to Mark, the plane landed and they got up to leave. As they did so, two businessmen who had been sitting in the seat behind them said, almost in unison, 'Hello. Aren't you Tony Hamilton's brother?' They were two of my clients and I loved them ever after for that. But it was the only time such a reversal happened and generally I was accosted in trains, pubs, restaurants and anywhere else I went! It amused me greatly to be asked for my autograph and if anybody told me how much they enjoyed the programme I would say, 'Oh, thank you so much.' If, on the other hand, there was a hint of criticism I would say, 'Oh, that's my brother.'

A presenter who joined *Gardeners' World* at this time was Nigel Colborn, who was to become one of Geoff's friends as well as a colleague. They always maintained a healthy respect for each other, despite the fact that their views did not always align. They had first met when Geoff visited Nigel's small plant nursery in Careby in Lincolnshire, where they discovered an instant rapport and liking for each other. Nigel expressed an interest in getting involved with the television work that Geoff was engaged in, but at first Geoff didn't react to this at all. Some time later, however, in 1989, Nigel received a phone call from Geoff to ask him if he would like to appear in a *Gardeners' World* programme, to show viewers how to plant and naturalise bulbs. Nigel told Geoff that he had something else he had to do on that date and Geoff, employing his typically light and diplomatic touch, said, 'Don't be bloody ridiculous, man. Here's a chance to get into television. Get yourself over here!' So he did.

During that programme Geoff very quietly let Nigel know, just as Graham Rose had done for him, that Mark Kershaw, the producer, was looking for another presenter to team up with Geoff. After some gentle pressure from Geoff, Nigel was invited to do a full screen test and he was accepted as a regular contributor.

Geoff scared him when he first began to present. He recalls the second time he ever visited Barnsdale, when he knocked at the front door, which was opened by Geoff, who said, 'Nigel, you silly bugger, nobody knocks at Barnsdale. You just walk in.' This scared him even more, but once he saw that all the other members of the crew did the same he became less diffident.

Nigel was one of the very few people to whom I talked during the research for this book who didn't find Geoff easy to work with. Geoff, he says, was very competitive and liked it to be known that he was the lead presenter and that the others should watch their Ps and Qs. He would also make sure that he was always in control of how the programme was going. However, Nigel didn't see Geoff as being a control freak, but felt that this was just a sign of his professionalism and pride in the programme.

Nigel says that his time at *Gardeners' World* was, of all his broadcasting experiences, the happiest and most fulfilling, because Geoff was not only funny and mischievous during the making of every programme and a highly skilled communicator but he also knew his subject inside out. His secret was his direct and unassuming approach to his viewers. He would identify with them by making the point that, like the majority of gardeners, he knew what it was like to be not very well off and unable to afford a 'designer' approach, his soil was impossible, so he had to make it work for him and he hadn't got all the time in the world, so whatever he would do would be cheap, straightforward and easy to accomplish. His viewers loved him for recognising and accommodating their needs.

I am glad to report that Geoff and Nigel only ever disagreed on technical matters. Geoff was vociferous in his defence of pure organic gardening and he despised the use of peat, the exploitation of which is steadily depleting our stock of wildlife as a unique habitat is destroyed. Nigel took the opposing view, believing that a mix of chemical and organic methods was more sensible and that peat was a valuable horticultural commodity that was worth the attendant losses. I just held their jackets.

When the programme was put out to a private production company (of which more in the next chapter) Nigel was dropped, even though Geoff dearly wanted to retain the team that had worked so well together.

Nigel describes Geoff as the person who perhaps had the greatest effect on the promotion of gardening in the twentieth century, and was surprised that he had not been awarded the Victoria Medal of Honour in Horticulture (VMH) by the Royal Horticultural Society. Celebrated gardener Valerie Finnis is equally upset that they never saw fit to honour Geoff's achievements with this medal, as he was loved, as she says, by millions of people and able to make gardening accessible to those with small gardens, a window box or even a single pot. She saw this as a great injustice and campaigned to get it put right, unfortunately to no avail.

Gordon Rae, who was the director general of the RHS during most of Geoff's television career, expresses his bemusement at this notable omission and he cannot give a reason for it. He could find no trace of antagonism at all towards Geoff amongst his colleagues at the RHS.

He explains that twenty years ago the RHS was a very conservative organisation and that gardeners who appeared in the media were, somewhat curiously I think, not considered suitable subjects. (Percy Thrower didn't get an honour either. Poor old Percy.) Apparently Geoff's name was never proposed to the awards committee. I suspect that this was partly because of Geoff's uncompromising approach to the people he thought to be contributing to the destruction of the environment – chemical gardeners, peat users, limestone rock exploiters and the like. He was never afraid to take a stand against the establishment and it could be that this made him less acceptable than the blander proponents of less forward-looking views. It is seldom that rebels get the recognition they deserve, and, though they may change the world for the better they are only recognised after the event. Geoff was surprised that although he was the inspiration behind Gardeners' World Live, the best-attended gardening show in the country, which is now run by the RHS, he never seemed to be accepted as a valued contributor. However, he was quite the last person to feel aggrieved about it, particularly as he had had some notable disagreements with the RHS in the past, and simply shrugged it off with a resigned sigh. Ah well, perhaps a posthumous award is already winging its way in the post.

Mark Kershaw continued to produce the weekly programmes and he also produced the series. These usually went out in six parts, which could be shot during the year and screened during the winter. The first that Mark produced, in 1989–90, for screening during the winter of 1990, was called *The Ornamental Kitchen Garden* and was based on the ideas of the old-time cottage gardeners who would mix flowers and vegetables in the same beds. Not only was the design and the landscaping of the garden interesting and architecturally brilliant; it was also radiant with colour and form. Geoff chose to plant vegetables that complemented the other planting perfectly. There was red cabbage with striking red and white foliage, carrots with their fern-like foliage, brilliant red ruby chard, globe artichokes standing proudly in one corner and lots of others. He also demonstrated how pests could be kept at bay by hiding the plants they normally attacked by surrounding them with flowers. The programme was a triumph and it became the precursor for many more.

Television reviewers seemed to be greatly attracted to Geoff and wrote many pieces about his performance, the vast majority complimentary and nearly all of them amiably tongue-in-cheek. Though there are far too many to record here, none wrote so eloquently of Geoff as the glorious Nancy Banks-Smith of the *Guardian*, that Dorothy Parker of British criticism, who wrote of *The Ornamental Kitchen Garden*:

The question which agitates the nation today is what are we going to do about Geoff Hamilton's trousers?

I would describe them as organic. Unlike sprucer presenters, whom you could take anywhere, Geoff of *Gardeners' World* looks as though he has just arrived from mucking out his marrows and can't wait to get back to them. The trousers have a battle-hardened air, like a soldier returning from the 100 Years War. They are deeply furrowed at the top as if with thought and the knees, surprisingly, seem to be half-way down the calf. Either Mr Hamilton has very amusing legs or the trousers have a life of their own and can, at a pinch muck out the marrows on their own. A surreptitious inspection this week during a press day at Barnsdale showed that they not only look green, they are green. But then so is Geoff Hamilton.

He is very forceful about fitting in with nature, not fighting her. *The Ornamental Kitchen Garden* ... is well worth the price of admission for the sight of him picking up vegetables in a supermarket and flinging them aside with a muffled oath. Made-to-measure carrots 'No thanks!' Ageing corn on the cob 'No thanks!' 'Every one of these vegetables has been raised on a diet of chemicals. No thanks!' he said and flung them about a bit more. Even the organic vegetables were dismissed as overpriced.

In the ornamental kitchen garden at Barnsdale he uses no pesticides. In a glasshouse some tomatoes are growing in solitary.

These are California Supreme, a fistful of tomato like a small red boxing glove. Half of them have been grown from seeds which were in space for six years aboard NASA's Long Duration Exposure Facility satellite. Nobody could anticipate how they would turn out and those who had seen 'Attack of the Killer Tomatoes' rather wished they hadn't. The space tomatoes grew heartily ...

Three people work regularly at Barnsdale. Carol, who knows no fear, tried the space tomatoes and says roundly that California Supreme tastes revolting, irradiated or not. Ian didn't try them. He doesn't like any kind of tomato. Geoff went over the boxing gloves with a geiger counter. There was no radiation but for all that he thought perhaps he wouldn't. Personally I take my hat off to any tomato which has survived six years in space. It says something for the glorious persistence of life.

I was alone in the greenhouse. My fingers twitched a bit. Eve had much the same twitch, and look what happened to her.

Geoff laughed, as they say, like a drain when he read this. He was delighted because he felt it had captured the whole essence of what he was about. He was down-to-earth and yes, this did make him dirty. He was also prepared to be forthright about what he believed and he was right at the forefront of technology. He was also funny and this zest for life came across right into his viewers' living rooms. No wonder he was successful.

The new magazine format for *Gardeners' World*, with less gardening and more consumer journalism and design, introduced by Cyril Gates in 1989, was not proving very successful. Since Geoff had joined the programme the viewing figures had increased: in 1983, when he moved into the new Barnsdale, they were an average of 2.7 million, and by 1989, 3.2 million. Now, however, the programme was losing viewers at a fairly high rate of knots, mainly because it had lost its strong identification with Joe Public and taken on the 'arty-farty' style so much despised by Geoff. Computerised graphics, electronic music and a fast-moving style of presentation were simply not appreciated by Geoff's loyal audience. It was rescheduled to an earlier, less favourable slot. It featured twice on *Points of View* and many times in the newspapers, with viewers asking what on earth had happened to *Gardeners' World*. Before too long Mark was 'permitted' to exercise his judgement in favour of returning to some of the older core values of the programme.

At about this time, Stephanie Silk joined the newly expanded Gardening and Leisure Unit. She was a former producer of *Pebble Mill at One* and *On The House*, an innovative and practical home improvement programme which ran for four successful series. But then came the era of Alan Yentob, who had come from the arts side of BBC2 and was keen to have more arts programmes and make everything highly contemporary and 'distinctive'. He began to wield his axe and *On The House* was one of his victims, along with *One Man and his Dog*.

In the spring of 1990, Stephanie was asked to produce the coverage of the Chelsea Flower Show, so she became much more closely involved with the horticultural output. She was delighted by this, partly because of a new challenge and partly because she was a keen amateur gardener. She became aware of proposals to take *Gardeners' World* off the air in June and bring it back in the autumn. I don't believe Geoff ever got a sniff of this plan, because had he known he would immediately have mounted a fight-back. The show that was planned to replace *Gardeners' World* for the summer was to be a brainchild of Cyril Gates, called *Gardens by Design*, produced by Nick Patten.

Nobody seemed to support this idea, but nobody seemed capable of influencing the decision. One fortunate day in April, Colin Adams, the head of Network Television, happened to pass Stephanie in the corridor and asked her opinion about dropping *Gardeners' World* for the new programme. Stephanie, bless her, expressed the view that it was utter madness to rest *Gardeners' World* in high summer, just as it was beginning to find its feet again and replace it with a completely unknown quantity that had been filmed at the end of winter and would look bleakly out of place. It wasn't fair to either programme.

The idea was dropped and because Mark Kershaw was scheduled to complete *The Ornamental Kitchen Garden* Stephanie was asked at very short notice to take on the production of the programme herself, which she then did for the next two years.

Stephanie was the first woman producer that Geoff had encountered on his home ground and she felt that she would definitely have to prove herself to earn the respect of this horticultural legend. They didn't always see eye to eye but he accepted that she was a good practical 'hands-on' producer and gardener who cared about the best interests of the programme and was in touch with the audience. In turn, she had the greatest respect for him – indeed, she feels that Geoff was the first, and to date the last presenter who was able to enthuse his audience with an idea of what *they* could do both to improve their gardens and to halt the damage we are doing to the environment.

Geoff and Steph formed a good, friendly productive working relationship. Geoff returned to his old familiar style, while she concentrated on producing a balanced and varied mix of subject-matter for Geoff's co-presenters. This balance ensured that viewers could retain that sense of personal contact they had always had with Geoff, while at the same time benefiting from the expertise of a variety of presenters. The combination was a great success, the ratings began to climb again and the letters to the press changed from complaint to praise.

In 1991, Mark Kershaw and Geoff collaborated on a series called *Old Garden – New Gardener*, which was jointly presented by Geoff and Gay Search. The series was made from gardens in Rugby, because Rugby seemed to be almost equidistant from the BBC at Pebble Mill, Barnsdale and London, where Gay lived. It was really the first 'makeover' programme, which took neglected gardens and turned each one into something beautiful and productive – but it wasn't done in twenty-four hours, as seems to be the requirement today. Geoff and Gay worked well together and strove to demonstrate that whatever your starting point it is possible to conquer all adversities and come up with something stunning. They worked on gardens with impossible slopes, gardens that were swept constantly by Siberian winds, gardens that started with nothing but a pile of builder's rubble or a wilderness of nettles and brambles, gardens that were nothing but an uninspiring square of soil and stones and rubbish. In fact they would take on any challenge and the result was always a delight to the new owner of the property. Geoff wrote a book to accompany the series and that too was very popular.

In his role as a presenter of *Gardeners' World*, Geoff would be inundated with garden supplies, even though he made it clear that he could give no guarantee that they would be used and, even if they were, the product name would be obliterated because the rules on advertising on the BBC were then much stricter than they are now. I can remember him telling me that he once received a telephone call from a well-known manufacturer of a very wide range of tools asking if he would like any tools this year. 'Well, if you have anything new,' said Geoff, 'you can send it to me, but I can't promise that I'll use it.' 'What would you like?' said the salesman. Geoff said, 'Oh, I'll leave that to you. Anything that's new and interesting.' A few days later a huge truck arrived, carrying every single product the company manufactured – not just gardening tools but woodworking tools, building tools, engineering tools, the lot. So his barn was stuffed with brand new tools of every type, which it would have been impossible to use, even if the programme had continued for a hundred years. Manufacturers knew the value of a free advert, with the tool implicitly recommended by a gardening guru of Geoff's stature providing exceptionally good publicity – even though the viewer would have to guess the maker's name.

He also got some very oddball products, supplied in the vain hope that Geoff might give the inventor a meteoric lift-off for a glittering career. There was the tiny hammer, allegedly for bumping off slugs (this may have been a joke, but you can never be sure), gnomes so numerous that he could have started a gnome home, concrete ornaments of such revolting taste that they would probably have sold very well, peculiar tools that were virtually impossible to use and all manner of other artefacts that Geoff was loath to part with because they came from his much-loved viewers. Eventually, I'm afraid, after they had hung about in his barn for a respectable period, they found their way into the scrap bin. On the other hand, if he was delivered of a worthy product he would promote it. He still had sharp memories of his own stumbling start, so he knew how hard it was to get going and he was keen to help anybody with a good idea and sufficient energy and enthusiasm to progress it. Now that no action can be taken against him, it can be revealed that he supplied his very closest friends and family with lawnmowers, tools, strimmers, spades, forks, hoes, etc. that had never been collected and had little chance of appearing, either because they were not good enough or because Geoff simply had too many.

As through *Gardeners' World* Geoff became more and more well known, journalists of all colours, shapes and sizes would seek out Geoff for an interesting snippet or two. Amongst his favourites was Gillian Thornton, a freelance writer who wrote a good deal for the magazine *My Weekly*. The first feature, which appeared in 1991, was organised by the press office at BBC Pebble Mill and was a general piece about Geoff and his work. She says that her first impression of Geoff was that he was 'a nice, warm, friendly man, who took me to lunch at the local pub and, at the end of the lunch it felt like we had been friends for ever' and she was 'very honoured to think that that friendship carried on'. She says that during the course of her work she meets a lot of so-called celebrities but feels that their warmth is only superficial. But Geoff always remembered you, asked about the family and showed a genuine interest in you as a person. She left after the interview bearing a box of plants from the nursery, which she cherishes to this day.

She found Geoff always very approachable, despite the fact that when she telephoned for an interview he would put on his exasperated tone, specially manufactured to milk the last drop of fun from the situation and say, 'Oh, not again. Are you writing my biography? What else can you find to write about me?' She even wrote a piece about his dog Moss for *Dogs Today* magazine and one about his cats Skippy and

Denis for *Your Cat* magazine, which were both very amusing as well as revealing something about the soft inner core of the man.

Geoff's role in *Gardeners' World* also led to his participating in Gardeners' World Live at the NEC in Birmingham (mentioned earlier). It was there that Geoff's friendship with Alan Titchmarsh was firmly cemented, as they worked together. I asked Alan to tell me about the unpleasant memories he had of Geoff and all he could come up with was 'Well, he was very generous. And he kept telling me not to work too hard.' Alan remembers that Geoff would always greet him with the immortal words, 'All right, then, boy?' and at the end of every shooting session he would say to the camera, and hence his viewers, 'Have a great weekend. Goodbye,' and then turn away and, unseen by the viewers would say, '*What* a nice man!' This was a typically self-mocking statement, and self-mockery was the thing that kept Geoff's feet on the ground. He never, ever played the 'star' and was always crucially aware of the importance of the people he was talking to and the respect and regard in which they should be held.

CHAPTER 11

Catalyst for Change

IN 1991, THE BROADCASTING ACT OBLIGED all broad-
casters, including the BBC, to put 25 per cent of their programming out to independent production companies. At the time, a
young producer called Tony Laryea (pronounced, disconcertingly,
'Lye') was working for the BBC but thinking about setting up his own
production company. He saw an ideal opportunity, so he put a case to
the BBC mandarins that he should take over *Gardeners' World* – but
only on one condition: he had to have Geoff. I think the BBC must
have realised that without Geoff the programme would be nothing, so
they agreed to Tony's proposition and so Catalyst Television was born.

Tony says that when he first met Geoff his overwhelming impression
was that he was the kind of man that any other man would love to
have a pint with and any woman would like to put up their shelves.
There were actually a lot of women he had a pint with and I don't
remember him ever putting up shelves for anybody, but I know what
Tony means. He means that Geoff had an almost universal appeal.

It now became Geoff's mission to convert Tony to understanding
the need to convey the practical aspects of gardening and to appeal to
a broad cross-section of viewers. Tony remembers doing a programme,
not using Geoff, from an Italianate garden that was full of what Geoff
would have called the 'arty-farty' and getting a blasting from Geoff
about straying away from the basic brief to meet the needs of the

ordinary gardener. Geoff saw the need for programmes of that kind but thought that they were well covered by people like Roy Strong, Christopher Lloyd and Stephen Lacey, who were more at home in that field. Nevertheless Tony feels that the tension that built between them was a healthy tension, which contributed rather than detracted from the programme. They certainly stayed the best of friends and a sense of great comradeship grew up between them.

Slowly but surely Catalyst began to build a reputation for being the company that made the best gardening programmes in the world. In fact this became a problem for it, because Tony began to feel that it was in danger of doing nothing else, so he was obliged to steer a course which expanded the company's interests beyond gardening. But what a nice problem for a young company to be landed with.

The first producer who worked with Geoff after Catalyst took over *Gardeners' World* was Rosemary Forgan. Having trained in production with Thames Television, she was running her own production company, Bamboo Productions, but when she saw Catalyst's advertisement for a producer, she couldn't resist the temptation to work with *Gardeners' World*. When she was interviewed at Catalyst, she was surprised to find Geoff there. It is not usual to see the star of the show at a production interview, but she hadn't reckoned with Geoff's intense professionalism. Geoff had had to cope with a number of new producers, most of whom he had liked and enjoyed working with. But not all! This had made him very cautious about new arrivals on the scene and he was anxious to make sure that the chemistry between them was right before he agreed to work with them. Neither had Rosemary bargained for the difficult questions he threw at her. 'OK,' he said, 'it's January and we're filming at Barnsdale. We do one day and on the second you come down to find it's snowed in the night. How would you proceed from there?' Rosemary, intensely professional herself, simply refused to answer the question there and then and asked for five minutes to think through a running order. This clearly impressed Geoff and Tony, and they offered Rosemary the job.

It was a potentially difficult assignment because the waters had been muddied by rumours of dramatic change to the programme – so much so that there had even been questions in the House about it. Why politicians should concern themselves with *Gardeners' World* I cannot imagine. *Blue Peter*, yes, but *Gardeners' World* – that is beyond me. In fact, what Tony was seeking was evolution not revolution and he saw Rosemary as the person to bring that about. He was looking for a wider variety of locations and co-presenters with the solid core of gardening expertise still put across by Geoff from his base at Barnsdale.

A self-confessed 'sucker for a sense of humour', Rosemary was delighted by Geoff. It saddened her that she was never able to get his off-screen hilarity across in the programme. My own belief is that Geoff had become cautious about being too joky on the screen because John Kenyon and warned him about the difficulty of pulling it off and very rarely allowed jokes. Certainly there is nothing worse than a contrived joke that may have been repeated in front of a camera three or four times before it's finally delivered. However, although his audience may not have realised that he could have people doubled up with laughter at times, I think his light-hearted approach *did* come across.

Whilst Rosemary never found Geoff to be unpleasant or unkind, she did find that he would sometimes get quite agitated about what he was asked to do and would often just refuse, if it didn't align with his views. But his greatest agitation arose if he felt that other people working on the programme, away from Barnsdale, had said something technically wrong or something out of step with his quite trenchant views about organics or peat or the like – then Rosemary knew she could expect a furious phone call. Ever anxious to preserve the integrity of the programme, he could sometimes be a difficult adversary.

After a year's work together, which they both thoroughly enjoyed, Rosemary left to take up an offer that her company, Bamboo, had received to make *The Lost Gardens of Heligan* series.

After Rosemary came Laurence Vulliamy, in 1993. You will not find many Vulliamys in the telephone directory. It is a Huguenot name of great antiquity. Laurence comes from a distinguished line of horologists – clock makers who, during the eighteenth and nineteenth centuries supplied clocks to the gentry, some of which are still on show in Buckingham Palace. But Laurence is a freelance television producer and director of no mean repute.

When he first met Geoff, he says, he was bowled over by his charm and his generosity, and his instant impression was 'Here is a man I can work with' – easy-going, down-to-earth and very, very knowledgeable. Laurence is an innovative man, who saw that the basic ethos of the programme needed to remain the same but felt it had to move on. So once again the idea of a 'magazine format' for the programme was introduced, with less of Geoff's basic gardening skills and more shot, often by a variety of other people, at locations other than Barnsdale, including stately homes and the gardens of the great and the good. Geoff resisted this and there was some disagreement. He resisted not because he objected to other people being brought into the pro- gramme – that had always been the case – but because once again he saw them getting further and further away from what he saw as the purpose of the programme – to show the ordinary man and woman on the Clapham omnibus, their core audience, how the basics of gardening should be carried out. He wanted to be able to introduce people gradually to more exciting and innovative ideas that they could execute themselves, without specialist help and without vast expend- iture. What he didn't want was to be forever visiting stately piles that the majority of his audience wouldn't identify with and couldn't replicate. In fact the programme began to attract some criticism for just this reason and Geoff made sure, from that point onwards, that the programme always contained enough core gardening to keep the central audience satisfied. If asked to visit a stately home, he would always bring back a few ideas and show how they could be executed on a small scale in a garden on a typical housing estate.

When it came to contract renegotiation time, Laurence had to face up to Geoff's battling spirit. Geoff asked for a fee that was three times greater than the previous year's. There were spin-offs to his work on *Gardeners' World* – books, personal appearances, consulting fees, etc., but Geoff, now confident about his value and knowing his worth, felt that his basic fee was too low. Geoff could never be called a greedy person, but he saw the costs at Barnsdale beginning to mount as the demands on it became more complex and he felt the stand he made was perfectly justified. He didn't get three times the amount, but he got well over twice.

Laurence stayed with the programme for two seasons and then, much to Geoff's regret, he left for pastures new. The producer who made Geoff's final weekly programmes (as opposed to the series) was John Percival, an experienced independent documentary maker with a yen to get into gardening.

When John and Geoff first met, John felt that he was being 'eyed up' and ruthlessly appraised. If you wanted to work with Geoff you had to be good at what you did, you had to respect each other's areas of expertise and, above all, whatever you did had to be fun. John picked up this tacit requirement immediately and felt that with a presenter of Geoff's ability there was no reason to question his style and certainly not the content, and that all he had to worry about was the visual impact of the work. The initial meeting went well and before it was over they were firm friends.

John found Geoff to be very 'preoccupied with this work', as he tactfully put it. As others had found before him, Geoff didn't suffer fools gladly and, whilst he would never be hurtful to or dismissive of them, he would not allow them to influence the two things that were of most value to him – his family and his work. What I think John means is that Geoff was sharp-tongued if diverted from what he thought to be important by something he regarded as trivial. This was verified for me by my wife Carol and by several of the other people who worked at Barnsdale. Woe betide the pitiful innocent who would interrupt his pre-shot walk, when he was constructing the scene in his head, with shouts of 'Where did you leave the chain-saw, Geoff?' or the like. His most frequent response was, 'Not now. Not now,' at which some hasty backing-off would be wise.

Life for a programme-maker is not always a smooth ride, particularly if giving advice, and John and Geoff survived a couple of nasty moments. During one programme, Geoff suggested that bundles of barley straw should be thrown into a pond to clear the green algae that every pond owner has to contend with. The plan was to come back a few weeks later to demonstrate the effect of immersing the straw. But before this could be done John received a telephone call from an extremely irate man. He had followed Geoff's advice and, as a result, his £25,000-worth of exotic fish had turned belly up and died. Threats of legal action and letters to *The Times* followed, so John, by now in a state of some distress, contacted Geoff, who explained that their death was almost certainly caused by pesticides and/or herbicides which had been sprayed on to the straw. John quickly reran the tape of the programme and was relieved to find that Geoff had explained this during the programme and recommended that the straw must be obtained from an *organic* farm. So he took a strong line with the complainant and his legal action, like his fish, died.

A much more distressing episode followed a programme in which Geoff collected hellebore seed for propagation. He simply picked them off the plant and sowed them into a small pot. A few days later John got a call from a man who said that his wife had followed Geoff's advice and, as a result, had come out in the most fearful rash. John, of course, expressed his concern and immediately rang Geoff, who said that he had been handling hellebore seeds all his life and had never had a problem. So John rang the RHS, who put him on to the toxicology department of one of the big London hospitals, who confirmed that, in a few rare cases, there could be a toxic reaction. As a result they had to broadcast a warning that all avid propagators should remember to invest in Marigolds before handling hellebores.

John's abiding impression of Geoff was that he was a true pro, who had an immense knowledge as well as the ability to get it across as though he was just the bloke next door. He made everything achievable and, whenever he did something more adventurous and expensive, such as the Vegetable Parterre, he would always show a smaller, cheaper version, to accommodate the needs of his most highly valued form of wildlife – the ordinary working man.

It was during the Catalyst years that Geoff was asked to work with a production assistant called Marcia Kirby. The irrepressible Marcia is a larger than life, roundish, outrageous lady; nobody can walk within a hundred yards of her without coming under her spell. She has a line in expletives that made even Geoff blush and a disarming disregard for celebrity and all its ephemeral trappings. They first worked together in 1992. Marcia had the usual qualifications – a complete lack of knowledge about gardening and a 'townie's' naïvety about the rigours of living in the country. For the first shoot, in early spring, she turned up in high-heeled shoes and a genteel spring outfit, to face the biting winds and mud of Barnsdale. Lynda, a country girl herself, was as amused as the rest of the crew but, always compassionate, fixed her up with boots and jacket and a short lecture on how to dress for Barnsdale.

As soon as they met, Geoff's kindly but teasing sense of humour came into play – but he discovered that he got every bit as good as he gave. This gave rise to a whole new era of hilarity. For instance, Marcia had an infallible knack of getting the technical content wrong. After Geoff had to break off a piece about pulmonarias, as she was responsible for continuity she helpfully reminded him that he had been talking about 'pool malarias'. Geoff took several minutes to collect himself, only to be reminded during his next piece about anemones that he had been talking about 'enemas'.

Geoff, to Marcia, was the perfect gentleman, down-to-earth and professionally demanding but never unkind or inattentive. The rapport – indeed warm and loving relationship – that grew between them was based not only on their ability to joke so easily with each other but also on respect for each other's professionalism.

In parallel to the weekly *Gardeners' World* programmes, the series continued to be made. This was, I think, the work Geoff enjoyed doing most, particularly because he could have more control over its conception and subsequent implementation. He also liked the continuity that was implicit in this type of work; he could gradually develop something that, week by week, would become an achievable reality to his viewers.

Geoff was a dreamer, but a dreamer of the most positive kind. He would slowly develop a vision of a programme and his excitement would grow until he could speak of little else. Then he would begin the detailed design, thinking all the way through the process of how best it could be presented. With this ammunition he was always able to sell the idea to the BBC, especially as they were so confident in his ability to win a good audience that they were eager to accept almost anything he suggested.

In 1992 he had the idea for a series called *The Living Garden*. Here his purpose was to combine the innovative technology of wildlife photography with his own presentation and design skills to show how gardens could be made into habitats for a whole host of insects, butterflies and moths, birds and mammals. He could sense and see the movement away from regimented rows of allysum and lobelia and a move towards gardens which, whilst possibly retaining some degree of formality, could be made into a haven for a great profusion of animal life. And he believed that this could be done even in the smallest suburban garden or a new housing estate, which would be the suburbia of the future – that anyone could nurture their own small piece of the British countryside, or something as close as they could get it.

The series was produced by Mick Rhodes, an inspirationally imaginative man with all the technical knowledge of wildlife photography at his fingertips. Mick was originally an academic zoologist who had turned to scientific journalism. He then moved into BBC radio, working on science programmes, and from there to television, working on the highly prestigious *Horizon* and *QED* programmes, with the Natural History Unit in Bristol. Finally, after a sojourn in America working in the same sort of area, he returned to head up the Science Unit of the BBC. So Mick came with a lot of credentials and a kitbag full of experience, which excited Geoff no end. This was to be an entirely new departure for Geoff, in which he would move away from straight gardening and demonstrate the wonders of nature that most of us don't even realise are going on in our gardens. It would also enable him to reinforce his organic message (of which more later).

Geoff built a small wildlife garden and then demonstrated what would happen in it during a typical year. Mick was a specialist in all the techniques of time-lapse and microphotography, so in addition to shots of the construction of a garden with wild areas (but still containing all the usual amenities required by the normal household), there were astonishing sequences of bees pollinating, birds nest-building, ladybirds and their larvae feeding on aphids, hedgehogs feeding and an entire David Attenborough-worth of fascinating pictures. This kind of work is very expensive to accomplish, so it was a costly series, but the sight of wildlife performing their delicate ballet in the garden that Geoff had built at Barnsdale was not only moving and joyful but also very convincing for those who doubted Geoff's argument that nature thrives in a plot gardened organically. And what's more they were all pictures that could have been reproduced in any small garden, provided the habitats were provided and the chemicals were banished back to laboratories, where they should be serving life sentences.

Mick describes Geoff as 'a honey to work with', which would have made Geoff smile, and says that he had an easy time working with him. If for some technical reason they had to ask Geoff to do another take, or even another three, there would never be a grumble and he would say the lines *exactly* as he had said them the first time. Any presenter will tell you that it isn't easy to do that.

A very perceptive man, Mick instantly recognised Geoff's idiosyncrasies, such as his stubborn streak and his passionate political views. He observed his curious preference for taking his own vehicle to a site, even if it was just up the road and there was space in somebody else's. Those of us who were closer to him knew that he was, in fact, quite a solitary man, who liked his space, so that he could relax, think through what he had to do next and be comfortable with his own company.

The series was an instant success, as was the accompanying book, which was co-written by Geoff and Jennifer Owen, a biologist who had been actively gardening and studying garden wildlife in this country, the USA and Africa for twenty years. Thus, through both the book and the series, Geoff did a great deal to raise the public's awareness of what they can do in their own gardens to enrich their own little corner of Britain. Mick has now retired and has a cottage in France, lucky man. It has a piece of land attached to it that is currently overgrown and wild, but Mick intends to tame it and turn it into his own Geoff Hamilton Memorial Garden. What a wonderful tribute.

During the shooting of *The Living Garden* Geoff had seen some enchanting old-fashioned cottage gardens, which were his most prolific source of material for each programme in the series. This set him thinking that his next series should be about cottage gardens, for they must be the most rewarding kind of garden for any small gardener to establish. Certainly the formal garden was an option as a subject for a programme, but it could only be made to be really dramatic if done on a large scale. Most of Geoff's gardeners were small gardeners, as were the cottage gardeners of old, albeit they lived on an estate instead of living in a quaint thatched cottage. Even if you lived in a large house the idea was appropriate. The more Geoff thought about it, the more enthusiastic he became about the idea, believing it would appeal to a wide range of people, so in 1994, he put the idea to the BBC.

The BBC hummed and hawed, as is their wont, but eventually saw the attraction of the programme and agreed to put up the money for Catalyst to make it. Catalyst sent Geoff a producer called Andrew Gosling, who had been a colleague of Tony Laryea's when they both worked for the BBC. Andrew had made every kind of programme in the past – drama, fairy stories, documentaries, ghost stories, the lot – except for gardening, so he says, he felt he was eminently qualified. Andrew is a tall, Eton-educated, slightly hippie, bearded man who has an upper-crust accent, and a predilection for clogs and huge, engulfing waterproofs. Geoff's suspicions were immediately aroused and I can imagine the hair on the back of his working-class neck bristling like an angry dog's.

But Geoff was not a man for stereotyping people and they talked amicably, if cautiously, about the proposed format for the programme like two gladiators slowly circling each other. Andrew never pretended that he knew anything about gardening, but he certainly knew an awful lot about production and Geoff had a nose for quality when he saw it. So it was not long before their relationship began to build a firm foundation, and they became good friends and developed a healthy respect for each other, though Geoff would tease him mercilessly about his accent, explaining, for instance, that the word was not 'problim' but 'problem'. After Geoff died I had the privilege of working with Andrew, and I can vouch for Geoff's judgement.

Andrew says, 'Geoff was an extraordinary act. We would rough out how the shot might work and then he would say, 'OK, Andrew, just give me a moment.' Then he would literally walk the scene into his head. Up and down. Up and down – away from the rest of the unit. Then he would come back and say, 'OK, let's go,' and, to the amazement of the crew, he would do it perfectly, in one take.' On one occasion Andrew trapped Geoff behind a bench in a greenhouse, with heavy rain outside, so that he couldn't do his walk. Andrew had never seen him need so many takes before he got it right. He never made that mistake again.

Their relationship strengthened when they went on a trip to Sri Lanka to film the production process of coir. It was a tough shoot with a very heavy schedule and Andrew wanted to pull out of one location to give the crew a rest. Geoff was incandescent with rage and insisted that if they were going to do it at all it *had* to be right. In the face of this onslaught, the crew agreed and Andrew was obliged to back down. This was the only real disagreement they ever had. The situation was defused by an official reception, to which they were invited by the Sri Lankan dignitaries. Andrew claimed that the difficulties of the shoot had exhausted him but Geoff claimed that he had had a few drinks too many. Whatever the reason, Andrew had to be supported on one side by Geoff and on the other by the cameraman while he shook hands with all the 'suits'.

During the making of the *Cottage Gardens* series, Geoff and Andrew capitalised on this very easy friendship, enjoying a lot of banter and a lot of fun. They were both very confident about what they wanted to do and the work was made much easier for Andrew by the fact that Geoff's vision of what he wanted was so strong. It took him some time to realise that Geoff's mission was much more than just telling people how to garden. He believed that people could use gardening and all the fulfilment that comes with it to take control of a part of their lives and Geoff saw himself as a kind of enabler. Andrew finally realised this when Geoff turned *him* on to gardening. 'When I'm out working in my garden now,' he says, 'I like to think the old bastard is up there saying, "See, I got you hooked in the end!"'

But, Andrew found, life with Geoff also had its difficulties. He would get really irritated if he was asked to reshoot a piece that he felt was perfectly all right. On the other hand, the reverse would also apply. Andrew recalls a time when he and John Couzens, the cameraman for the series, had planned an amazingly complicated tracking shot that started on Geoff and wandered over some artefacts he had made and back to finish on Geoff again. It was very ambitious and took a long time to achieve. Andrew was happy to let it go after several takes because he thought it was near enough and he didn't feel he could keep Geoff out there any longer. But not Geoff. I can imagine him having a vision of Cy, our old dad, in his mind, wagging a finger and saying, 'Geoffrey, near enough is not good enough!' He insisted that they did it again and again until it was perfect.

Cameramen came and went during Geoff's career, but John Couzens was the one whom he enjoyed the most. John was a skilful operator who added a lot to the quality of the programmes. John worked originally for the BBC, but when the major reorganisations came he decided to go freelance. So he often worked on *Gardeners' World* when the programme was made in-house and was then asked to continue after Catalyst took over. It took a little while for their friendship to blossom, as they both cautiously fenced around each other, but when it did it was as firm and as mutually respectful as Geoff's friendships with his other colleagues. Camera work requires a lot of patience because every time a mistake is made the shot has to be retaken and John, fortunately, was endowed with this quality in full measure. I remember watching an out-take one Christmas which would have tried the patience of a saint. It was the opening shot, over which the titles and credits would be shown, and the camera was placed in a tall hydraulic lift so that the whole of Barnsdale could be seen. The camera began to roll, the music played and the titles drifted across the screen as the camera slowly, slowly zoomed in on Geoff, who started as a pinprick and eventually came into full view. The shot seemed to take an age and when it finally reached Geoff he looked up at the camera, gave one of his beneficent smiles and said, 'Oh bugger, I've forgotten what I was going to say!'

Another incident that still brings a smile to John's lips was Geoff coming out of his office brandishing a cheque that had just been sent by the BBC and muttering, 'Well, now I've seen it all.' The cheque, made out for £2,710. 95, didn't seem to align with any of the invoices he had submitted. So he phoned the BBC's finance department who, after a lot of investigation, discovered the cause of the mistake. They had not paid the amount shown on one of his invoices – they had paid him the date!

Sarah Greene, the production manager on the *Cottage Gardens* series, remembers Geoff with enormous affection. She used to call him 'Winnie the Pooh' because when he was taking his pre-shot walks he would wander round in ever-decreasing circles, with his head on his chest, muttering to himself, until Sarah would shout to him, 'Come on Winnie. Trot on.' He used to call her 'Robert Post's Child' after the character in *Cold Comfort Farm*, because she was bossy, capable and entertaining. They developed a wonderfully warm relationship, based on mutual respect and laughter. Sarah says that she laughed for a whole year and it was a gloriously exhilarating tonic. She feels that his public persona didn't entirely reflect the real Geoff. Although his warmth, humour and professionalism came across in abundance on the screen, few of his viewers would have believed the Anglo-Saxon language that would echo over the set when he got something wrong. If they were at the bottom end of Barnsdale, close to Nick's nursery, they would sometimes have to hide in the hedge bottom to escape the outrage of the nursery customers while they were all doubled up with laughter.

Sarah was the organiser and, undaunted by Geoff's celebrity, she didn't necessarily arrange things precisely to suit him. When she was making arrangements for anything, her name was a great advantage because if it was linked with the word 'television' everybody assumed that she was *the* Sarah Greene who used to present *Blue Peter* from 1980 to 1983. So, if booking a hotel, she always found that, miraculously, it was she who got the four-poster and the jacuzzi while Geoff was dispatched to the small room over the generator house. Geoff would protest and fume and fulminate, but Sarah would stick to her guns and point out that the room had her name on it and was thus rightfully hers, and Geoff would trudge sulkily back to his room muttering about Germaine Greer and her evil influence.

She remembers affectionately how Geoff would always wear jeans and a checked shirt, both of which would gradually get dirtier as the programme progressed. There had been a move by one producer to get him into 'fleeces' and designer clothes, but Geoff just flatly refused. Sarah recalls a day when Geoff had to meet his bank manager for lunch, as the bank manager was retiring and wanted to introduce the new man. Geoff set off in his jeans and checked shirt, amid howls of protest from Sarah and the crew, who strongly advised him to wear some smarter clothes. 'Look,' said Geoff, 'I'm a gardener and he's a bank manager. He'll turn up in his working clothes and I shall turn up in mine!' I'm not sure he would have been quite so confident some years earlier when the bank manager was a very important figure in his life.

For the *Cottage Gardens* series Geoff built two gardens at Barnsdale – the Gentleman's Garden and the Artisan's Garden. In the first he allowed a large proportion of the budget to be spent, recognising that there were viewers who had a bob or two to spend, and in the second he concentrated on cheaper materials and a budget that would fit most people's pockets. In addition, they travelled the country visiting some of the most enchanting gardens you could possibly imagine. In the course of their travels they also found some amazing people. Geoff loved them all, but his favourite by far was old George Flatt.

Andrew's parents live in Suffolk and they had a woman from the village who came in to clean for them. When Andrew mentioned to her that they were keen to find a real, genuine old cottage gardener, she said, 'Oh, you ought to meet my Uncle George.' Uncle George was eighty-seven and had been a farm worker all his life. He had created the most wonderful cottage garden around his old thatched cottage on the edge of the village. It was all done with no money. He let his flowers self-seed, collected his own vegetable seed and just let his garden grow on from one year to the next. Geoff asked where he had learned his skills and he said, in his rich Suffolk accent, 'From my old dad, boy. He told me, always dig with a spade, boy.' That was really his only gardening tip, but he was one of the most successful gardeners Geoff had met. When he was working on the farm he would come home and dig by moonlight – the 'parish lantern' he called it. Everything was home-made, from a potting bench covered with an old carpet to a treasure-trove of a shed, stuffed with old implements and machines of every description, and even a wartime Anderson shelter that he used as his tool shed.

Both Andrew and Geoff told me that they thought George was the happiest man they had ever met. He'd never travelled far from his comfortable Suffolk village and was quite content with his old house and his glorious garden. Andrew asked Geoff about his gardening techniques and Geoff, in some puzzlement, said, 'Well, he does everything wrong. But somehow he just gets it to work for him.' So if you are ever perplexed and troubled about your garden just think of old George. Just get on and do it!

Andrew says that the *Cottage Gardens* shoot was one of the best he's ever done. The weather was beautiful, the gardens were exquisite and the result was extraordinarily good. The programme was a major success and the book that Geoff wrote to accompany it was in the best-seller list for months and is still in good demand. It's good to think that through this classic book Geoff helped people in all walks of life to build sanctuaries of peace and calm for themselves.

Geoff's last programme was *Paradise Gardens*, which was produced for Catalyst by Ray Hough in 1994. Ray was chosen more by chance than design. He happened to be coming out of the Algerian Coffee Shop in Soho in London when Tony Laryea, the head of Catalyst, happened to be passing in a taxi. He stopped the cab and said to Ray, whom he knew of old, 'I've got a job for you – it's a gardening programme.' 'No, I don't do gardening,' said Ray. 'I'm an old man.' 'No, you won't actually have to do any gardening,' Tony assured him. 'It's with Geoff Hamilton and he's good. You'll enjoy it. Come and talk about it.' So they did and Ray was convinced.

Ray is a larger-than-life cockney with a craggy, life-worn face, an outrageous sense of humour, a wicked propensity for practical jokes and more creativity stuffed inside him than most Hollywood directors. You'd love him as soon as you looked at him. When Geoff first met Ray at Barnsdale, having recently finished working with Andrew Gosling, the cultivated public-school man with an upper-crust accent described earlier, he said as they shook hands, 'Blimey, you lot go from the sublime to the bloody ridiculous, don't you?' Ray took this in good part, but nevertheless felt strongly during that first meeting that Geoff was eyeing him up and had not yet decided on his suitability. But after a good lunch and the discussion of some ideas he was more than satisfied – and what a good decision that turned out to be. Geoff was pleased about Ray's lack of knowledge about gardening, because it would give him more freedom to do the things he wanted to do; but Ray is an uncommonly experienced documentary film maker, who knows everything about making films, and Geoff didn't know at that stage what interesting and inventive tricks Ray had up his sleeve.

There was, nevertheless, quite a bit of adjustment to do when Ray started work. Ray says that when he turned up, Geoff would give him a detailed briefing about what he was going to do and that he wanted this backdrop here and that path leading diagonally to it etc., and Ray thought, Jesus, I'm going to be directing drama here – with things that don't move! Geoff was actually just testing Ray, probing to find any weak spots in his technique, because he was ardent in his desire to get it right.

In turn Ray, in his first session, saw an expanse of bare soil and, seeing little opportunity for exciting work, committed the dreadful solecism of calling it 'dirt'. Geoff bristled and pointed out in trenchant terms that this 'dirt' was their raw material and he was about to make it into a beautiful garden. Gradually, however, they got used to each other and began to respect the attributes that each could bring to the programme and the work settled into an enjoyable and effective pattern. From then on Ray became fascinated by Geoff's ability to take simple materials and to turn them into something clever and beautiful.

Two Paradise Gardens were built at Barnsdale, both designed and constructed by his very able young landscape specialist, Adam Frost. The first was a town garden, which was enclosed within high brick walls and the second was a country garden, bounded simply by hedges and some fencing. These two gardens formed the basis for the programme, a six-part series, and there were also location programmes. One was done from a sumptuously planted roof-garden in London that drowned out the murmur of the traffic with recorded birdsong. Another episode was filmed in a flat in the East End of London, which had nothing but a balcony and a window box. But what a window box it was – overflowing with bright, tumbling flowers that covered the drab walls with an absolute riot of colour and shape. The balcony could have come straight from the African jungle – banana plants, breadfruit, figs, the lot, giving a feeling that you would have to hack your way through with a machete should you want to see the traffic below.

The team visited a wonderfully constructed water garden with interconnected ponds that ran from one end of a long, downward sloping site to the other. It was engineered in a way that would have done justice to Telford, the canal builder, or to Brunel, the engineer. The garden was owned by a Mr Guppy and I regret to report that Ray, like a small boy at school, stood making fish faces at Geoff from behind the camera, unseen by Mr Guppy, causing Geoff great difficulty in keeping control of the interview.

This disgraceful episode aside, one of the things that Ray noted was how much sheer pleasure Geoff got out of other people's gardens, and how much he felt at home with people with a common interest. It didn't matter if they were 'luvable cockney sparrers' or the landed gentry: if they were gardeners it was all the same to Geoff and he didn't differentiate one from the other. And he met some wonderful people during this series – such as Millie and Horace Hunt, a simple retired couple, from a working-class background, by now both retired, who lived in an idyllic country cottage, and who were totally unaffected and sincere. Millie was talkative and lively, with a cheeky look that reminded you of the cocked head of the robin that perches on your spade, and Horace was quiet and philosophical, often silent and deep in thought. These were the kind of people who demonstrate the happiness the love of a garden can bring.

One of Ray's innovations was to try to give the impression, at the end of each programme, that Geoff's own Paradise Garden was located in a hostile position, just to show that paradise could be found even in hostile surroundings. So he decided to project on to a large blue screen at the back of the garden a scene of heavy traffic or aeroplanes taking off or some similar unpleasantness, with Geoff sitting in a cool and leafy bower, able to ignore it all. Geoff volunteered to make the screen, which was a huge plywood structure. What the viewing public didn't know was that behind the screen were a desperate gang of riggers and staff from Barnsdale, all struggling to keep the damned thing upright, often in howling winds, whilst Geoff sat unmoved and smiling in front. But, like so much else in *Paradise Gardens*, it was dramatic, effective and memorable and the series was a great success.

During the early filming for the *Paradise Gardens*, Geoff had his first heart attack, but, true to form, he was back again after a few short weeks, as though nothing had happened. Ray, however, could tell that all was not well. Geoff began to worry more about his performance and, although Ray did his best to calm his fears, he would fret over their schedule for the following day, a thing he had never done before. To me he seemed his old self, but I too was worried about his future.

Geoff had accepted the very heavy workload imposed on him by the BBC – in Lynda's opinion, partly because of vanity and partly because he still harboured a residual fear of being poor again. That year he had started filming *Gardeners' World* in February, going on to make the *Paradise Gardens* series, during which he had to travel all over the country and write an accompanying book. And then he was asked to do a daytime show for BBC1. There had never been a gardening programme on BBC1 before and Geoff was keen to do it because he knew that if it was well received it would get a prime-time slot. He planned to give up his demanding role on *Gardeners' World* to take up the new programme, as he felt it would be easier and less stressful because he could plan and direct the work in exactly the way he wanted. So, on top of all his other work, including his writing for the *Radio Times*, the *Daily Express* and *Country Living*, he began the preparation and planning, including building extensive gardens, for the new programme. Lynda feels that all this must have added to the strain on his already weakened heart. She tried hard to dissuade him but it was difficult: she didn't want him to feel she wasn't supporting him but, on the other hand, she was trying to keep him alive. But Geoff was a stubborn old devil and would have it no other way.

He was never to make the new programme and he died very shortly after *Paradise Gardens* was made. Unfortunately, whilst he had done all the filming he had not completed the voice-overs and I had the great honour to be asked to do them in his place. I can't tell you what a privilege it was to finish what I considered the finest piece of work that my brilliant brother had ever done. It was a very small contribution but it meant a very great deal to me.

CHAPTER 12

The Environmental Crusades

I N T H E E A R L Y D A Y S O F G E O F F's career, he behaved as all innocent gardeners behaved. He burned all his garden waste, unknowingly polluting the atmosphere; he gave his household waste to the dustman, unknowingly filling landfill sites; he sprayed every pest, disease or weed he could find with noxious chemicals, unknowingly polluting our watercourses and killing off his would-be insect friends; he covered his erstwhile tasty vegetables with poisons, unknowingly killing himself; he used literally tons of peat, unknowingly destroying our precious wetlands; and he filled his gardens with hardwoods, limestone, Yorkstone and all manner of materials with which he was, unknowingly, destroying valuable habitats for wild flowers and animals of all sorts.

Wow! What a list! Geoff did a lot of gardening, so in his early days, the more he did the more devastation followed in his wake. So was this some kind of rural guerrilla we had let loose to do all this damage? No, it wasn't. It was just an ordinary gardener doing what he thought was right – because nobody knew any better. Of course, this wasn't only true of Geoff: we were all pursuing the same path. Put us all together, remembering that the keener you are the more damage you do, and you have a powerful gang of despoilers and rural rapists.

But Geoff left college in 1959, and at that time nobody outside a small band of scientists, who were largely ignored, understood what pollution was or how the industrialised methods we were beginning to employ could devastate our delicate environment. As for global warming, if it had been envisaged in those days of harder winters it would have been positively welcomed by most people. The M1, which was the first major motorway, from St Albans to Birmingham, had only just been opened and when you drove along it you were lucky to see another car. The first stretch of motorway to be opened, a year before the M1, was the Preston bypass, which nobody from our part of the world had even heard of, let alone worried about. I wonder what we would have thought had we known it was about to turn into the infamous M6, a road to be travelled only by those with lungs like leather and plenty of time to spare.

Geoff had learned at college that by far the most efficient way to get rid of pests and diseases was to squirt them with chemicals and that the best way to ensure good growing conditions for plants and hence good yields, was to lather them with artificial fertilisers. So not only was that what he did himself but also he advised everybody else to do it too.

Little by little, however, Geoff's awareness began to awaken. And it grew into a concern for the environment that informed all the writing and programmes he did later, which I have described in earlier chapters.

Initially his awakening was not environmental but economic. He would write, for that's all he did in the early days of his career, about grand landscaping schemes, well-equipped greenhouses, expensive garden machinery and the like, and he would receive letters from his faithful following complaining that, for them, his ideas were unaffordable. So he began to realise that his prime audience was not the upper- or middle-class person with money but the ordinary working man with nothing but an almost primeval desire to feed his family and to get outside with his hands in some soil. I think he understood a truth about gardeners that remains true today. Things have changed a little now because more and more people *can* afford five tons of paving and two tons of decking but I don't think the current band of television presenters should be complacent about that. The primeval urge will not go away. However affluent we get people will still want to know the basic horticulture – how to dig, sow seeds, take cuttings, prune, etc.

Geoff began to devise simple methods using second-hand materials to make cloches, frames, compost bins and even seed trays and flowerpots. Without it really dawning on him at first, this was the beginning of his campaign for recycling – his very first step on the environmental ladder. He put these simple methods into *Practical Gardening*, when he was the editor, and they were immediately well received. When he began to hear about the shortage of landfill sites and how Britain was becoming swamped with rubbish, he wrote about it in his 'Last Word' column for *Garden News*, in which he regularly confronted such issues – and Geoff could be pretty confrontational when aroused. Circulation began to rise while he was writing the column, and his own popularity with it.

Some of Geoff's more conventional professional gardening contemporaries tended to laugh a little behind their hands at his somewhat Heath Robinson ideas. But his contemporaries' views didn't deter Geoff one iota, and their views were not shared by his readers or, eventually by his viewers, even though at first they were interested not so much in reducing environmental damage as in finding refreshing new ways to make their gardening less expensive and more satisfying. Geoff believed in what he was doing and whenever he had a firm belief he would pursue it relentlessly. It was an attitude that was to lead him into a few confrontations with some powerful people, often with vested interests, which he took on like David facing Goliath.

Geoff's and his producer John Kenyon's quest for new ways to make the garden easier, cheaper and more productive for everybody, regardless of income, eventually led to the series of pieces he presented on *Gardeners' World* in 1984, aimed at showing a family of three how they could garden for a year, providing an ornamental garden and keeping them in fruit and vegetables, on a budget of no more than

£104. This was supplemented by a book called *The Two Pound Garden*, which, though small and less lavish than his later books, was very widely read. It made an assumption that they already had basic tools and a small greenhouse, but he met his budget, with about £4.50 to spare, and reckoned that he'd made a profit, over the cost of buying provisions, of £45. Not enough to make him a tycoon, but enough to leave him with an immense sense of satisfaction.

This enterprise involved him in making compost in plastic rubbish bags, making tubs from plastic containers cadged from restaurant owners and hanging baskets from wooden roofing laths, collecting seed and scrounging cuttings, making large cloches to cover a deep bed from alkathene water pipe and plastic sheeting and a whole host of other brilliantly simple ideas, which could be done for next to nothing – or less. My first view of his idea was, I regret to say, that I wouldn't want my garden covered in plastic and old bits of wood and metal, but I was startlingly, and all too predictably, wrong. I was to prove to be wrong about many of my innovative brother's concoctions and, at first sight, zany ideas, but if I was to laugh at anybody, who better than Geoff? After all, I'd done it all my life. He actually turned out to be a master of disguise. By the time it was painted in matt paint and planted up nobody would have guessed that the plastic drum was plastic; and the hanging basket and the plastic rubbish bags were cleverly hidden from sight with planting. And the thing that excited and interested most people was not only that they were cheap but also that they cleverly re-used innumerable throw-away items that would normally end up in a smelly, ugly, poisonous hole in the ground.

It was during this feature, incidentally, that Geoff made the only joke that John Kenyon ever allowed. Geoff was pricking out some lettuces into foil Chinese takeaway trays, when he looked up at the camera and said, 'Of course the only trouble with pricking these out into Chinese takeaway trays is that an hour after you've pricked out one you feel the need to prick out another one.' John allowed him that one but wagged a cautionary finger at him and said, 'In future, leave the jokes to Morecambe and Wise.'

When Geoff began to look at cheap ways to grow flowers, fruit and vegetables, it was necessary to abandon the convenient tricks he'd learned at college using chemicals and artificial fertilisers and to rely on some of the more old-fashioned methods. So he had to turn to cow muck and other organic materials to enrich the soil, resistant plants to guard against disease and the build-up of predators to deal with pests. Always diligent about getting his facts right he sought the advice of the people who knew about organic growing methods – organisations like the HDRA at Ryton, the Soil Association and the RHS – as well as visiting some noted organic gardeners.

What he had expected to find was a motley collection of bearded and be-sandalled people in chunky Arran sweaters who saved their urine for the compost heap. He was surprised to find that they were just like all the other gardeners he met – enthusiastic, interesting and pleasant. (Geoff thought *all* keen gardeners were nice people. With almost religious fervour he would view anybody who had a spade in his hand as a good egg – oblivious of the fact that they may be about to beat their next-door neighbour to death with it.)

The thing that impressed him about the organic brigade was their genuine respect for nature and their passion for protecting and harmonising with it. He could find no argument against the fact that it was senseless to kill off beneficial insects, mammals and bacteria when, if allowed to build up naturally, they would munch through most of the harmful pests without you having to lift a finger – or a sprayer. Nor could he dispute the fact that feeding the *plant*, which is what chemical fertilisers do, rather than feeding the *soil*, which is what organic methods do, seemed like good sense. He understood the dangers of not feeding the soil, as Barnsdale was situated next to an arable field that had grown corn crops, without significant rotation and without the return of any organic matter for years, and its soil was hard and lifeless, without so much as an earthworm in sight.

He was also influenced by the argument that heavy doses of chemicals leach out of the soil and get into watercourses, damaging fish and other wildlife as well as clogging them with dense weed growth. Again, he understood this from what he had seen locally: Rutland Water, just half a mile from Barnsdale had twice been poisoned with algae which, when ingested by sheep, dogs or other animals, had killed them. And this was the water we are asked to drink. Whilst I'm quite certain that it is treated to ensure that there is no possible danger to the public, the sinister sight of the spreading blue-green mass on the surface of the water does tend to undermine confidence just a little.

So he was left floundering with only the argument that there was no organic treatment for fungal diseases, except to replace vulnerable subjects with resistant varieties. But when he thought that one through he came to the conclusion that it wasn't a bad practice in any case. Whilst it may deny the planting of some favourite varieties it would at least ensure that no damage was done to friendly creatures. Also, increased demand for disease-resistant varieties would put pressure on the plant breeders to develop more subjects.

Geoff's great ally and mentor in his initial sorties into the organic fray was Bob Sherman, the head of Horticulture at the HDRA (the Henry Doubleday Research Association), the Organic Organization.

Geoff met Bob through Alan Gear, the chief executive of HDRA, whom he first met when Alan was asked to do a piece for *Gardeners' World*. Alan remembers being constantly interrupted by jet fighters from RAF Cottesmore, just up the road, and fuming about the way they were damaging the environment through their emissions, their noise and the way in which they disturbed the wildlife – not to mentioned the civilised life – for miles around. (Geoff eventually rang the station commander who, when he understood the problems he was causing, changed the flying schedule so that it didn't coincide with BBC shoots. Nice man.) Alan says that he and Geoff 'got on like a house on fire'. He meets a lot of so-called celebrities in the gardening business and he has a particular nose for frauds and for people pretending to be what they are not, but what struck him about Geoff was that here was a guy from whom you got it straight. He was honest and down-to-earth, with a good sense of humour and no pretensions, and Alan immediately warmed to him. From that initial meeting there developed a very close relationship, which gave Alan a chance to talk about HDRA on television whilst Geoff, in return, made frequent use of the technical team based at Ryton, which included Bob Sherman, fount of all knowledge on all things organic.

Bob advised Geoff, as he launched into organic growing methods, that it could take up to five years for the level of natural predators to build up to the point where they would be in control. So, although there were some interim controlling measures he could take until then, Geoff would have no option but to stand by and watch the greenfly, mealy bugs, woolly aphid and the like forming up in close ranks outside his garden gate preparing for the attack. But by this time Geoff was hooked; he believed it would be worth the short-term disadvantages and he determined to give organic methods a try.

Nevertheless, he was a cautious man where his garden and the gardens of his viewers and readers were concerned, so he felt the need to satisfy himself completely, under controlled conditions, in his own plot, that what he was about to put forward he could personally back from his own experience. So he decided to conduct a series of trials at Barnsdale, which could be shown on *Gardeners' World*, and which would deliver both the good news and the bad news, so that his viewers could make their own judgements. Initially John Kenyon was cautious but, after a few retirements to the boardroom (actually the local), a little lubrication and a lot of persuasion it was eventually agreed – on condition that Geoff hid *nothing* from his viewers, whatever he claimed did not contradict the evidence of the trials and that whatever he suggested was not outside the means of the viewers.

Four trial beds were set up to demonstrate the results of every combination of growing methods – one fertilised and sprayed chemically and one organically, one using a mixture of organic and chemical methods, and one control plot which used none of these methods. They were all sown or planted with exactly the same varieties – at this stage using vegetables only.

The first year's results were a disaster! The vegetables produced on the plots on which entirely chemical methods had been used were far and away better than those that had been grown under organic methods, which were smaller, more shrivelled and eaten away with bugs and diseases of all kinds. Also, if the experiments were going to work at all, Geoff had had to bite the bullet and stop spraying in the rest of Barnsdale, to give the useful predators a chance to thrive. So, during the first year everything suffered except those plants that had received the toxicologist's attention. It looked ominous for the fighter in the green corner. But the seconds got to work and the plots were prepared for the following year.

In the second year, there was a noticeable improvement and the fighter from the green corner was beaten only on points, as opposed to a direct knockout the year before. By the following year the match was declared a draw and by the end of year four the positions were completely reversed. Plump, healthy vegetables overflowed the organic beds, far outdoing those raised chemically. And what's more, it was the opinion of all who ate them that they tasted better too. There was no evidence to say that this was due to the fact that the plants had not absorbed chemicals – it probably wasn't – but it seems reasonable to me to believe that a healthy, robust plant is likely to taste better than one that hasn't achieved its full potential. Sure, he was pained to see his roses covered in black spot in a bad year or his Michaelmas daisies suffering from mildew, but he knew that it was only an occasional problem and that the rewards outweighed the disadvantages. And if a new variety, more resistant to fungal attack, was produced he would 'rive out' (an expression he got from Geoffrey Smith) the old one and replace it with the new. The added bonus was that Barnsdale became alive with the chirruping, buzzing and rustling noises that are associated with a garden full of wildlife as well as the sight of colourful butterflies, bees working away at the pollen gathering, squirrels bouncing exuberantly through the trees and hedgehogs snuffling their way round the garden in thoughtful appreciation.

Many people I spoke to when researching this book made the point that Geoff's organic trials were more observational than scientific. Denis Gartside (the producer mentioned in Chapter 10), for instance, feels that if he was going to do it properly, he should have divided the garden in two and made one half organic and the other inorganic. I disagree, as the difficulty here, I'm sure, would be that the insects and other predators of pests would be inclined to disregard the boundaries between the two plots. There is no fence yet made that will keep a bee or a ladybird confined to one place. In any case, what is wrong with observation?

Most of Geoff's media colleagues thought his ideas cranky and inefficient, and the vested interests – pesticide, fungicide and herbicide manufacturers as well as the enormous chemical fertiliser companies – with one voice, rose up against him. He had some minor spats with the press and publicity departments of some of the big companies, but that was a price that Geoff thought well worth paying.

A company that was no friend of Geoff's was ICI. He would often write about ICI's contribution to the pollution of the North Sea and the atmosphere, as well as playing perhaps the leading role in persuading gardeners to use chemicals with seemingly gay abandon. Geoff's first encounter with Gordon Rae, then general manager with the professional gardeners' division of ICI, was not exactly a meeting of minds. Gordon says that their first meeting took place at Chelsea, when he attended a lunch given by the *Express* newspaper. Both Geoff and Gordon arrived early and as soon as he realised Gordon's role Geoff launched into a heated debate. They happened to be asked to sit opposite one another and the argument continued throughout the lunch, getting more and more acrimonious. I don't think either of them enjoyed it very much.

Later, however, when Gordon was appointed to his exalted post as director general of the RHS, he visited Geoff at Barnsdale. Geoff was never one to bear a grudge for more than five minutes, so they began to make friends again, albeit with some tongue-in-cheek comments and jibes at each other. For example, Gordon remembers being shown into a potting shed to watch a girl taking cuttings. Before putting them into the pot she would dip them into a little pot. 'What's in the little pot?' asked Gordon. 'Hormone rooting powder,' said the girl. ' Not chemical, of course,' said Gordon, at which Geoff grunted, 'Stop harassing my staff!' But eventually they became good friends on a personal level, although Geoff always harboured some ill-feeling towards the RHS as an organisation for its refusal to move more quickly towards what he saw as a sensible, environmentally safe approach to gardening.

True to form, in his organic campaign he resisted all opponents to his views like Joshua at the battle of Jericho and sure enough, the more he blew his horn, the more the walls began to crumble. He continued to write about his organic experiences, as well as to broadcast them. He also stood out against the wishy-washy, cautious stand almost all writers and presenters take about 'using a mixture of both, where appropriate', preferring the whole-hearted approach to organic growing.

Whilst Geoff would never have claimed to have started the organic movement, or indeed to have been the major player, there is no doubt that he did more than most to get over the message about eating well and protecting the environment through organic means. Like many others I spoke to, journalist Gillian Thornton, for instance, believes that Geoff was able to get his then quite radical views across because he came over as an ordinary bloke but with a great deal of horticultural knowledge who was able to demonstrate that what he was advocating actually worked. The result of his efforts, and others', is that there is now a huge and growing demand for organic produce of all kinds, which seems to be sweeping aside all the old prejudices and stereotypes that were attached to organic growers, and a huge and growing enthusiasm for gardening organically.

Barnsdale is still organic, Geoff's son Nick stoutly defending his father's principles, and it is perhaps a good indication of the value of his approach that, of the hundreds of thousands of visitors the gardens have received since Geoff died, there has been no sniff of a complaint about the plants being infested with pests or diseases – largely, perhaps, because they aren't.

Whilst it would be hard to claim that it was due entirely to Geoff, because HDRA were also to run their own television programme called *Muck and Magic* in the late eighties, subscriptions to the association certainly rose dramatically during the period of Geoff's association with them. Alan Gear feels he was highly influential in raising the awareness of ordinary people of the importance of preserving what we have.

When Geoff died, Alan initiated the building of a memorial garden, designed by Gabriella Pape and Isabelle van Groenigen of Land Art. It was called a 'Paradise Garden', partly because that was the name of Geoff's last programme and partly because it was just so appropriate. It is now visited and admired by the thousands of people who visit HDRA each year and is a lasting monument to Geoff's work.

One of the questions I asked Alan about Geoff was, 'Did you like him?' 'Oh yes,' he said, 'a great, great bloke.' Geoff would have liked to have been described and remembered like that.

Another of Geoff's conversions, and perhaps the best known of his crusades, concerned the use of peat. Geoff had always been a peat man, ever since we got our first inkling of the pleasures of gardening in the back yard of our parents' house in Broxbourne. He had always used it, had been educated to use it at college and had used it during his early days in commercial horticulture. He took it for granted, never questioning its value or its origins.

But during the course of his writing career, he began to hear mutterings about the depletion of the small area of the raised peat bog that remained in this country. He began to hear from eminent environmentalists about what they regarded as a serious erosion of an important wildlife habitat. Geoff began to envisage it as a possible subject for his contentious 'The Last Word' column in *Garden News*, but, keen as always to check his facts before getting on his soap box, he talked to the specialists about it and he would not be satisfied until he had seen for himself.

So in the early eighties he set up a meeting with the Board da Mona, the Irish Peat Board, to go and see peat cutting in action. The Irish peat bogs are wild, windswept places that at first sight appear desolate and lonely, but more careful inspection will reveal an amazing collection of wild flowers – the glorious scarlet elf cup (*Sarcoscypha coccinea*), the insect-eating sundew (*Drosera intermedia*) and dozens more. Birds also thrive in these unspoiled places – nightjars, curlews, meadow pippets, harriers, red-throated divers, etc., as well as other animals such as the Irish hare and even the humble dor beetle. The sight of a new plant would always have Geoff on his hands and knees, gently lifting its head, running his hands lightly over the foliage and exclaiming about the wonder of it like a small boy with a Christmas present – and he loved wildlife. So he was enchanted and excited by what he saw – until, a little further on, he saw a huge machine tearing at the peat, the peat mill, carving great swathes of it away and leaving a trail of destruction.

This experience changed Geoff's life for ever and began a campaign that was to change the face of gardening in this country for all time. I am quite sure that the whole of the British peat industry rues the day that Geoff was invited to see the peat bogs of Ireland because his impact on it was crucial and devastating. He was by no means the only person to raise his voice against the destruction of our rare wetlands, but he was certainly one of the most powerful. He had the means and the authority to communicate his views very widely indeed, through television, newspapers and the journals for which he wrote, and he used them with a dogged determination.

He also gathered together the views of the people who shared his stand against what he saw as environmental vandalism – Professor David Bellamy, Dr Jane Smart, executive director of Plantlife, an organisation dedicated to the preservation of wild plants and their habitats, Neil Bragg, a renowned soil scientist, at the time with the Agricultural Development and Advisory service (ADAS), David Border, an active environmental campaigner for many years, and a number of others.

By the time he had spoken to all these eminent people, whose views he greatly respected, he was in no doubt about the rightness of his cause. Now was the time to plan a campaign. He was aiming to convince the ordinary gardener – not the horticultural trade or local government, who used vast amounts of peat, and certainly not the peat producers, who he was well aware would bring all their might to bear on him as soon as he rode into battle. So he knew he had to be convincing and he knew he had to make his proposition attractive to his readers and viewers.

His first step, therefore, was to set up a series of trials, showing the results obtained with environmentally friendly peat alternatives with the results obtained with peat or peat-based composts, used under exactly the same conditions. Hurdle number one was to find a suitable alternative. He tried everything. Chopped straw was too coarse, garden compost was too variable, leaf mould was prone to harbour fungal diseases and mushroom compost was too alkaline. He experimented with the commercial peat-free products and, whilst he found they were as good as peat-based composts they were no better, and therefore would not provide a strong enough argument to persuade people to change. He decided that he should work only on alternatives for propagation and for potting because there were so many good, cheap alternatives available for soil conditioning that that aspect should be a secondary consideration.

He worried the problem like a dog with a bone – until he discovered coir. Coir is a waste product of the Sri Lankan coconut industry. After the coconut fibre has been removed for the manufacture of doormats and brushes, etc., a fine material called 'pith' is left and this is piled into enormous heaps and composted for several years, sterilised, baled up and shipped abroad. It is then re-wetted, a slow-release fertiliser is added and it is bagged up for sale to gardeners. At that time gardeners, because they were used to using peat-based composts and because they were not aware of the damage that peat extraction causes, steadfastly refused to buy it. So the garden centres put the price up – despite the fact that the raw material is cheaper to buy than raw peat – and it had become a niche market, for use only by the few gardeners who had taken all this on board.

This was Geoff's challenge: to persuade gardeners, to stop buying peat and use coir instead; he also wanted them to try to force the price down, first by badgering the trade and second by buying enough to get it out of the 'niche market' bracket and into the mainstream. I knew, right from birth, that if you really want to defeat a challenge, do so with somebody other than Geoff. Once he got the bit between his teeth he would put his head down and go – and woe betide anybody who got in his way. A man of considerable courage, an implacable determination and a strong streak of bloody-mindedness is a powerful adversary, as the peat industry were to discover.

At first Geoff's trials with coir were something of a disaster. Coir is a light, open compost and so needs frequent watering, which washes all the nutrients out of the bottom of the tray or pot. So, whilst the peat-grown plants flourished those grown in coir were spindly and weak. All this was shown on *Gardeners' World*, which wasn't good for the cause.

Then Geoff realised that the solution lay in the way the watering was done. He transferred all his trays and pots on to a bench in the greenhouse covered with capillary matting, which is very cheap to buy and which will absorb the water. With the containers standing permanently on a damp surface, the coir sucked up the water as it needed it, leaving all the nutrients available to the plant. The results were brilliant. He was able to proudly show on television strong, healthy plants grown in coir next to slightly less strong plants grown in peat. The peat was good, but not *as* good, so he had proved his point. During his campaign, Geoff spoke to a nurseryman with a very large enterprise who said, 'I don't care about the peat bogs, but I wouldn't go back to peat for a pension – the results with coir are so much better.'

Geoff took every opportunity he could to publicise the cause, writing about it in the press and in journals and pushing it remorselessly on television. In 1991, he spoke at a Commission of Enquiry into Peat and Peatlands, organised by Plantlife and supported by English Nature, the World Wide Fund for Nature and the Joint Nature Conservation Committee. He gave a presentation demonstrating the alternatives to peat he had tried and that they worked.

Denis Gartside criticises Geoff – though it was the only criticism Denis could level at him – for using his celebrity to push his own ideals – particularly his organic views and his abhorrence of the exploitation of peat – unmercifully, often at the expense of other, more all-embracing philosophies. When he said this to me, I sprang immediately to his defence and asked what he was supposed to do about such issues. If he had simply said, for instance, that the use of peat was wrong but if you feel like it you should use it, I can hardly see it making much impact. It would be like a rabbi saying that eating a pork sandwich was OK at home but don't do it in the synagogue. Nonsense! I agree with Geoff. If you truly believe it, let your voice be heard. It is a sad fact that, even after all Geoff's work and the undoubted rightness of the cause, the sales of peat are again rising. I was unable, recently, to buy coir compost at any of our local garden centres, because nobody is now asking for it. It seems that Geoff's was a lone voice, crying in the wilderness, and if so the destruction of the last of our unique raised peat bog habitats will be completed. I hope and trust that his loyal followers will now rise up and rally to the cause. Gardening fundamentalists unite! Throw down your gardening glove and challenge the heretics!

Neil Bragg first met Geoff in June 1990, when he was invited up to Barnsdale to talk about peat and peat alternatives. He was surprised, a few minutes after he arrived, to hear Geoff saying (and this was typical of Geoff), 'Oh, Neil, we've got a crew here. Would you like to come out and do a piece to camera?' So poor Neil suddenly found himself thrust in front of a camera explaining his views about peat, the disadvantages associated with its extraction and the alternatives that were available to gardeners. But Neil, a good presenter himself and a firebrand for peat alternatives, did an excellent off-the-cuff piece. Geoff followed it up with a visit to the ADAS trial grounds in September 1991, where they looked at the practical results.

Geoff received a lot of inflamed criticism from companies like Fisons, who make Levington compost (which is peat-based), and perhaps that could be expected – just as the cigarette manufacturers claimed for years that smoking did not cause cancer, until the irrefutable truth caught up with them. It also brought him into conflict with individuals whose views were diametrically opposed to his – for example, the well-known writer and television presenter Peter Seabrooke.

Also an ex-Writtle student, Peter had worked with Geoff during his short career at Anglia Television, where their ideas first clashed. Geoff sang the praises of bare-rooted plants whilst Peter was all for container growing, which resulted in some mild confrontation on television and never ended in agreement. Peter had worked as a presenter of *Gardeners' World*, in tandem with Arthur Billett, at Clacks Farm for about five years before Geoff came on the scene, but when the programme was shifted by the BBC, to be managed by the Agricultural Unit, with John Kenyon as director, Peter decided that farming and horticulture didn't mix and, he says, he and John Kenyon didn't mix either. So he saw the year out and then got out, although, he says, he subsequently felt uneasy about Geoff moving into a programme that he had presented before.

Peter worked as a peat salesman for about five years during the early part of his career and is still not convinced by the argument that peat extraction is damaging the environment; nor does he believe that the opposite side of the argument has ever been put. So Peter is a peat enthusiast and it was here that Geoff's views collided with his. In his campaign for the use of coir as a peat replacement and in his writing particularly, Geoff criticised Peter for promoting peat. There is no doubt that this put considerable pressure on their relationship. When I asked Peter what the atmosphere was like when he and Geoff would meet at press conferences or shows, he gave me a one-word answer: 'Frosty.'

But Geoff won praise for taking the flack for promoting the cause he believed in. Professor David Bellamy would probably top Geoff's list of top-flight professional gardeners, plantsmen and environmentalists whose company he revelled in. An ebullient academic, with an infectious enthusiasm for all matters environmental, he lifts the spirits with his sheer joy of living. (When I spoke to him and asked him how I should refer to him in this book, he said, 'My God, boy, I've got five doctorates and four professorships. Just call me an itinerant botanist. That's really what I am.') He enthuses (as he has a tendency to do) about Geoff's campaigns against the use of peat. 'He was up against a lot of people who would claim to have always used peat, although peat only began to be used in 1960 and digging peat into your garden is a stupid thing to do anyway. But Geoff stood up to them and really began to make a difference. The thing about Geoff was that his knowledge was so profound that nobody could call him a crank, so people listened to what he had to say – and found that it worked.'

While Geoff's peat campaign was in full swing, he was approached by Jane Smart, a very well-respected ecologist who had done intensive research at Sheffield University on the destruction of peat bogs, on behalf of Plantlife. She was seeking Geoff's help in the promotion of Plantlife's conservation aims. They were particularly gratified to get a very positive response, because in those days they were a very small organisation. There was no kudos attached to a connection with Plantlife, but Geoff wasn't interested in kudos, despite what some of his detractors may have said; he was completely dedicated to his beliefs and would do anything constructive to further them. He and Jane became good friends because, she says, he was exactly the same as he was on television – no posing and no air of self-importance. He was a little perplexed that they had not got further than they had, because he could see how compelling the arguments were, so he offered them lots of advice about how they could advance the cause and freely offered his help – which perhaps reached its highest profile during the great peat campaign. David Bellamy, who is president of Plantlife, says, 'Now we're going great guns. If it hadn't have been for Geoff, Plantlife would not have risen nearly as fast.'

After Geoff died Plantlife received sufficient donations in his memory, with some help from the shampoo manufacturer Timotei, to enable them to buy Seaton Meadow, some ten miles or so from Barnsdale – not a peat-land site but a flood meadow of considerable beauty and an almost unique history. It is one of the few remaining flood meadows that is still managed as a flood meadow, never having had chemical fertilisers used on it and managed in the old-fashioned, non-intensive way that encouraged the growth of myriad wild flowers. Whilst still farmed by the brothers who owned it, it is managed by Plantlife in a way which will ensure that the flowers remain as a perfect memory of Geoff's good work.

* * *

The blame for Geoff's limestone pavement campaign can be laid squarely at the door of his good and faithful friend Roy Lancaster. At the end of a television session they were shooting together in Carnforth, Lancashire, Roy invited Geoff to walk up to the towering limestone pavement just behind the garden in which they were filming. He wanted to show Geoff some of the rare and beautiful specimens of flowers that grow there. Limestone pavements are huge areas of flat stone or 'clints' divided by myriad cracks and crevices, called 'grikes', which shelter unique plants – harts-tongue ferns, wood anemones, bloody cranesbill, dog's mercury and many more, all sharing their space with high-brown and pearl-bordered fritillary butterflies, marsh harriers, bitterns and many other exotic species. Geoff was entranced by this sight and enthused with Roy over its unexpected richness.

Then Roy told him about the exploitation of yet another rare habitat for a fast buck. Limestone pavements are being systematically destroyed so that the stone can be carted away and sold for considerable profits to gardeners who wish to make rockeries and other hard landscaping features. Clearly Geoff would never wish to try to deprive people of the chance to pretty up their gardens – that's what he was in business to try to encourage – but he doubted they knew what a price was having to be paid in the wilds of Yorkshire for a rockery in Surbiton. He was convinced that if they did know they would shrink from the thought of despoiling a beautiful natural environment in one place just in order to make an unnatural one in another.

So, once again he confirmed his views with the environmental experts, all of whom backed his proposed stand. And again he decided that if he was going to ask people to stop using stone, he had to be able to offer an alternative – something easy to make or acquire, cheaper than the real thing and every bit as attractive.

This was when the experiments started and the time when I began to seriously worry for his sanity. I knew he worked under considerable, largely self-imposed, pressure and I saw him, at last, slipping into the final stages of senile dementia. He began to dig holes of peculiar, random shapes, line them with plastic and fill them with concrete, dyed in various rainbow hues. 'What are you doing, Geoff,' said I gently, sensing the dangers of upsetting the seriously deranged. 'Making stones,' he grunted, and my concern mounted. He grunted more as he struggled to get the hardened stones out of the hole. They were just lumps of concrete. 'Geoff, nobody is going to use these in their gardens,' I said. 'They're just lumps of concrete.' 'I haven't finished yet,' he grudgingly growled. 'Give me time.' I drove home concerned and amused. The old boy's lost it at last, I thought.

The following week I went back again and there, resplendent in its stony glory was a small group of large and quite attractive rocks. They were now not made of concrete but a mixture of concrete, sand and coir, with a dye to ensure a suitable colour. Now it was my turn to be grumpy. 'Still don't think they'll look any good,' said I, with the uncomfortable feeling that the inventive old bugger had done it across me again. This time he had his usual, intensely irritating grin of confidence on his face as he said, 'Wait till I've got them in place and planted up. You'll like them then.' And sure enough they looked wonderful. The whole operation was televised in Geoff's by now familiar step-by-step style and he received hundreds of letters of congratulation. And once again he took every opportunity he could find to reinforce his point and to buttress the case for using artificial stone instead of robbing our heritage.

It was very gratifying and heartwarming that after Geoff's death Plantlife were able to complete the purchase of Winskill Stones in North Yorkshire, largely through donations from the public, received as a result of the lead he gave to the campaign to raise the money to buy it, so that it could be preserved for ever from the depredations of the bulldozers. David Bellamy opened the site, looking like Moses as he cried out his message of hope against a howling wind and driving rain. The pavement is now dedicated to Geoff in perpetuity and our family is proud to have a notable connection with such a beautiful county.

★　★　★

When I interviewed the producer Laurence Vulliamy, who was a great admirer of Geoff's battling spirit and fully supported his very firm views about the gardeners' responsibility for the preservation of the environment, he wondered what Geoff's stand would have been on genetically modified foods and feels sure that had he been alive today he would have been right up there in the forefront of the debate, lobbying, arguing, debating and generally making his voice heard. I wished he'd lived long enough to be able to comment, because that would have torn him in half. On the one hand, he would have applauded the prospect of being able to feed the world, but on the other, he would have shrunk in horror at the idea of pest-resistant plants, which he would have seen as the end to all insects. That's an argument we were never able to have in the pub, but what a night that would have been!

Epilogue

ON THAT DREADFUL DAY, 4 AUGUST 1996, when Geoff took part in the tragic cycle ride which ended his life he was accompanied by Sibylle Riesen from Sustrans, a charity who are dedicated to the provision of sustainable transport. She rode with Geoff all the way on what was to have been a ride of twenty-five miles along the Taff Trail in the Brecon Beacons in south Wales in order to inaugurate the trail.

Although she had watched Geoff on television, because she and her husband are both keen gardeners, she had never met him before, but found a warm, smiling, fit-looking Geoff in the car park from which the ride was to start. When he opened this stage of the trail, he gave a short speech which focused mainly on a sculpture that had been dedicated to visually impaired people who, because of the trail's clever construction, would be able to ride it without assistance. Geoff spoke eloquently about this endeavour, saying how delighted he was to find people who cared so much about enabling such a wide cross-section of society to enjoy the countryside.

Sibylle knew he had recently had his first heart attack, so she enquired about how he felt and whether or not he was sure he should ride the full twenty-five miles. Had she known Geoff as I did, she wouldn't have asked that question because the stubborn old devil was always going to say yes. When he had told me about his proposed cycle ride a couple of days before he did it, I had tried desperately to dissuade him, pointing out the perils of riding on forty-five-degree slopes just after a heart attack. I pleaded with him to hide his car in the trees and ride the last half-mile. But if Geoff had made up his mind to do something in pursuit of one of his passions, no argument was eloquent enough to change his course.

When they started, Geoff, perhaps remembering his old rowing days, went off like a bat out of hell, but gradually fell behind as the trail got steeper. Sibylle stayed with him all the way, chatting about gardening as they rode and even offering to swap bikes with Geoff because he had only three gears and she had twenty-four. But Geoff, true to form, was determined to ride his own bike and refused. They stopped at a particularly breathtaking view, which Geoff sat and admired, soliloquising about its beauty. Sustrans have now erected a memorial seat at this point, with an inscription which acknowledges the sacrifice he made, albeit involuntarily, for his beliefs.

Eventually they got to the top of the hill, where there was a refreshment point, so they stopped for a cup of tea. Sibylle didn't think he looked well at this point and repeatedly asked him if he wanted to go on, but once Geoff set his mind on a target there was no dissuading him, so he got back on to his bike and pedalled off. He had only gone a few yards before he suddenly collapsed in a heap with his bicycle on top of him. Sibylle, seeing the seriousness of his condition, pedalled furiously to the nearby medical point and a nurse rushed back, within three minutes, and tried to resuscitate him, but to no avail. By the time he arrived at the hospital, his life had slipped away and Geoff was no more.

Lynda was waiting expectantly for him at the other end of the trail and was devastated to hear the news that he had collapsed and been taken to hospital. She drove off to the Prince Charles Hospital in Merthyr Tydfil, not knowing whether or not he had survived, only to receive the news that he had not. Advised to return to the hotel she tried valiantly to compose herself and telephoned me. I can't describe the effect this shattering blow had on me, but somehow the rarely present rational side of my brain took over and I knew the situation had to be managed. I contacted his three boys and asked Nick to drive me down to south Wales immediately so that we could rescue Lynda and bring Geoff's Land Rover back to Barnsdale.

I am immensely glad that I spoke to Sibylle during the research for this book. I now realise what a dreadful shock it must have been for her and how very well and sensitively she handled it. I am sure the awful nature of the event will stay with her for ever, but I and the rest of the family are immensely grateful to her for making the last hour or so of Geoff's life so pleasant and fulfilling.

Each of Geoff's three boys was devastated and filled with grief, which each dealt with in his own way. Steve expressed his sorrow in anger with his father, shouting at him, kicking the furniture and expostulating at his stupidity in accepting the invitation to ride a bicycle for twenty-five miles after he had already had one heart attack. Nick internalised it in public, but expressed it in volumes to himself, in private. When he and I drove down to south Wales to pick up Lynda he seemed calm and even detached, but he told me that when he was on his own driving Geoff's Land Rover back to Barnsdale, he cried through every mile, with the result that he could hardly see the road. Chris, as he put it, 'blubbed' uncontrollably, not, he felt, because of the loss of a sentimental attachment; it was a more mature kind of sorrow at the passing of a good man. Each of them felt some consolation in the thought that he had died at the peak of his career and that had he lived to be ninety and unable to pick up a spade or plant another plant he would have died of frustration and fury.

Lynda, who bore the greatest part of the loss and sadness, is now coming to terms with it; Geoff's presence is always with her, sometimes a heartache, but more and more often a joy and a source of immense pride. Sometimes she feels that every nerve is raw, but this is always mitigated by a sense of his strength, his ability, even through all the trials of his early life, just to get on with it.

Our relationship with Lynda is now loving but sensible and down-to-earth, as Geoff would have wished. She, Carol and I see a lot of each other and together manage the Geoff Hamilton New Gardeners' Foundation (although Lynda does almost all the work). Lynda has contributed masses of information and inspiration for this book and I am truly grateful. She is a worthy carrier of Geoff's banner and I am very proud of her.

The Foundation was the brainchild of Tony Laryea, who was conscious of the unparalleled contribution that Geoff had made to the popularisation of gardening and knew that he was always keen to give back some of what he took out. So he made a compilation video called *The Barnsdale Collection*, which is now on sale at Barnsdale and many other gardens and garden centres throughout the country. The proceeds of the sale (all of them) are put towards financing needy students who wish to study at Geoff's old college, Writtle, in Essex. A fitting tribute from one generous man to honour another. We are very grateful to Tony for his foresight.

Geoff died too early but we can console ourselves with the fact that he had used all his many talents to the full and had contributed more than his fair share to other people's lives. In my opinion, he also provided the launch pad for the enormous explosion of enthusiasm for gardening. He made a major contribution to raising the awareness of gardeners to the action they could take to improve the environment – avoiding the use of peat and limestone; using organic methods to retain pest predators and prevent the extinction of friendly animal life, not to mention reaping the benefits of not ingesting noxious chemicals; recycling materials to cut costs and reduce the amount of rubbish we put into landfill sites; and a whole range of other measures. He was also responsible for raising the profiles of Plantlife, who do excellent work in the preservation of wildlife habitats, and of Sustrans.

The view of John Kenyon, who worked with Geoff for so many years as producer of *Gardeners' World*, is that it was Geoff who laid the foundation for the present resurgence of interest in gardening. 'After all,' he says, 'how many gardening programmes were there on television in the early eighties? There was one. *Gardeners' World*. And how many were there by the mid-nineties? There were thousands of them, all over the place. And who made that possible? It was Geoff Hamilton, because he appealed to the *generality* of gardeners – from Mrs Joe Soap who just wants her garden to look nice to Lady Muck, who is fearfully excited about her chrysanthemums.'

Alan Titchmarsh feels that Geoff made a significant contribution to the environment by dripping away at his viewers and readers so that, as if by osmosis, they became more responsible for and responsive to the needs of the environment. He also feels he's a great loss to the gardening fraternity. He says that when Geoff died, and Alan took over *Gardeners' World*, he had had a wonderful letter from a lady who said, 'Please give yourself time to breathe. You've lost a friend.' That letter clearly touched Alan, as his telling of it did me. When Geoff died, so many people felt they had lost a friend.

Alan Gear, chief executive of HDRA, feels that Geoff did more to influence the move towards organic production than anybody in the country. He transformed the old stereotyped image of organic gardeners being cranks with beards and sandals and gave the whole practice of organic growing and environmental protection an authority and substance that it had never had before.

David Bellamy, 'itinerant botanist' and president of Plantlife, is himself an East Ender by extraction, a race of down-to-earth, practical people, and believes that Geoff was a gardener of that ilk. He understood plants and where to put them, and he knew how important it was to get the soil right. Gardening now, he says, seems to be filled with cardboard cutouts and, in his opinion, Geoff was the gardener of the era. 'To have Geoff's ability and knowledge is a wonderful thing but to be able to get it across so that people turn on the television and say, "Hi, Geoff" is a golden gift. My Mum loved him, my mother-in-law loved him, and now it's all gone and gardening programmes just aren't the same.' He feels that Geoff had given a new prominence to gardening and performed the vital task of raising people's consciousnesses about the need to preserve the environment. He speaks of Geoff as a part of the renaissance of gardening that has happened over the last thirty years and puts him alongside people like Gertrude Jekyll who did so much to enthuse people about their gardens in the latter part of the nineteenth century and the early part of the twentieth.

One of the country's leading rose growers, David Austin, who was a particular friend of Geoff's and told me of the immense respect and affection they had for each other, describes Geoff as a true gardener who loved his subject. David sees gardening as an ever-changing, dynamic environment that depends on plants, rather than pure design for its beauty and makes the point that the type of gardens that are shown at the Chelsea Flower Show might be very beautiful, but they are the work of designers rather than gardeners; for a short time they may be wonderful but once the one or two plants they actually put in them are over there is no more movement. Geoff, on the other hand, put across in his gardens the true gardener's sense of the simple enjoyment of growing plants, being surrounded by beauty and being able to eat from God's table. David feels that we now need another Geoff, to influence people in the way he did, but he doesn't see one on the horizon, partly because television is now devoted more to entertainment than to instruction.

David honoured Geoff by naming a new rose after him, called *Rosa* 'Geoff Hamilton', and it is a sure sign, not only of the outstanding beauty of the rose but also of Geoff's acclaim, that it has sold more than any rose in David's list. He named the rose after Geoff because he felt he had made an outstanding contribution to horticulture and to the 'common man's gardening', and because he found him to be a generous-hearted and kind man.

David was not the only person to honour Geoff in this way. Woodfield Brothers of Stratford dedicated a striking blue and white lupin to Geoff – *Lupinus* 'Barnsdale'. Clive and Kathy Gandly of Cullompton named a deep carmine penstemon after him. Geoff invited the celebrated sweet pea growers Diane and Terry Sewell, who produce some of the country's best plants from their nursery at Over in Cambridgeshire, to appear on *Gardeners' World* after he had visited their nursery and they became firm friends, so much so that the first sweet pea hybrid they ever developed themselves they called *Lathyrus odoratus* 'Geoff Hamilton'. He was touched and delighted by this but, though never a shrinking violet, he expressed to me his wonderment that anybody should feel so strongly about the quality of his work. I, of course, said that I was surprised as well, but that wasn't what I really felt and he knew it.

Geoff had always been a vigorous character, a risk taker and an optimist – indeed these characteristics were the foundation of his attraction, the things that made him so good to be with, even in a vicarious way through television and writing. So maybe his premature death was inevitable; maybe, one way or another, it would have happened anyway. His life was too short and he left a lot of sad people behind him, but on the other hand he achieved more in his short life than ten of us ordinary folk could have done. He was perhaps the country's best television gardener ever; he was a stimulating writer; he made a momentous difference to the way people regard the environment; he left a lot of friends better off for having known him and he left his family a legacy that not only provides for them but which fills them with pride and gratitude.

I was reading *Dubliners* by James Joyce recently, and I came across a quotation which I feel sums up my feelings about Geoff's death much better than I ever could (I suppose one should expect that from James Joyce). It ran: 'Better pass boldly into that other world, in the full glory of some passion, than fade and wither dismally with age.'

He now lies in a tiny country churchyard, surrounded by trees, flowers and animals. He is buried beneath his favourite cersidiphyllum, a tree with pale green leaves in spring, changing to blood-red in autumn and smelling strongly of the sweet taste of honey. His gravestone bears the simple inscription 'Geoff Hamilton, Gardener of Barnsdale'. That's how he would have liked to have been known: no pomp, no frills, no expression of his achievements – just a quiet exit, as his entrance had been all those years ago in London.

Index

271